Jesus,
the
Crucified
People

"And the word became flesh . . ."

—JOHN 1:14

The Cross in the Lotus World

A trilogy by C.S. Song

Jesus, the Crucified People
Jesus and the Reign of God
Jesus in the Power of the Spirit

Jesus,
the
Crucified
People

C. S. SONG

Fortress Press   Minneapolis

JESUS, THE CRUCIFIED PEOPLE
C. S. Song

First Fortress Press edition 1996.

The cover art is from *Sketches of Christ from a Chinese Brush* by Shek Kai-Nung and Olaf K. Skinsnes, copyright © 1956 Augsburg Publishing House.

Library of Congress Cataloging-in-Publication Data

Song, Choan-Seng, 1929-
    Jesus, the crucified people / C. S. Song.
      p.   cm.
    Originally published: New York, NY: Crossroad Publishing Company, © 1990.
    ISBN 0-8006-2969-8
    1. Jesus Christ — Person and offices. 2. People of God.
  3. Christianity and justice. 4. Feminist theology. I. Title.
    BT205.S766   1996
    232 — dc20

Manufactured in the U.S.A.   AF 1–2969

00   99   98   97   96   1   2   3   4   5   6   7   8   9   10

To New College, the University of Edinburgh,
which initiated me into the mystery of Christian theology
and honored me with the invitation to deliver
the Gunning Victoria Jubilee Lectures
in the Autumn of 1989

Contents

Preface

While the present work was in progress, one question kept coming to my mind: Did Jesus, born in Palestine two thousand years ago, expect his influence to go beyond the land of his birth and his impact to long outlive him? The answer is probably no. He burnt himself out totally, like a candle, to give light to the people living under the power of darkness. He lived, toiled, and died solely for that purpose. But unlike a candle he did not just melt away, leaving no trace behind him. And though a candle is unable to prevent the return of darkness as soon as it is extinguished, Jesus' light has burned on and has ignited countless new lights in the world, becoming the source of courage and hope to millions and millions of people during the past two millennia. The question that I had to ask again and again shaped this discourse on Jesus into testimonies, rather than a treatise, a doctrine, or a theological system — testimonies of men, women, and children who live and die so that the light kindled by Jesus will go on burning until that time when God will bring all things to fulfillment.

And there was a thought that inspired me along the way, the thought that perhaps Jesus waited, for these past two thousand years, to hear something different about him from the parts of the world now called Third World. Who could blame Jesus if he has grown a little tired of hearing over and over essentially the same thing about him said, taught, proclaimed, and preached by traditional Christianity for so many centuries with only slight variations from time to time? He himself strove to bring fresh air into the traditions of his own religion. He must have been unable to suppress a sense of irony to know that the churches established in his name have come to revere him as a tradition that allows little fresh air to enter. Now that new voices are being enunciated about him by those churches and Christians outside the traditional framework of Christianity, he must be experiencing an emancipation from the confinement of orthodoxy that has immobilized him.

What has been attempted in the following pages is a humble addition to these voices that have been growing in both volume and power in recent years. It has a specific orientation toward Asia, the vast continent the author comes from. That Asian orientation has shaped the contents and even the style of what is now in the hands of my readers. Some, or even much, of what is said may sound alien to the Christians whose ears are attuned to the familiar "christological" music of traditional Christianity. But my hope is that they will be willing to exercise their theological imagination and put themselves in the continent of Asia dominated not by Christianity but by other religions and cultures. Then the voice they hear in this book may not be so strange to them. They may also realize that perhaps Jesus himself will not mind at all to hear some different things said about him and different emphases made about what he must have done. But my earnest hope is that Jesus, the subject of this study, will recognize in these pages even just a little of what he must have been and of what he had actually attempted during his all too brief life and ministry.

Jesus, according to the Gospels of Matthew and Luke, was born in Bethlehem and grew up in Nazareth. He was not a divine principle, but a person of flesh and blood. In due course the passage of time came to be measured and recorded as B.C. (before Christ) and A.D. (*Anno Domini*), beginning backward and forward in relation to the time of his birth. Jesus as a historical person can be identified within a particular cross-section of space-time.

That particular cross-section of space-time proves, from the Christian standpoint, to be an extraordinary segment in human history. That space-time of Jesus was not a mere thirty years limited to the small confine of the land in which he was born. His time seems to stretch to eternity and his space extends to all the universe. In the words of the Letter to the Hebrews, "Jesus Christ is the same yesterday, today, and for ever" (13:8). John, the author of the Fourth Gospel, in a flash of penetrating theological hindsight grasped the meaning of Jesus in relation to the world when he said: "The Word became flesh" (1:14, RSV). What a mystery is packed into this brief statement! The Word that was in the beginning of time now comes into the thick of our time. The God who filled the space of chaos with creation now fills our space of suffering, strife, and death with the Word-become-flesh.

The secret of grasping the meaning of the Word-become-flesh for us today lies in our learning to say it in one breath. We must also learn to say it with crescendo reaching the climax at the "flesh." The flesh must be so accentuated that we can hear the Word in it, that we can perceive the Word bursting from it. Otherwise, the Word-become-flesh is just another abstract concept invented by theologians insulated from the world of flesh, the world filled with the noise, sighs, and tears of women, men, and children whose flesh the Word has become. To learn to say the Word-become-flesh in one breath with crescendo reaching the climax at the "flesh" is a theological adventure we wish to embark on.

Most of the material in this volume was given as lectures in the course "Christ in our World Today" at the Pacific School of Religion and the Graduate Theological Union at Berkeley in the United States. I am grateful to my students who wrestled with me in an effort to make Jesus speak once again, not just out of the past, not only out of the familiar settings of the West, but out of our culturally pluralistic world today, and especially out of Asia, which has remained outside the orbit of the influence exercised by Christianity.

Words of warm thanks also go to my Alma Mater, New College the University of Edinburgh, Scotland, which honored me with the invitation to deliver the Gunning Lectures, from October 16 to 27, 1989. I chose chapters from the manuscript of this book and was to share my "christological" effort in eight lectures. I went to Edinburgh with both excitement and trepidation — excitement because the invitation enabled me to visit, after thirty years, the community of theological learning that awakened in me zeal for God's truth, and trepidation because my theological journey has taken a considerably different direction since those relatively innocent days. But after I gave two lectures, on October 17 the earthquake that measured 7.1 on the Richter scale shook San Francisco and brought me back home to be with my family and with the people of the San Francisco Bay Area devastated by the fury of Mother Earth. Subsequently I returned to Edinburgh from November 27 to December 1. I am grateful to Principal Duncan Forrester, Dean David Wright, and Professor J. C. L. Gibson, chairperson of the committee on visiting lectureships, for the hospitality shown me during my stay and particularly for making it possible for me to return to Edinburgh to fulfill my commitment to the Gunning Lectures.

The present work was originally planned and written as one volume. But it has grown into a three-volume work under the general title *The Cross in the Lotus World*. The word "lotus" is of course symbolic of Buddhism. Although a great part of Asia has been under Buddhist influence for centuries, Asia as a home to other religions and cultures cannot be described entirely as a "lotus world." Still, this general title expresses in a symbolic way a theological effort to understand Christian faith in the part of the world not dominated by Christianity. *Jesus, the Crucified People* is the first volume, to be followed by *Jesus and the Reign of God* and *Jesus in the Power of the Spirit*.

I am indebted to editor John Eagleson for the suggestion that the original manuscript could be expanded into three volumes, and for the excellent editorial work he and his staff have done I am very grateful. My thanks also go to Audrey Englert, the Pacific School of Religion's faculty secretary, and her assistant, Allyson Platt, for transferring my original manuscript into the personal computer and thus making the work of revision and expansion infinitely easier. Audrey Englert initiated me into the "mystery" of the computer age and made me realize that manual typewriters are, alas, things of the days gone by.

And when I think of the sacrifice the writing of books and other academic activities demand on my family, my heart-felt thanks have to go to my wife and my daughters for the publication of this work on Jesus. Many a family trip had to be eternally postponed and much of the family vacation became a promise with no fulfillment. This work, just as the works already published, is therefore the fruit of their love and understanding as much as the outcome of my theological labor. From time to time in our life together I am reminded that in Jesus I am not dealing with a theological system, a christological formula, or a metaphysical principle, but a person of flesh and blood who has embodied in himself what God must be. After all, Jesus had so much to do with life. How could, then, an effort to understand him become detached from the life we live together as a family, as a community, and as a nation? This is the theological wisdom I continue to learn in the school of faith called family.

Throughout the book I have made a conscious effort to use inclusive language. Freedom from sexist language is a theological freedom as well as social and cultural freedom. It is with such freedom that I have usually made the biblical quotations inclusive in language. After all, "God created Adam in God's own image ... male *and female* God created *them*" (Gen. 1:27). As to the quotations from other authors, I have taken the liberty to render some of their language to be more inclusive whenever possible. I had to leave some non-inclusive language unchanged when the change proved difficult. In an exercise such as this I also experienced again and again the power of the "inclusive Word" become flesh.

Unless otherwise indicated, the scriptural quotations are taken from the New English Bible.

PROLOGUE

Oh, Jesus, Here With Us!

The Gold-Crowned Jesus is a play written by Korean Christian poet Kim
Chi Ha, who is "a recidivist, seized and tortured again and again, tried
again and again, always charged with the same crimes — crimes of the
tongue, misuse of the pen."[1] As the curtain rises, a Christ-pietà figure can
be seen in silhouette and a song accompanied by guitar music is heard in
the background:

> That frozen sky
> That frozen field
> Even the sun has lost its light
> Oh, that poor, dark, dark street
> Where did you come from
> People with emaciated faces...?
> Running around in search of what?
> Those eyes
> Those emaciated hands
>
> There is no native earth
> There is no place to rest your tired bodies
> There is no place even for a grave
> In the heart of winter
> I have been abandoned
> I have been abandoned...
>
> Where can it be?
> Where is the heavenly kingdom?
> Over on the other side of death?
> Green forest of the four seasons?
> Can it be there?...
>
> Endless winter
> Darkness of the abyss that I cannot bear

1

This tragic time and tide
This endless, endless poverty
This empty, cold world
I cannot bear it any longer

Where can he be?
Where can he be?

Where is Jesus?
That frozen sky
That frozen field
Even the sun has lost its light
That dark, dark, poor street
Where can he be?
Where can he be?
He who could save us
Where can he be?

Oh, Jesus
Now here with us
Oh, Jesus, with us ...[2]

What a world! What a life! The world in the powerful grip of darkness
and life exposed to the cruel winter and sapped of its vitality! Is this the
world created by a poetic fantasy born of a soul chained to the prison
wall? Or is this the world of chaos with which God has to contend at
the beginning of time and at all times? Is this a life painted in despair
by the conscience tortured in the police interrogation room? Or is this the
life of pain and suffering God also has to endure in the midst of history
and at the end of time? It must be both. In this world and in this life
God and human beings become engaged in the search for meaning, fulfillment, and destiny. This is a huge operation called salvation. But who is
the savior? Where is Jesus, the one who is said to come to save the world?
Where is the Christ, the one anointed to redeem humanity?

Where Is Jesus?

The frozen sky. The dark, dark, poor street. And people with emaciated
faces. Where can Jesus be, the Christ who comes to save and redeem?
All power of the pen released in *The Gold-Crowned Jesus* is poured into
probing the question. And of all people, it is Beggar and Leper who ask
the question — two wretched souls, the scum of society, not theologians
who teach Christian doctrine, not Christians who know their catechism
inside out. And that makes all the difference!

When a theologian raises the question, it becomes a theological question to be settled with massive knowledge of biblical interpretation and church teachings. When an informed Christian raises it, the question turns into the defense of Christian faith against other faiths. But when a beggar turns to the question, it is not his head that turns to it. It is his stomach, his empty stomach! The one who saves must save his stomach first, must first fill his empty stomach. And when a leper bothers to ask the question, his immediate concern is not defense of faith and correct doctrine. What is at stake is his humanity — humanity eaten away by the horrible disease and excluded from human community. Leper and Beggar do not have in the question "Who is Jesus?" a theological axe to grind. For them it is a question of life and death, the question of whether love is rich enough to fill an empty stomach, strong enough to restore a disfigured humanity, and powerful enough to create life in the midst of death.

Leper seeks Jesus from his troubled humanity. This is where the search for the savior must begin, not only for Leper, but for us all. We have studied the history of Israel hard and long to discover the traces of the savior. We have poured intently over the Hebrew Scriptures to hear footsteps of a messiah. We have made great efforts to recapture the image of Jesus from the witnesses of the early Christian community. We have also searched diligently that strange book of Revelation in anticipation of the coming of Christ in power and glory. But most of the time we are afraid to look into our own selves nagged by deep anxiety and unable to make a christological sense of Asia populated with millions and millions of hungry stomachs and disfigured human beings. We also feel uncomfortable with those longing souls looking for salvation from the suffering of this world in their gods and lords. Our Jesus Christ is still to be linked up with the life of the vast Asian world.

But Leper sees and feels something very different. He sees his own tormented self and not an abstract ideal humanity. He feels in his own person the broken world of injustice and not a heavenly kingdom of peace and harmony. He shivers in the cold winter where the ethical idealism of a Christian community does not apply. He knows something must be wrong, terribly wrong. He bursts out:

> When your house gets torn down, "Stay silent, don't fight, turn the other cheek, obey the masters, the gentlemen, the police," they tell you. "Obey them, for these are the *true* believers." This is what the people who wear luxurious clothes, eat rich food, and prove their high station by displaying their wealth like to say to us. They manipulate and sweet talk us, deny us our souls, tame us into dumb unquestioning dull-heads, well-trained pups, while they enjoy their

glory, their power. Isn't it true, Jesus? Tell me if I lie. Tell me I say this because I am stupid, because I know no better.[3]

These are desperate words. They are also words of protest. And they are charged with a moral force demanding an answer, a response.

What, I wonder, would Jesus' answer be? What would be his response, he who said: "If anyone strikes you on the right cheek, turn the other also; and if anyone wants to sue and take your coat, give your cloak as well; and if anyone forces you to go one mile, go also the second mile" (Matt. 5:39–40, NRSV)? Could it be that Jesus had in mind the situation where someone still had the other cheek to turn, a coat to give, the energy to walk the second mile? But Leper has no other cheek to turn, no coat to give, and no energy left to walk the second mile. What would Jesus say to him?

Asia is a huge mass of human beings who are such lepers. And the Aborigines of Australia are an example of such human beings. They have lived in their own land for more than thirty thousand years. But since 1770 the British "claimed Australia and began to send settlers. They used it first as a penal colony, then encouraged the development of the sheep industry and agriculture, and eventually expanded into additional areas with the discovery of gold and mineral resources.... [They] negotiated no treaties, made no purchases of land, and paid no compensation. As the invaders covered the land with sheep, cattle, and crops, the Aborigines were pushed aside, their food supply destroyed, their sacred rites violated. Individuals and whole groups were massacred. By 1933, the Aboriginal population, which had been 300,000 in 1788, was reduced to 60,000."[4] A heart-breaking story! Listen to what they say about their land taken away from them and alienated from them:

> The land is our Mother.
> It is the source of our
> existence, our religion,
> our identity.
>
> To us land is a living
> thing. We are part of
> it, and it is part of us.
>
> For many, many years
> Aboriginal people have
> been losing a little bit
> of themselves. We are
> determined we will not
> lose anything.

> Until our land rights
> are recognized, we cannot
> be free and equal citizens
> with white Australians.[5]

This is a lament of a religious soul deeply wounded. Can you hear it? This is an indictment of a human being helplessly overpowered. Can you see it? And this is a cry of a human spirit awakened to claim back the rights given by God the Creator. Can you understand it?

"The land is our Mother," says the poem. When we think of life, we think of mother. Life begins within the mother. It grows in her. It is nourished by her. It receives flesh and blood from her. It moves within her. It breathes with her. It is securely, tenderly, and lovingly embraced in that mysterious womb filled with vital power. It is there that life takes shape, forms personality, and develops identity. What is involved is much, much more than a mere biological process. A life growing in the mother's womb is a matter of the spirit, an event of faith, an act of religion. Essentially, religion has to do with life. Is it, then, not natural that religion basically has the "mother-character," the feminine vitality?

Life is an act of faith. To live is to believe. And to believe is to hope. That is why we must look for light in the midst of darkness. That is why we must struggle for freedom when bound in bondage. That is why we must believe in the victory of love over hate, justice over injustice, and life over death. Here is a poem written on the Democracy Wall in Beijing at the height of struggle for human rights in China after the fall of "the Gang of Four" in 1976:[6]

> While I am imprisoned in a cage of pitch darkness
> Still able to endure the pain from torture,
> I will struggle to rise, bite open my fingers,
> and with my blood write on the wall: Believe in life!
> After I have gone through all hardships of life
> Dying at dawn surrounded by my posterity,
> I will summon my last breath with all my strength,
> Crying as loudly and clearly as I can: Believe in life! ...
>
> If the earth goes round and round without ceasing,
> If history has a new journey to make,
> If my children and grandchildren go on living,
> Then I: Believe in the future! Believe in life![7]

What a powerful ode to life! What a strong faith in tomorrow despite bitter disappointment of yesterday and cruel realities of today! And what a magnificent hope in the power of life reaching out to eternity! This is the ode of the people. This is their confession of faith. And this is their hymn of hope. Do we not hear in this people's ode Jesus' ode? Do we not recognize in this people's faith Jesus' faith? Do we not encounter in this people's hope the hope of Jesus?

Australian Aborigines also echo such ode of life when they say: Land is my Mother! There is something sacred about their land. It is deeply human. It is profoundly religious. It is inviolable. In the land they reach down to the roots of their life. There they are in tune with the rhythms of life. There they are in communion with the source of their life. When they work the land, they are engaged in the sacred act of bringing life into being. And when they return to the land at the end of their life's journey, they return to the womb of the mother-earth, not to die, but to live. To rob them of their land is, then, to rob them of their life. To rape their land is to rape their Mother. To destroy their land is to destroy their eternity. Land is their right to life, power, and eternity. "Land is my Mother!" Jesus would say amen to this. He would never say to the Australian Aborigines: "Give up your claim to the land."

Jesus' Statue Is Not Jesus

"Isn't this true, Jesus?" asks Leper. "What do you say?" But Jesus does not reply — the Jesus pietà encased in cement with a gold crown on his head. This Jesus looks rigid and stiff; he cannot move. He is not a bit like Mary's son who walked the length and breath of Palestine. This Jesus is silent; he cannot talk. He has lost the power of speech. He bears no resemblance to that workman who talked a lot to the crowds that thronged him. And the eyes of this Jesus! These eyes do not shine with light, wisdom, and love. They are cold, without fire and passion. They are not the intense eyes of that man from Nazareth who relentlessly saw through the hypocrisy of the religious leaders and looked at beggars, prostitutes, and outcasts with infinite compassion.

There is one thing, though, in this Jesus pietà that shines, moves, talks, and impresses. It is the gold crown on his head! The crown shines with golden splendor in the cold wintry night. It commands adoration from the people who worship gold. It speaks with authority in the world in which all that glitters counts. It impresses vain church leaders, autocratic rulers, and greedy company presidents. But it defeats lepers, beggars, and prostitutes. The motionless and emotionless Jesus wearing a dazzlingly brilliant gold crown. What a grotesque combination! What a cruel irony! If this is not a crude invention of religious piety gone astray, what is it, then?

"Isn't it true, Jesus?" Leper asks the Jesus statue in a beseeching voice. If only Jesus would answer and say yes, or just nod his head in agreement. But from that gold crown on the head of the Jesus statue Leper seems to be hearing something different. It seems to be saying to him: "Stay silent, don't fight, turn the other cheek, obey the masters, give your land rights away, forget your human rights, fear the military authorities!" Is this what Jesus is really saying? Is this what he is urging us to do? Is this the *real* Jesus speaking?

Leper rubs his eyes and looks at the Jesus pietà once again. He cannot believe what he is hearing is true. For he remembers that Jesus began his work with a powerful proclamation in the synagogue of Nazareth, his native town:

> The Spirit of the Lord is upon me
> because he has anointed me;
> He has sent me to announce good news to the poor,
> to proclaim release for prisoners
> and recovery of sight for the blind;
> to let the broken victims go free,
> to proclaim the year of the Lord's favor.
>
> (Luke 4:17–19)

This is a strong manifesto for social and political change. This is the powerful message of God's reign, the good news that also has been making a lot of difference to a lot of people in Asia.

There is a painting called *Freedom* by Abubakar from Indonesia. In the painting a prisoner stands erect against a dark prison wall, his outstretched hands almost reaching the iron bars above. The outside world is partly visible through those iron bars. In contrast to the gloomy prison cell, the prisoner's body, though thin and bony, seems bursting with the energy and power of the spirit within, declaring at the top of its voice "Freedom!" against all forces of tyranny. Freedom in bondage, faith in the midst of adversity, and strength when robbed of all power — this is what the painter himself experienced in his own imprisonment. This is a confession of faith through an art form. Seeing it, how can we not believe in the power of life over against the power of death? How can there be no resurrection from the depths of death on the cross?

It is the powerful message of God's reign to which the painting *Freedom* testifies. The same testimony also comes from a leader of the peasants in the Philippines:

> You know, before we heard all these things about God wanting us to be free, we were like dumb beasts, like our own carabaos. In the morning you wake up and lead the carabao to the water or to the fields, and it obeys. You put a yoke on the carabao, and it just stands there. You tie the plow, you bring the beast to the furrow, and it goes along. A dumb animal, with no mind or will or purpose of its own. But now it's different. We understand something of what human dig-

nity is, of the dignity of God's children. We know we can think, too. Decide, too. That we can say Yes; we can say No. That not all the decisions and plans and ideas of those who are "above us" are right and compatible with our dignity and rights as human beings.[8]

We are not like our own carabaos! What a liberating thought after centuries of servitude! An exciting future beckons. Social, political, and religious bondage must now be broken! Those Philippine peasants are not unlike the peasants of Jesus' day who tried to devour and digest each and every word of his message of God's reign. "Now it's different," they say. "We understand something of what human dignity is, of the dignity of God's children."

Isn't it true, Jesus? Leper continues to ask, for it is still his lot to suffer. In spite of the difference the awakening of the people has made to Asia today, the world of Asia is still a prison of suffering. No matter where you turn, you are confronted with human tragedies — personal, national, and regional, staggering you and making your heart sink. There is nothing to boast about in suffering. Suffering is the pain we feel in our flesh and bones. There is nothing virtuous about suffering. It is a vice that like sulfuric acid destroys the beauty and grace of humanity. And suffering is an evil force mobilized by a satanical power to stop the flow of time, to deprive the world of future, and to take away hope from human beings. Suffering is of course no monopoly of Asian peoples. It strikes men, women, and children in the East and in the West, in the South and in the North. The entire world, even the whole creation, lies exposed to the assault from the destructive power of suffering. As Paul so poignantly puts it: "Up to the present, we know, the whole created universe groans in all its parts as if in the pangs of childbirth" (Rom. 8:22). He could not have been more right.

But suffering in Asia has a particularly sinister and ugly face. "More Asians are hungry, homeless, unemployed and illiterate," it is reported, "than all the rest of the world put together. More men and women are despised, humiliated, cheated; more suffer the tyranny of governments and oppressive elites, and the fear and shame that tyranny brings, than all the rest of the world combined."[9] This is the Asia betrayed by the prosperous Hong Kong, the orderly Singapore, the industrialized Japan, and by pseudo-democracy in most Asian countries.

This is our Mother-Asia. But she has not lain prostrate before the tyranny of suffering. Suffering has given the peoples of Asia their history. True, it is the history of suffering and pain. But it *is* history. We remember the history of our own nation by the sufferings our forebears went through. We feel history in our own person through the pain that disfigures the face of Asia today. And we entrust our history to the future generations, knowing that suffering and pain will fall upon them also. Suffering makes our history really historical. It makes our history truly contextual. It exhibits the saddest and the ugliest in humanity, but it also calls forth the best and the noblest in us to create room in the space of pain and to strive for a new time of joy within the old time of mourning. History is not just dates and places. History is people. History is the story of how people live and die, love and hate, suffer and hope. If this is history, Asia is abundant with history, as abundant as the enormous numbers of its inhabitants.

Here is a Thai song that tells us what the history of the people in Asia can be like:

> At dawn I rise
> Look at the earth, gaze
> at the sky.
> A farmer in the wind, I
> eat off the land.
>
> Unnumbered seasons pass.
> The fields
> crawl with our children.
> Ages that fade into each other
> undisturbed, now end.
> From cities come
> the men who think they're
> God —
> They scrape, they gouge
> and suck me out —
> my buffalo, my ox,
> the piece of earth I stand on;
> a landless beast that sells its sweat
> and gets just half of what it makes.
> Numbed, sick at heart I am
> a man no different from an ox.
>
> I wait for my luck to turn.
> I wait for fate to change.
> I starve and wait for earth
> and wait
> for heaven —
> fields overgrown with
> debts.[10]

History happens when people's luck refuses to turn, when their fate shows no sign of change, and when their fields are overgrown with debts. His-

tory is not created by an empty trust in heaven. It is not forged by
messianic pretensions of religious and political leaders. History is hatched
in people's suffering. It grows in their instinctive will to live and die
as human beings. And it bursts into the world through people's power
to hope.

Is this not true, Jesus? Leper looks up at the Jesus pietà hoping for
a yes answer. But that Jesus stays silent. His mouth is shut tight. His
eyes look in the distance. His ears do not seem to catch Leper's question. Leper feels a little embarrassed. Am I asking a stupid question?
he wonders aloud. The silence puzzles and confuses him. If only Jesus
would break the silence and say something! Then his suffering would be
somehow more bearable.

Who Is the Real Jesus?

But the gold-crowned Jesus does not seem interested in the least in that
Thai farmer waiting for his luck to turn. Nor is he moved by the pathetic
sight of Leper begging him for an answer. That Jesus is absurdly out of
place in the history of Asian peoples. Is he an imposter? Is he a pretender?
Is he a fake? If he is an imposter who does not see why God has much
to do with the people of Asia, then where is the real Jesus? If he is a
pretender standing for a God who remains aloof from the histories and
cultures of Asian nations, then where can the real Jesus be? And if he is
a fake incapable of hearing the suffering humanity in Asia, where, then,
must the real Jesus be?

At last it begins to dawn on Leper that the gold-crowned Jesus is not
the real Jesus. This is a very important discovery for him. He must help
Beggar, his fellow sufferer, to realize this. He puts a question to the latter: Who is Jesus? Beggar takes the question in jest. But even in jest the
earnestness of the question becomes very poignant.

BEGGAR: Hah! Your stomach has been empty for so long your head's become empty as well. Jesus is the one standing over there with open
hands (*points to statue*). Now do you understand? See, that guy over
there (*points to the Jesus statue again*).

LEPER: That's Jesus! You talk like the biggest fool in a village of fools.
That's cement made to look like Jesus. That's not what I mean. I
mean the *real Jesus*.

BEGGAR: Real Jesus. Who is the real Jesus?

LEPER: Do you know or don't you?

BEGGAR: Hell, if I know, would I be squatting here with you, living like
this in this shit? Do you have to act as a leftover cowhead?[11]

Who is the real Jesus? Beggar wants to know. If that cement Jesus with a gold crown is not the real Jesus, then who is?

The search for the real Jesus is soon to take an astonishing turn. A dramatic moment arrives when the cement Jesus at long last opens his mouth and speaks to Leper:

> I have been closed up in this stone for a long, long time . . . entombed in this dark, lonely, suffocating prison. I have longed to talk to you, the kind and poor people like yourself, and share your suffering. I can't begin to tell you how long I have waited for this day. . . . this day when I would be freed from my prison, this day of liberation when I would live and burn again as a flame inside you, inside the very depths of your misery. But now you have finally come. And because you have come close to me I can speak now. You are my rescuer.[12]

"You are my rescuer," Jesus says to Leper. This has not been heard of before. Leper must be dumbfounded. Why has Jesus said such a thing? What does he really mean? Why am I important to him? Why does he count on me to live and burn again as a flame?

The real Jesus and the people in suffering. The real Jesus and men and women striving for freedom and justice. The real Jesus and human persons longing for life, for eternal life. Jesus cannot be Jesus apart from such people. Jesus is not real unless he is with them in their daily struggle. This is the meaning of what Jesus said to Leper. Here is, then, a clue to the question of the real Jesus. Here is the secret of the historical Jesus. And here is an entry into the mystery of the "messiah" who enables people to have faith in the God of love and compassion in the world of greed and selfishness. Ordinary people like you and me, like Beggar and Leper, are part of this clue and this secret. Is this not a most exciting discovery in the quest for the real Jesus?

Of course that cement Jesus with a gold crown is not the real Jesus. That is the false Jesus adulterated by the riches of this world. That is the pseudo-Jesus venerated through pompous liturgy. That is the doctrinaire Jesus encased in a system of rigid doctrines. That Jesus has no heart for the people. That Jesus cannot understand the Asian spirituality that lives in hope in the midst of suffering. That Jesus cannot make sense of Asian history filled with human tragedies and aspirations. In short, that Jesus stands aloof from history as people, culture as men, women, and children, and religion as human persons.

But the real Jesus has spoken at last! "I have waited for this day," Leper hears Jesus saying, "this day when I would be freed from my prison, this day when I would live and burn again as a flame inside you, inside the very depths of your misery!" The gold-crown has vanished

from his head — the gold-crown that has separated him from the real
world, made him inaccessible to the people, and created a terrible distortion of God's ways with suffering humanity. The real Jesus who has
spoken wears now a crown of thorns. His emaciated face seems no longer
able to hold back the passion of his pain. And his words are those of the
dying Jesus on the cross, mustering the last drop of his strength, beseeching God for help: "My God, my God, why have you forsaken me?" What
a cry! On the cross confronted with death inflicted on him by unjust political and religious powers, Jesus utters the cry of Leper and Beggar, the
cry of those who suffer oppression, the cry of human beings who refuse
to believe that injustice, bondage, and death have the last word.

People Hermeneutic

A decisive change has taken place — change from the cold, muted, gold-
crowned Jesus to the Jesus of passion who speaks. And Leper and Beggar
have something to do with the change! This is strange, is it not? It is
strange to those of us who have known Jesus in traditional theology as
"the very God and the very Man," a metaphysical concept difficult to
grasp in a historical sense. But the change is decisive. *People are now
clues to who the real Jesus is* — people who are poor, outcast, and socially
and politically oppressed. What Jesus has said and done is not compre-
hensible apart from men, women, and children who suffer in body and
spirit. The life and work of Jesus grow out of the close relationships developed between him and the people. "Because you have come close to
me," he said to Leper, "I can speak now." People come so close to him
that he has to speak the truth, to point to where God's reign is, and to walk
the road of suffering. Jesus the messiah is not made in one day. Jesus the
Christ is not called into being out of the blue. Jesus comes into his own
as the savior and as the Christ as he becomes more and more deeply absorbed in the impacts that men, women, and children, troubled in body
and spirit, make on him. Christological hermeneutic has to be "people
hermeneutic."

People touch Jesus' heart. Jesus' heart is vulnerable to people's
touching. In turn Jesus touches people's hearts. People's hearts are also
vulnerable to Jesus' touching. This is not a casual touching between
strangers. Nor is it a ceremonial touching on a state occasion or on a religious occasion. It is a touching that reaches the source of our life, that
evokes the power of life, that signals the hope of life. In this touching we
touch the heart of God — the source, the power, and the hope of life.

The moving story of the death of Lazarus (John 11:1–44) tells us how
powerful such "heart-touching" can be between Jesus and people. Lazarus
is dead, Jesus was told. The news of Lazarus' death and the extreme sor-

row of his sisters must have touched Jesus' heart deeply. Death renders a person into a nonperson. It turns a living life to a dead memory. It marks the victory of decay over growth. It puts an end to hope and future. With death hope vanishes and future ceases. In the death of Lazarus Jesus once again stared at the abyss of emptiness and the futility of life.

Four expressions in the story describe how deeply Jesus was touched by Lazarus' death. Jesus "sighed heavily" and "was deeply moved" when he heard the weeping of Mary and her companions (John 11:33). He "wept" when they confirmed the death of Lazarus by offering to take him to the grave (11:34). And he "sighed deeply" as he reached the tomb (11:38). How could death destroy life? How could it make life-less? Jesus sighed heavily and deeply. The power of death to create fear and sorrow among the living, the power to render the world colorless and joyless — Jesus was confronted with that power. And standing in front of the tomb where life is extinguished and death reigns, Jesus wept. Death is the space where God seems absent. Death is the power that defies life. Death is the eternal pause and silence of life born in the midst of hope and excitement.

Facing such death, Jesus "was deeply moved." What could be going on in his mind? Was he hearing an echo of the cry of God's forsakenness — the cry he himself was to utter on the cross? Was he muttering to himself, "it is finished" — the last words he himself was to say before his own death? Death of Lazarus, death of human beings, his own death, death of the creation, and death of God — for a moment Jesus must have felt himself sinking into the abyss of pitch darkness. All movements come to a standstill. All creation ceases to whisper, speak, and sing through trees, birds, insects, mountains, rivers, and human beings. The only thing audible is the tomb. The tomb could be heard in the weeping of the bereaved, in the sighing of the friends, in the solemn faces of the bystanders. Death reigns from the tomb.

But Jesus finally broke the silence ruled by death. From his mouth these words rang out: "I am the resurrection and I am Life" (11:25). What powerful words! They echo God's words of creation in the beginning. They anticipate the words of a new creation at the end of time. Life is pronounced in the world seized by death. Resurrection is declared from the very place terrorized by death. Jesus' message of life does not come from a paradise that knows no death. It comes from within the world threatened and tyrannized by death. It sums up the will of the people to live and to live eternally. It carries God's power of life promised to all humanity.

The messianic contour of Jesus becomes increasingly sharpened as he absorbs more and more into himself the struggle of the people to live in faith, hope, and love. *God is the story of Jesus. And Jesus is the story of the people.* "Who is the real Jesus?" Beggar asked Leper. The real Jesus is not that cement Jesus pietà with a gold crown. The ready-made Jesus encased in a statue, enshrined in a cathedral, dictated by church traditions, or crystallized in doctrine is not the real Jesus. The real Jesus is the love of God that creates miracles of life in the world. He is the pain of God mingled with the pain of humanity. He is the hope of God that people manifest in the midst of despair. He is the eternal life of God that people live in spite of death. Jesus is, lives, and becomes real when people, with unflagging faith in God, engage each other to bring about a new world out of the ruins of the old world. The real Jesus is the light of God's salvation that men, women, and children kindle in the darkness of hell. The real Jesus is that power of God's truth that people manifest in the face of the power of lies wielded by the powers and principalities of this world. Jesus is the story of such people. And being the story of such people, Jesus is the story of God.

NOTES

1. See Kim Chi Ha, *The Gold-Crowned Jesus and Other Writings* (Maryknoll, N.Y.: Orbis Books, 1978).

2. Ibid., pp. 85–87.

3. Ibid., p. 119.

4. See *No Place in the Inn*, Voices of Minority Peoples in Asia (Hong Kong: Christian Conference of Asia–Urban Rural Mission, 1979), pp. 32–33.

5. Ibid., p. 15.

6. "The Gang of Four," led by Jiang Qing, wife of Mao Zedong, got China involved in the horrendous chaos of the Cultural Revolution of a decade beginning in 1966.

7. Kuo Lu-Seng, "Believe in Life," see *Peking Spring and Other Selected Poems*, Wei Chin-Sheng, ed. (Hong Kong: P'ing Ming Publishing House, 1980), pp. 293–295. Translation from the Chinese original by C. S. Song.

8. This quotation and the reference to Abubakar's painting come from *Living in Christ with People*, twelve meditations on the theme of the Seventh Assembly of the Christian Conference of Asia (CCA) in Bangalore, India, 1981, Ron O'Grady, ed. (Singapore: CCA, 1981), p. 6.

9. Ibid., p. 99.

10. This song appeared in the *Bangkok Post*, August 23, 1981, and was reproduced in *In Clenched Fists of Struggle*, Report of the Workshop on the Impact of TNC's in Asia (Hong Kong: Urban Rural Mission–Christian Conference of Asia, 1981), p. 91.

11. Kim Chi Ha, *The Gold-Crowned Jesus*, p. 107.

12. Ibid., pp. 121–122.

CHAPTER 1

Controversy with God

What do you make of Jesus? This is the main question that preoccupies us here. But why the question again? Has it not been answered already in the history of Christianity? Has not the Christian church been about the business of Jesus for all these centuries? Have not the best, and also not so best, theological minds told us what Jesus must mean for us? Have not "these witnesses to faith around us like a cloud" (Heb. 12:1) been testifying to Jesus not only through words but often with blood? The question, it seems, may turn out to be not about Jesus, but about faith in him and our faithfulness to him. Certainly, the question has a lot to do with ourselves, our world, and how human beings live, believe, struggle, and hope; it should at the same time lead us to a deeper experience of him who, like us, also lived, believed, struggled, and hoped in the world of conflicts and pain.

It can be argued, and it has been argued, that there is nothing more to say about Jesus other than what the Creed of Nicaea (325 C.E.) has to tell us about him. As a matter of fact, most churches in East and West, in North and South, consider these words of the Creed as standard in their confession of faith in Jesus:

> And [we believe] in one Lord Jesus Christ, the Son of God, begotten of the Father as only begotten, that is, from the essence of the Father, God from God, Light from Light, true God from true God, begotten not created, of the same essence as the Father, through whom all things came into being, both in heaven and on earth; who for us human beings and for our salvation came down and was incarnate, becoming human. He suffered and the third day he rose and ascended into the heavens. And he will come to judge both the living and the dead.

The language is lofty and beyond the comprehension not only of ordinary believers, but perhaps also of fine theological minds. But it seems to have said all that is needed to be said about Jesus. The fact of the matter, however, is that this authoritative statement on Jesus has not put to rest theological curiosity of the succeeding generations of Christians. Today the question about Jesus still preoccupies not only Christians but an increasing number of people who do not profess the Christian faith.

Or take another creed almost universally recited by Christians at worship service. I am referring to the Apostles' Creed, which took its definitive form around 700 C.E. "And [I believe] in Jesus Christ," the voice rises from the pews in unison:

> God's only Son, our Lord, Who was conceived by the Holy Spirit, born of the Virgin Mary, suffered under Pontius Pilate, was crucified, dead, and buried. He descended to hell, on the third day rose again from the dead, ascended to heaven, sits at the right hand of God the Father almighty, thence He will come to judge the living and the dead.

This is a truly ecumenical creed. Christians, whatever their ethnic background or confessional identity, recite it in their respective languages. It is not as theologically heady as the Nicene Creed. Although there is a big jump from Jesus' birth to his suffering, leaving his ministry entirely unaccounted for, the Creed still admirably summarizes Jesus' life in the language close to that we find in the Bible. What more light, we are prompted to ask, can be shed on Jesus? But again, the fact of the matter is that the quest for the real Jesus has not ceased. And as we are more and more exposed to the world of pluralism that both bewilders and excites us, we feel compelled to ask again what we can really make of Jesus.

Whatever we may make of Jesus — prophet, messiah, Lord, or Son of God — there is one historical fact that cannot be ignored, the fact called Jesus of Nazareth. As a village in Galilee in Jesus' time Nazareth was not a significant place. This is fully reflected in Nathanael's surprise when he was first told about Jesus from Nazareth (John 1:43–51). "Nazareth!" he is reported to have exclaimed. "Can anything good come from Nazareth?" Politically, economically, and even religiously, Nazareth might have nothing to boast about as Jerusalem or Samaria did. But as a human community it has to be as important as other villages and cities. It also stands for a world in which human dramas are played out in an infinite variety of ways, exposing conflicts and contradictions in human relationships on the one hand and, on the other, revealing the power of healing within individual souls, in families, and in society.

Nazareth, an ancient village in which Jesus grew up and still identifiable as a village in today's Palestine, cannot be replaced by any other village or city. It has its own particular place in geography and history. Nazareth is no Jerusalem. For that matter, it is no Bangkok either. Nor is it Manila. But as a world of human dramas of conflicts and hopes, a community in which love and hate struggle for supremacy, Nazareth is no different from other human communities. It is another Jerusalem. It is another Bangkok, another Manila. In this sense Nazareth plays a twofold role in our effort to understand the profound theological insight of "the Word that became flesh" in Jesus of Nazareth. On the one hand Nazareth calls us to focus our attention on Jesus in relation to the world of human dramas in which he lived, labored, and died. It, on the other hand, inspires us to find in Jesus of Nazareth someone who both commands the faith of Christians and shares the historical destiny of all human beings. If, then, we must speak of Jesus of Nazareth, we must also speak of Jesus of Bangkok, Jesus of Manila, for example. What would this Jesus of Bangkok mean? Who would this Jesus of Manila be? This is what we are going to explore here.

At this point we are prompted to make our approach to Jesus different from that made by traditional Christian theology. Can we not, we ask, begin with Jesus of Manila, Jesus of Bangkok, Jesus of Taipei, or Jesus of Colombo instead of always starting out with Jesus of Nazareth? In these cities of Asia we are dealing with worlds different from the world that is Nazareth. This is obvious. But these worlds, old or new, Pacific or Mediterranean, are parts of the one world of God with common human tragedies and aspirations. For those of us with our roots in Asia is it not, then, right and proper to begin our approach to Jesus from where we are, from Colombo for instance? From Colombo to Nazareth, and back to Colombo again. This is the theological movement we want to attempt here. As this movement back and forth continues, we may discover much deeper meanings of Jesus for us today. Here is, then, an invitation to join a "christological journey" that begins with a story from Sri Lanka, from that Buddhist part of God's world. What you are about to hear is a story of human cruelty, a story bearing the extreme anguish of the human soul that develops into a controversy with God, at least with the kind of God fabricated by those who hold political and religious power.

A Letter to the Prime Minister

The island-nation of Sri Lanka, situated in the Indian Ocean and separated from India by a narrow stretch of water, was disrupted by communal strife and ruptured by racial violence. On political, religious, and economic grounds the majority Sinhalese community (72 percent of the population) vented its hatred on the minority Tamil community (20 percent). Words of protest, written in the form of a letter to Prime Minister Jayewaredene by an anonymous Tamil, give a glimpse of racial conflict in that land of Buddhist culture:

When my father Manikkam's house was ransacked and he was slaughtered to death in the South five years back — just one month after you came to power; when my cousin Parvathy was defiled, deflowered, by five thugs in the old Estate; when my brother Inpam was rudely awakened in the middle of the night, taken in a jeep, and his skull abandoned on the Pannai causeway; when just a few weeks back, my younger brother, Davidson, was assaulted and sent to the nerve-tingling Panagoda; at these times, out of my loneliness, despair and desperation I longed avidly to hear from you. One word from you would have given me hope to face an environment which is hostile, inhuman, and frustrating. Why were you silent?...

To be frank, I was highly honored by your concluding invitation to join you and "travel together to the goal of a Free and Just Society." But after five long years of travelling with you I find we are far, far away from our goal. And many are the times you have abandoned me in the middle of the road. So adieu! I realize I must travel alone now if I am to reach that destined goal, and the path may be lonely, rugged, and bloody![1]

This is a sad and angry letter from a victim of racial violence. It is full of forebodings for the society of that tropical South Asian country torn by strife between two human communities divided for reasons of race, religion, and political interests. The tragedy portrayed in the letter is not Sri Lanka's alone. It is the tragedy of human community both in the East and in the West from ancient times to the present day.

Reading the letter, we cannot but ask: Why such senseless killings? But the fact is that human history is filled with such senseless killings. Inscribed on the pages of history are horror stories of human "holocausts." The most recent example still vivid in our memories is the Nazi holocaust of millions of Jews during World War II. It was a hideous political crime that happens again and again in the annals of history. But the crime is not committed in the name of politics alone. It can be a religious crime too. In the name of religion and on behalf of its God, human community has committed holocausts. Practically no religion is innocent of religious persecutions. This is a supreme irony. A religion that preaches love can turn itself into an instrument of hate. It can resort to destruction of lives in defense of salvation of the soul. And when politics and religion join forces in the destruction of the enemies and opponents, fear and anguish fill the hearts of people and stifle their humanity. This, as we shall see, is the story of Jesus' crucifixion. The sad reality is that the story is repeated over and over again in human history with almost predictable regularity. It tells us that we human beings seem destined to be at enmity with one another even for religious reasons. The atrocity described in the letter of an anonymous Tamil person to the prime minister of Sri Lanka is but one of the latest human tragedies symbolized by the story of Jesus' death.

History of course has a brighter side. It records human achievements in arts, literature, science, and technology. It also testifies to the genuine religious devotion of women and men who dedicate their lives to the well-being of suffering people and to the betterment of a society. This is all true. Prophets in ancient Israel come to mind at once. It was they who upheld the love and truth of God as the most fundamental principles of human life and community. But for them the history of Israel would have been just another history buried in the ruins of the past with no message for us today. The massive concentration of indomitable prophetic spirit makes it stand out in the records of humanity. Other religious communities are also capable of producing their own prophets who make truth and love shine in the darkness of power politics and debasement of basic human values. They ennoble the pages of human history and retain our faith that life and history have meanings beyond insane acts of violence and destruction. And the fact of the matter is that the world has been under the powerful impact of the redeeming power of that obscure Jesus of Nazareth ever since he, like a comet, appeared on the horizon of the Palestinian world two thousand years ago. His impact has grown steadily "in Jerusalem, and all over Judaea and Samaria, and away to the ends of the earth" (Acts 1:8). And how he has inspired and continues to inspire men and women to be bearers of the torch of love in the midst of hate and the light of truth when lies prevail! Because of him God continues to be the living presence in the world of suffering and tribulations.

Still, the fact is that redemptive power at work in human community has to take account of history as testimonies to human sinfulness. I am not saying that there must be an inevitable relation between human sin and God's redeeming love. I am not advocating a crude theology with an assertion that human beings must sin in order for God to reveal God's saving love. There is no biblical and theological justification for the kind of Christian faith that predicates paradise regained on paradise lost. God's boundless love does not have to presuppose the heinous sinfulness of humanity. This is a muddled sort of theology that has dominated the teaching of the Christian church and the piety of Christians for centuries. There is no theological ground for a causal relationship between sin and grace. God's grace is grace even if human beings do not sin. Grace does not derive its efficacy from sin. Such derivative grace is no grace. It would in fact become an accomplice of sin. To be unclear about this, to be confused about the relationship between God's saving grace and human sin, is to vitiate our understanding of who God is and what God does in the world. Perhaps because of confused theology such as this, we as Christians have tended to distort our perception of people of other religions as people living entirely in sin and wholly deserving God's wrath.

What, then, is this sinister thing called sin? What does its sinisterness consist of? What does the story such as told in the letter from Sri Lanka tell us about sin? What is in sin that restrains us from having naive faith in human progress? And what does it teach us about human ability to bring about the best possible world for the greatest number of people? Such questions have to lead us to a closer examination of the Christian church's teaching on sin. They help us to remove the religious camouflage of sin and stare it in the face.

Sin is one of the main Christian concepts. Repentance as the basis of religious conversion and renewal of life presupposes sin. Traditionally, it is understood as disobedience to God when religious laws are broken, sacred taboos violated, and moral codes established by the religious community infringed upon. Sin is primarily offense against God. "Against thee, thee only, I have sinned," says the psalmist in a prayer of repentance (Ps. 51:4). Crimes committed against other human beings, injustice done to them, are all too quickly transferred from the human court of justice to the divine court of appeal. The result is elaborate rituals of sacrifice to induce God's pardon and to avert disasters as divine punishments. Out of this are developed, as will be discussed later, the concept of God as the God of retribution and the idea of atonement as having more to do with satisfying God's glory and restoring the right relationship with God than facing the social consequences of sin and working toward healing human relationships. We can, then, go away from the rituals of repentance and forgiveness only to continue the practice of discrimination on the ground of race, sex, class, or creed. Is it by accident that a most infamous form of racism is practiced in South Africa by the whites who justify the apartheid on the basis of Christian faith? Is it also accidental that a political ruler could be a dictator and a Christian at the same time as in the case of the Philippines under Ferdinand Marcos and Chile under General Augusto Pinochet?

To relate sin exclusively to the so-called disobedience to God does not get to the heart of sin. It does not touch the terrible nature of sin — its ability to destroy not God but human beings. Sin, however powerful, cannot destroy God. It is not capable of such a feat. The God who can be defeated, overcome, and destroyed by human sin is not God. Traditional Christian theology has created an image of God who is morbidly afraid of human sin. That God is not the true God. It is an idol made by human hands. Throughout human history many such idols have risen and fallen, sharing the same fate as the rise and fall of the nations. These idols are projections of human interests, masks of religious power, or personi-

fications of political ideology. The history of such idols is the history of
human sin.

Here the terrible nature of sin — its destructiveness — is fully disclosed. Sin with the horrendous power of destruction is not just a religious
concept. It is not merely a metaphysical construct. Nor is it no more than
a philosophical idea. It is a demonic power hidden in the depths of human
beings and lurking in the abyss of human community, biding its time to
strike and to destroy. For its work of destruction it employs all means at
its disposal — political, military, economic, ideological, even religious.
Sin is human power turned demonic, inflicting pain, terror, and death on
human persons and tearing apart human community. In that letter to the
prime minister of Sri Lanka we see how the demonic power of sin is at
work. And it is the work of the same demonic power of sin that the world
witnessed in the crucifixion of Jesus.

How deeply sin touches and affects human beings! That is why it also
touches and affects God so deeply — God who made human beings to be
in the relationships of love, justice, and peace. The story of the cross has
to be, first and foremost, the story of Jesus of Nazareth. It then becomes
the story of God. It has to unfold itself on earth and not in heaven. One of
the most powerful indictments against sin as the demonic power of human
self- and mutual destructiveness comes from the pen of a Chinese writer
by the name of Lu Xun (1881–1939) at the time when China was going
through one of the most turbulent periods of its history.

Human Power of Destructiveness

Lu Xun was a preeminent writer, powerful essayist, and biting political
satirist during China's years of national humiliation at the hands of foreign powers and of internal corruption perpetrated by those in power in
the early part of the twentieth century. "His pen," it was said, "was like a
rapier. With one sudden stroke it would fatally pierce the very heart of its
objective."[2]

It is in one of his short stories entitled "A Madman's Diary" that Lu
Xun exposed the history of China in a most penetrating fashion as a history of human destructiveness. As the "Madman" saw it, demonic power
was at work in China throughout its history, corroding Chinese humanity, corrupting Chinese society, and threatening the Chinese nation with
destruction. Lu Xun let the Madman speak thus:

Desperately unsleeping, I carefully look it [the history of China]
over again and again for half the night, and at last find between
the lines that it is full of the same word "cannibalism"!... Having

unconsciously practiced cannibalism for four thousand years, I am
awakening now and feel ashamed to face a genuine human being![3]

Lu Xun could have added that he equally felt ashamed to face God because of the terrible fact that his reading of Chinese history had disclosed
to him. The history of China, often extolled as a glorious history of five
thousand years of high civilization, is in fact a history of cannibalism!
Is this not also true of the history of other nations? Is this not the history of humanity as a whole? And does not the cross of Jesus stand out
in that history of cannibalism as a most hideous manifestation of human
sinfulness?

The story of the Madman unfolds in this way. The Madman asked a
friend of his a point-blank question: "Is it right to eat human beings?"
To his friend the question must have sounded silly. He replied, smiling:
"Where there is no famine how can one eat human beings?" At least he
admitted that there was cannibalism in the extremity of famine, but beyond that the question meant to him nothing more than a joke. Or does
the question come from a deranged mind? Is it for no reason that the man
who asked the question is known as "the Madman"? The friend must have
wondered. But the Madman was not to be put off by the reaction of his
friend. He persisted and summoned up courage to repeat the question: "Is
it right?" The friend realized that the Madman was serious. At last he
"looked disconcerted and muttered, No . . . "

> "No? Then why do they still do it?"
> "What are you talking about?"
> "They are eating humans now in Wolf Club Village, and you can
> see it written all over the books, in fresh red ink."
> His expression changed. He grew ghastly pale. "It may be so,"
> he said staring at me. "That's the way it's always been . . . "
> "Does that make it right?"

Ours is a society made up of "eaters" of human beings. It was Lu Xun's
self-appointed mission to expose this brutal reality and lay it before the
conscience of the nation.

The story is an allegory, of course. Lu Xun was referring to the oppression, exploitation, massacre, and mass murder abundant in China
throughout its history. He made that history of sin speak out in this
poignant story. Even the Madman's friend had to admit finally: "That's
the way it's always been." The Madman followed that admission at once
with a question: "Does that make it right?" Of course it doesn't. In that
question of the Madman we perceive the deep sadness, profound bitterness, and irrepressible anger of a prophetic mind weighed down by

mountains of human tragedies accumulated in the long history of the past and repeated in the socio-political turmoils of the present time.

The conversation proved to be too much for the Madman's friend. He turned away to go, but before leaving he said to the Madman: "I refuse to discuss it with you. Anyway you shouldn't talk about it. It's wrong for anyone to talk about it." In this way true history gets suppressed, especially by those in power. Official history is all too often fabrication of the court historians and government officials who practice the art of "reporting only what is good while concealing what is unpleasant" (*pau hsi pu pau yu*), to use a Chinese expression. It takes the courage and foresightedness of people such as the prophets of the Hebrew Scriptures, for example, or writers like Lu Xun, to recover the suppressed history, correct the history falsified by the rulers, and bring to light what actually happened in the past and what is happening now.

The Madman reacted to his friend's parting remark with uncontrollable emotion. As he tells it himself: "I leaped up and opened my eyes wide, but the man had vanished. I was soaked with sweat." Lu Xun did not make the Madman reply to his friend in so many words. Instead, his wide-opened eyes and his body soaked with sweat said it all — his chagrin, anger, helplessness could have consumed his friend. Through the Madman Lu Xun must have wanted to shout for all the world to hear: "It's wrong, utterly wrong, for anyone not to talk about it!"

What we see in this Madman is no other than Lu Xun himself, full of anguish for the malaise of his country. But he was not a prophet of doom. His was a call issued to men and women to wake up from their slumber in the tradition and civilization that dehumanized Chinese people for so many centuries. His ardent desire was to inspire them to strive for a better and brighter future for China and to struggle for their freedom and human dignity.

Later the Madman approached his brother and tried to share his concern with him. "Brother, I have something to say to you," he began.

It's nothing much, but I find it hard to say. Brother, probably all primitive people ate a little human flesh to begin with. Later, because their views altered, some of them stopped and tried so hard to do what was right that they changed into humans, into real human beings. But some are still eating people — just like reptiles. . . . When those who eat humans compare themselves with those who don't, how ashamed they must be. Probably much more ashamed than the reptiles are before monkeys.

In ancient times Yi Ya boiled his son for Jie and Zhou to eat; that is the old story. But actually since the creation of the heaven and the earth by Pan Gu human beings have been eating each other, from the

time of Yi Ya's son to the time of Xu Xilin, and from the time of Xu
Xilin down to the man caught in Wolf Club Village. Last year they
executed a criminal in the city, and a consumptive soaked a piece of
bread in the blood and sucked it. . . .[4]

Lu Xun, a sensitive writer full of anguish for the malaise of his country,
revealed in "A Madman's Diary" the monstrous power of destruction at
work in the life and history of all peoples and nations.

What Lu Xun as a writer encountered in his historical experience
is confirmed by psychoanalytical investigation of human persons. Erich
Fromm, an American psychoanalyst, makes this observation in *The
Anatomy of Human Destructiveness:* "Human history is a record of extraordinary destructiveness and cruelty, and human aggression, it seems,
far surpasses that of our animal ancestors, and the human being is, in
contrast to most animals, a real 'killer.' "[5] He then concludes with almost
a sense of helplessness: "Only human beings seem to take pleasure in
destroying life without any reason or purpose other than that of destroying. To put it more generally, only human beings appear to be destructive
beyond the aim of defense and/or of attaining what they need."[6] Is this
not the fact to which human atrocity in war testifies? Does not story
after story of human cruelty in prison and torture chamber, both past
and present, give witness to it? Even religious institutions are capable of
such human destructiveness "beyond the aim of defense." The traditional
teaching of the Christian church on sin has not faced this satanic power of
destruction and cruelty that brings endless tragedies to individual persons
and to the human community as a whole.

No religion, in fact, can claim to have nothing to do with the power
of destructiveness in the course of its history. It is well documented
that human sacrifice was a common practice in ancient times. It is also
common knowledge that religious massacres have taken place between
believers of rival religions. Burning of heretics and witch-hunting have
disgraced the pages of the history of human spiritual development. The
supreme irony is that the satanic power of destruction becomes, under
religious sanction, a sacred power exercised by the religious authorities
against their own members and against members of other religious communities. A war waged in the name of religion can scarcely be less brutal,
less cruel, less horrifying, than other wars.

The God represented in such religious practices is a revengeful God,
a bloodthirsty God, a God to be feared rather than to be loved. It is an
experience of God such as this that shaped much of Christian teaching
of salvation and atonement and contributed to the prejudice of Christians toward people of other faiths and cultures. And here a strange twist
occurs in human religious piety: sin as disobedience to God is turned

around to become the religious virtue of obeying God even to the extent of committing violence against other people in the name of that God.

Small wonder that the Sinhalese community in Sri Lanka, deeply rooted in Buddhist spirituality, is capable of atrocity toward its Tamil neighbors. I have already referred to apartheid in South Africa. Small wonder too that the ruling white majority in South Africa practiced racial discrimination against blacks in the name of its "Christian" God. Is the situation less appalling in Northern Ireland, where Protestants and Catholics have been engaged in a religious-political war for years, in India, where enmity between Sikhs and Hindus breaks out in violence, or in Palestine, where Jews, Christians, and Muslims still have not learned to live in peace with one another? The God in whose name violence is committed, war is waged, and massacres are carried out must be exposed as a false God. That God is created by human political interest and religious prejudice. That God must be unmasked as the embodiment of the human power of destructiveness. This can be a frightening experience. The cost can be very high. To incur the wrath of that false God can be dangerous. It may cost you your freedom, even death. Still, the work of unmasking false Gods must be done. It is done often by victims of destructive power themselves when they are compelled to be engaged in controversy with God out of the depths of their suffering and pain.

Engaging God in Controversy

A religious faith at its deepest level is an earnest controversy between human beings and God. The controversy has to be earnest, as it often involves earnest situations of doubt, despair, and suffering. One will then find the formal language of rituals, ceremonies, or liturgies too slow, too indirect, too inadequate for a controversy with God. Suffering that breeds doubt and despair is not a leisurely matter. We cannot go through it as if we were having a tea party. The formal language of liturgy must turn into a passionate prayer said out loud for God to hear. This is the situation described in that "Letter to the Prime Minister." When my father is murdered, when my sister is abused, suffering becomes acute. When my body is emaciated with hard labor and malnutrition, when my spirit is exhausted by constant fear and uncertainty, then suffering turns my life into a bundle of meaninglessness; it makes no sense any longer to live. It is in an extreme situation such as this — the situation in which senselessness and absurdity fill one's life and threaten one's existence — that controversy between God and human beings becomes earnest and urgent. For here human beings are fighting for the last chance at life. Religion is no longer what we do in our spare time. It is not a pastime that does not have to be taken seriously. It has to do with the ultimate meaning of life. It concerns our destiny. The case has to be taken to the court of God.

Contrary to what the Christian church and its theologians have told us under the name of revelation, it is not God who speaks first in the controversy. It is *always* human beings who speak first. God seems infinitely patient and in no hurry to do anything. There seems to be silence surrounding God — silence ominous and terrifying. Revelation is always more a hindsight than a foresight. It is an afterthought rather than a forethought. Revelation is not something that God does to forestall us. It is not an answer God gives to a question we have not even asked. The understanding of revelation in traditional theology tends to minimize the role played by human beings. This does not quite correspond to our experience of life and faith. Nor does it entirely tally with ways in which some forebears of our faith came to discern the will of God.

And when they engage God in a controversy in the midst of their suffering, they do not whisper; they shout. Overwhelmed by agony and pain, they cannot observe the protocol prescribed by liturgical courtesy; they weep and cry. Confronted by calamities perpetrated by humans and created by nature, they do not ask God meekly why they suffer; they protest loudly for all heaven and earth to hear. But *mere* human beings questioning God and accusing God? Is this not presumptuous? Is this not sacrilegious? Not at all. For as long as human beings still turn to God to question God, the meaning of life is not yet completely gone. Insofar as they still dare to fight God, their faith in the power of God over the human power of destruction is not yet totally shattered.

Human controversy with God is an evidence that human beings are not self-explanatory beings. We are not creators of meanings. We do not possess the key to the ultimate meaning of life and history, the meaning from which all other meanings are derived. The key to that meaning is not in our hands. It must be in the hand of God. That is why we must ask God for explanation. We must press God to tell us why. We need God to be fully present in our search for the last word that explains all other words. We must insist, for example, that God tell us why human beings suffer. Did not Jacob wrestle and struggle with an angel of God until he obtained the promise of God's blessing (Gen. 32:22–32)? "I will not let you go," Jacob persisted, "unless you bless me." We want to pursue God until God unlocks the gate to the mystery of human life in pain. We have no peace until God gives us a glimpse of that vision of history that brings unfulfilled histories to fulfillment. We believe that God has created us human beings to be partakers of the God-meaning that makes sense of human life and enables us to locate human history in the purpose of God for the entire creation. Controversy with God becomes, then, an intense search for the origin and destiny of our life and history in God.

A mere human being in controversy with God! This seems to be what it amounts to. But is this not atheism? No, it is not. Atheists do not address God because they do not believe there is God. They do not bother themselves to question God, for they consider God a projection of human illusion. They do not need God's intervention in human affairs, because for them the only power that can change society and better human life is human power. God is not real enough for them to be engaged in controversy. Nor is God important enough to be included in their journey of life on earth. They will have no part in a religious faith that explains human life and history in relation to a "hypothetical" being called God.

The answer to this atheistic assertion is not more religion, more piety, more show of so-called spirituality. It is the "holier-than-thou" religious propensity that is partly to blame for alienating people from God in the first place. To engage God in controversy is not to be religious in a customary way. It is not just a matter of going to church every Sunday. It does not consist solely in observance of rituals and rites. It is quite different from reciting time-honored creeds and confessions of faith absent-mindedly. It is, in short, not a matter of "holding an incense stick and worshipping gods as others do" (giah hiu^n toe pai), as people in Taiwan would say. You know in your heart of hearts you are facing a formidable partner — a partner who has power over your soul, mind, and body, a partner in whose hand your destiny lies. You are aware that this may be an "all or nothing" contest — either God is for you or God is against you.

When, then, suffering impels you to address God, you are taking an enormous risk from which there is no return. You now have to wrestle with God twenty-four hours a day and seven days a week. Your soul is in turmoil and you draw God into that turmoil. Your spirit is in terrible unrest and you want God to feel it too. This is human faith in its most primitive, naked, and original manifestation. It is a religious expression that discloses the most authentic roots of human existence in God. It is such faith and such religion that we witness in Psalm 88, for example. In that psalm of lament the psalmist "in unrelieved anguish cleaves to God most passionately when God seems to have withdrawn...completely"[7]:

> O Lord, my God, by day I call for help,
> by night I cry aloud in thy presence.
> Let my prayer come before thee,
> hear my loud lament;
> for I have had my fill of woes,
> and they have brought me to the threshold of Sheol.
>
> Thou hast plunged me into the lowest abyss,
> in dark places, in the depths.

Thy wrath rises against me,
thou hast turned on me the full force of thy anger.
Thou hast taken all my friends far from me,
and made me loathsome to them.
I am in prison and cannot escape;
my eyes are failing and dim with anguish.
I have called upon thee, O Lord, every day
and spread out my hands in prayer to thee.

(Ps. 88:1–9)

We do not know what kind of suffering the psalmist is going through. Nor are we told why the person has to suffer. But the suffering must be very great; it must be terribly hard to bear. Otherwise, how could the psalmist dare to blame God for it? "Thou hast plunged me into the lowest depths!" the psalmist bursts out in agony and dismay. This reminds us of another psalmist who called to God "out of the depths" (Ps. 130).

These are called "psalms of lament." Yes, they are. But they are also psalms of protest! "Thou hast plunged me into the lowest abyss!" the psalmist must have shouted in the prayer. Words of protest such as these addressed to God cannot be heard in church any more. In public worship services and at prayer-meetings such protest-language is not tolerated. We have lost the courage to protest to God. We are afraid to be seen as unbelievers. We have been taught to be timid in relation to God, accepting everything as God's will. Is this not the reason why some churches today become socially inactive, politically tame, taking separation from the world as an expression of Christian spirituality? Timid Christians make a timid church. But protesting Christians make a protesting church, protesting what they perceive to be wrong within their own religious community and in their society. Christians who do not dare to protest are innocuous Christians and the church that can do without protest is a harmless church. Innocuous Christians and harmless church do not really know what suffering in the "depths" means. They have removed themselves from the realities of this world. In so doing, they have removed themselves from God as well. For where else can we encounter God except within the realities we face in our daily life?

As a matter of fact, nothing can be more horrible than suffering in the "depths." The "depths" are that underworld at the bottom of the ocean — that dark netherworld in which death, not life, reigns. The "depths" are the region where hope has no meaning, future does not exist, life is synonymous with death. To be abandoned by God in the depths means that God has turned God's back on you, that God is through with you, that God counts you as dead, eternally dead. Is this God still God, this merciless God? Is this God still your God, this apathetic God? Is this God still the Savior-God, this God without compassion? This God who plunges me into the lowest depths and abandons me there cannot be my God. How can I meekly keep silent? How can I refrain from protesting? The quest of a soul for a merciful God, the yearning of the heart for a sympathetic God, the longing of the spirit for a compassionate God, reaches the height of crisis.

This is the crisis of faith. All human beings, regardless of race, religion, or culture, share this crisis of faith. Here is a poem from ancient China in the ninth century B.C.E., composed by a king when a great drought devastated his country:

The drought is excessive
Its fervours become more and more tormenting.
I have not ceased offering pure sacrifices;
From the border altars I have gone to the ancestral temple.
To the [powers] above and below I have presented my offerings and
    then buried them: —
There is no Spirit whom I have not honored.
How-chi is not equal to the occasion;
God does not come to us.
This wasting and ruin of our country, —
Would that it fell [only] on me! . . .

The drought is excessive; —
I struggle, and fear to go away.
How is it I am afflicted with this drought?
I cannot ascertain the cause of it.
In praying for a good year I was abundantly early;
I was not late [in sacrificing] to [the Spirits] of the four quarters and
    of the land.

God in the great heaven
Does not consider me.
Reverent to the intelligent Spirits,
I ought not to be thus object of their anger. . . .

The drought is excessive; —
All is in dispersion, and the bonds of government are relaxed.
Reduced to extremities are the heads of departments;
Full of distress are my chief minister,
The master of the horse, the commander of the guards,
The chief cook, and my attendants.
There is no one who has not [tried to] help [the people];
They have not refrained on the ground of being unable.

I look up to the great heaven; —
Why am I plunged in this sorrow?[8]

Nature is in fury. The country is on the verge of ruin. People are dispersed in desperate search for food. The king has carried out his mandate of heaven responsibly. Still, he and his people are engulfed in this horrendous calamity. But God does not seem to care. God does not show signs of intervention. Who can blame the king if he starts to resent God?

This is an earnest prayer to get a response from God. If "God does not come to us," God must tell us why. If "God in the great heaven does not consider me," there must be a reason. God must not let us "look up to the great heaven" and make us wonder "why we are plunged in this sorrow."

A faith seeking an explanation from God in the depths of suffering! This is what it is. Human beings seem to be born with such faith. Faith facing a tragedy or a calamity more than we can bear, that faith begins to question the God confessed in the creeds, taught by theologians, and worshipped in the ways prescribed by the religious authorities. That faith laments. It pleads. It questions. And it also protests. In Psalm 88 these questions are put directly to God, God in the second person and not in the third person:

> Dost thou work wonders for the dead?
> Shall their company rise up and praise thee?
> Will they speak of thy faithful love in the grave,
>   of thy sure help in the place of Destruction?
> Will thy wonders be known in the dark,
>   thy victories in the land of oblivion?
>   (Ps. 88:10–12)

Questions such as these are not found in catechisms or in religious textbooks. They are irreverent questions that do not concern church leaders and theologians. But for ordinary believers they are life-and-death questions. For them suffering is their lot and not just somebody else's. They experience death in the loss of their loved ones, their relatives and their friends. It is not a concept others try to analyze and understand. Surely God must have answers for them.

And there are more questions to come in the psalm. They are even sharper, bolder, and more bitter questions:

> Why hast thou cast me off, O Lord,
>   why dost thou hide thy face from me?
> I have suffered from boyhood and come near to death;
>   I have borne thy terrors, I cower beneath thy blows.
> Thy burning fury has swept over me,
>   thy onslaughts have put me to silence;

all the day long they surge round me like a flood,
they engulf me in a moment.
Thou hast taken lover and friend far from me,
and parted me from my companions.

(Ps. 85:13–18)

Unlike many other psalmists who, after fretting, lamenting, and weeping, turn to God in repentance and for comfort, this psalmist lets the questions remain unanswered and the accusation unmitigated. Here we seem to hear that king in ancient China, that Tamil worker in Sri Lanka today, speaking through the mouth of a Hebrew-speaking Jew in those old days. This also echoes the cry of Jesus on the cross: "My God, my God, why have you abandoned me?"

What will be God's answer to all these questions? How is God to explain all these accusations? We do not know. But we do know that much is at stake both for God and for human beings. "Why hast thou cast me off, O Lord?" If God be God, God cannot be indifferent to the doubt, agony, and pain that fill a question such as this. Here again human beings have come into controversy with God.

If this is a crisis of faith for human beings, it is a crisis of credibility for God. In this crisis God is put on trial. The God who is nowhere to be found in the midst of human suffering — is that God a real God or an unreal God? The God who does not seem to mind the hardships women, men, and children are going through — is that God a loving God or an unloving God? The God who does not seem to hear cries of pain from the depths of human travail — is that God a living God or a dead God? And the God who does not appear to be affected by oppression and injustice rampant in the world — what kind of God is this? These are deeply theological questions that trouble many people both inside the Christian church and outside it. We will now turn to these questions and see if they can tell us something different about the God who has been the center of our life and faith.

NOTES

1. *Asian Issues* (Hong Kong, International Affairs/CCA), vol. 2, no. 1 (January 1983), p. 9.

2. Chow Tse-tsung, *The May Fourth Movement: Intellectual Revolution in Modern China* (Cambridge: Harvard University Press, 1960), p. 311.

3. See ibid., p. 308.

4. From *Lu Xun, Selected Works*, vol. 1, trans. Yang Xianyi and Gladys Yang (Beijing: Foreign Languages Press, 1956), pp. 39–51. "Yi Ya, a favorite of Duke of Huan of Qi in the seventh century B.C. was a good cook and sycophant. When the duke

demanded that he had never tasted the flesh of children, Yi Ya cooked his own son for him to eat. Jie and Zhou were kings of earlier periods" (see footnote in *Lu Xun*, p. 48). Xi Xilian was "a revolutionary executed in 1907 for assassinating a Qing official. His heart and liver were eaten" (ibid.). Pan Gu was creator of heaven and earth in Chinese creation myth.

5. Eric Fromm, *The Anatomy of Human Destructiveness* (New York: Fawcett Crest, 1973), p. 210.

6. Ibid., p. 211.

7. See *Peake's Commentary on the Bible*, Matthew Black and H. H. Rowley, eds. (London: Thomas Nelson, 1962), p. 432.

8. From the *She Ching* (The Book of Poetry), in James Legg, *The Chinese Classics* (Hong Kong: Hong Kong University Press, 1960), vol. 6, pp. 528–534. *How Chi* "may be treated as the name of the account of the House of Chou, 1111–249 B.C." (Legg, ibid., p. 697a).

CHAPTER 2

No to the God of Retribution

The heart of the matter here is God, not God in God's own self, but the God we have come to know through the traditions of our religious community, God worshipped in our church and taught by its teachers. The question we are constrained to ask is this: Is God in God's own self the same as the God the Christian church has taught us? This, I believe, is a legitimate question. It is not only legitimate; it is also necessary. After all, the language of faith is a human language with its possibilities and limitations. In the case of the language about God, its limitations are far greater than its possibilities. The reason is obvious: in God we are not dealing with a subject matter that can be seen, heard, touched, or felt directly. Religious language, particularly the language about God, has, then, to be an indirect language. Here the formula A = B that constitutes the basis of our daily communication does not apply. A direct knowledge of A and B acquired through experience, habit, convention, or scientific investigation is needed to establish the relation of A being the same as B. When, for example, we say, the dog is brown, we must already know dog is an animal and brown is a color.

Obviously, this is not the case when it comes to God. How can we *identify* God with something we know? Is this not what is condemned by the church as idolatry? We know how Paul vehemently inveighed against idolatry in his letter to the Christians in Rome. Those who worship idols, according to him, "boast of their wisdom, but have made fools of themselves, exchanging the splendor of the immortal God for an image shaped like a mortal human being, even for images like birds, beasts, and creeping things" (Rom. 1:22–23). Here passion and rhetoric combine to make a powerful theology against idolatry.

Much of Christian theology against idolatry has, since Paul penned these words in his letter to the Romans, been largely directed against people of other faiths and religions. It is a theology that forms the basis of

a Christian critique of other religions and justifies Christian evangeliza-
tion of people outside Christianity. It has not, however, been applied to
the teachings and practices of the Christian church with equal vigor and
severity.

We have tailored God to suit our limited imagination and created an
image of God that strongly reflects our cultural biases and our religious
experiences. How can we be otherwise as human beings? Yes, we cannot
be otherwise. But there is something that should have been utmost in our
mind — God as A and our knowledge of God as B are not identical. As
soon as we forget this, and how prone we are to forget this, that is to say,
as soon as we identify A with B or B with A, as soon as we make up our
mind that A = B, we commit the kind of idolatry that Paul talks about, the
same idolatry we as Christians are too ready to condemn in the people of
other religions. Is this alone not reason enough to examine whether the
God we have come to know in the tradition of our faith bears a close
resemblance to God in God's own self?

This is a soul-searching question. Take, for example, our perception
of relationships between God and human beings. These relationships are
shaped largely by the way we understand God. We understand God as
love, as mercy, as compassion. But is it not true that this loving, merciful, and compassionate God is often overshadowed by a revengeful God,
a God of retribution? Is not the God of love a compensation for the God
of retribution? Is it not our hope and prayer that the God of retribution
will somehow turn into the God of love? This, in my view, has affected
our religious piety on the one hand and our theological effort on the other.
What prevails in human society and in our relationship with one another
is, among other things, revenge and retribution in a variety of forms and
expressions. We then project the idea that relationships between God and
human beings must also be governed by revenge and retribution. Is this
not what is at the root of our fear of a wrathful God? Does this not develop into prayers and rituals to placate the revengeful God? And does
this not shape our theology of how our sins are forgiven, of how Jesus
atones for our sins? Is this not the way the Christian church has understood the meaning of Jesus' crucifixion and Christian theologians have
developed the theology of the cross?

The frightening thought is that when we direct our bitter complaints
and tearful prayers to our God full of wrath, a God who revenges the
wrongs we have done, a God of retribution, we are not dealing with God
in God's own self, but the God of our own creation and imagination. If
there is truth in this, it is necessary for us to unmask this God before we
can come to a different perception of how God — God in God's own self
and not God as a projection of what we human beings are and what we
do to one another — is struggling with us in the midst of our pain and

suffering as well as in our joy and aspiration. This unmasking is very central to our reunderstanding of what the cross of Jesus means and of how he is related to the crosses men and women have to bear in different times and at different places. As we pursue any controversy with God, we may realize that the God we are contending against may be a God of retribution who bears no resemblance to God in God's own self. To this God of retribution we must declare a loud and strong no. Liberation from this God of retribution is an important step in our fresh experience of the God of love.

Oh, God! What Hast Thou to Say?

From the God of retribution to God in God's own self — this is not an easy transition to make. From the God who controls our life like an autocratic ruler to the God who is in solidarity with us in our suffering — this is a big step to take. Involved in such transition is the struggle of the soul in deep agony. To take such a step we have to go through an experience of the spirit in great turmoil. A prayer from the wounded heart of a Tamil plantation worker caught in the racial conflicts in Sri Lanka referred to earlier seems an outcry for help in the midst of confusion and fear:

> What hast Thou to say, oh, God?
> Tell us, oh, Lord, what's in thy mind
>
> Ten decades of life for tea we have given,
>   Ten more decades we now pour out;
> All these years for our rights we have striven,
>   But our toil has brought us nought.
>   For all this, what sayest Thou?
>   Tell us, Lord, what is thy thought?
>
> As imported goods we were brought to these shores,
>   As worthless goods we're now returned;
> But for this land's wealth sweat poured from our pores,
>   Now without rights in camps we herd.
>   Seeing this, what sayest Thou, God?
>
> They promised new life to entice us out,
>   But all we saw were cemeteries;
> All our hope was gone, saved money ran out,
>   And lives became futilities.
>   Now what hast Thou to say, oh, God?
>   Tell us, oh, Lord, what Thou hast planned![1]

These words bring us deep distress also. They well out of an anguished soul and a tormented life. Years of labor have come to a tragic end.

Dreams for a better life are shattered. The power of hope becomes exhausted. Still this is not a prayer to end all prayers, not a cry to stop all cries. It is not a shout that echoes in eternal silence. It looks for a ray of hope from God who cares and redeems, God who hears and saves.

"Oh, God! What hast Thou to say?" This is not a metaphysical question expecting an erudite answer. It is a question of life and death groping for words of assurance from God in the midst of despair. This is not a philosophical question that demands an abstruse response. It is a question crying out to God to intervene in the world of injustice and cruelty. Nor is it an academic question dealing with God's providence in human affairs in the serenity of a theological study. It is a question of the meaning of life arising out of the personal experience of suffering, from the depths of a human community in conflict, and in the midst of the turbulent history of a troubled nation. This is a deeply religious question. Countless numbers of women, men, and children since the beginning of human history have been asking: "Oh, God, what hast Thou to say to this account of my life, to this story of my community, and to this history of my nation?"

But who is this God to whom this Tamil worker prays? The God from whom helpless people seek help — what is this God like? Questions such as these have seldom occurred to us before. And we are often perplexed why there is no answer from God. We feel our complaints, pleas, and earnest prayers are just like "rocks falling into the sea" (*she chen ta hai*), without a trace, as the Chinese would say. We are mystified by God's silence; we even despair because of it. And in the secret corner of our hearts we begin to have doubts about ourselves, not about the God to whom we pray and direct our hopes. Perhaps I am punished for the wrong I did in the past. I must have offended God so that God now turns away from me. We seem to take for granted that our God must be a God of retribution, a God who can get terribly angry and revengeful, a God who will not take an affront lightly.

From primitive religions to sophisticated religions there is a fear of a God who will not let us off scot-free. Most religions cultivate this fear and infuse it into the consciousness of believers. Is it because of this that side by side with this fearful God is developed a cult of a merciful goddess who intercedes for the believers, the goddess of mercy in Mahayana Buddhism, for example? It is to this goddess that most believers turn for help and protection. The cult of the Virgin Mary in Christianity seems to be part of this universal religious longing and practice.

To be liberated from the God of fear is, then, essential for people to have an experience of who God in God's own self is and to perceive how that God is related to them and to the world. This seems to be what that Tamil worker begins to do when he in his prayer asks God directly: "Oh, God! What hast Thou to say?" He must have been troubled by this question for a long time. He was afraid to ask it before. He could have been frightened by the thought of it. The very fact that the question came to his mind might be an evidence of his disobedience that deserved divine punishment. Is it a voice of the devil sowing in him a seed of rebellion against God? He might have wondered. He tried perhaps to put the question away, to forget it, to have nothing to do with it. But the suffering and pain he is going through will not let him suppress the question. In spite of himself he raises his voice and asks God what God has to say about his life of misery and despair.

Once the question is asked, our Tamil worker seems to be emboldened. Looking back on his own life and that of his people, he cannot believe they deserve all these hardships. "Ten decades of life for tea we have given," he says. That is the history of his people. His parents and grandparents were transported from the continent of India to this island nation to cultivate the tea plantation, to work for its economic development. And when their turn came, they did their share with equal fervor. This must be what he wants to say when he continues: "Ten more decades we now pour out." But he has to admit that "our toil has brought us nought." They are now faced with deportation from their home in the island back to the land where their forebears had come from — the land that has become strange and foreign to them. Can we blame the Tamil worker for demanding to know what God thinks of all this? "Tell us, oh, Lord," he says, "what's in thy mind? What is thy thought?" But God does not answer.

Perhaps I have not said enough to God? Or perhaps I have not said it loud and clear enough to God? If God is not fully aware of what our adversities are like, we must tell God. The Tamil plantation worker rekindles his hope and begins to recount the hardships they have gone through. Years ago they were "brought to these shores as imported goods." Yes, we are just goods and not considered to be human beings. Something was wrong from the very start. But we did not give up our hope. We worked very hard, "pouring sweat from our pores for this land's wealth." We did contribute to the economic development of this land of our adoption. Without our hard labor, how could this land have developed the tea industry that benefited its economy? But what have we got in return? "As worthless goods," laments the Tamil worker, "we're now returned." And waiting for deportation, "now without rights in camps we herd." This predicament of ours must move the heart of God. He desperately wants to know whether this is the case. He finds himself asking God again: "Seeing this, what sayest Thou, God?"

His mind keeps going back to the beginning of the long odyssey. People in the throes of suffering and pain remember how things began. Suffering makes us remember former things, especially happy things.

Pain takes us back to the world we left behind, the world full of joy and good things, real or imaginary. This is the experience of the people of Israel in the wilderness after they had made good their escape from Egypt, the land of slavery. When things got tough and difficult, when they ran out of food and water, when the endless trek in the wilderness under the burning sun began to wear them out, they looked back on Egypt with nostalgia. "If only we had died at the Lord's hand in Egypt," they complained and fretted, "where we sat round the flesh-pots and had plenty of bread to eat!" (Exod. 16:3). Never mind that these flesh-pots contained bitter herbs and that "plenty" of bread was in fact a mere pittance. The memory that idealizes away the miseries of the past and builds a history on the basis of illusory bygone days is a destructive memory. It destroys our will to struggle for a better present and dims our vision for the future.

When our Tamil worker says bitterly, "they promised new life to entice us out," he may not be totally free from that destructive memory that broke the will of some Israelites to press forward. Perhaps that "new life" existed only in the imagination of the Tamils who had left their homes for the strange shores in search of a better life. But imagination or not, their hope was betrayed and they have to face the harsh realities of discrimination on account of their race and religion. They become disposable merchandise to be deported from Sri Lanka. No memory of the past can alter the fact that "all we saw were cemeteries and [our] lives became futilities."

Faced with their predicament and misery, the Tamil worker does something besides harking back to the past that never existed. He turns to God and pours his heart out to God. "Now what hast Thou to say, oh, God?" he asks God. "Tell us, oh, Lord, what Thou hast planned!" We hear in this prayer something that perhaps the Tamil worker himself is not aware of, or only vaguely aware of. It can be his anger toward God, the God who allows all this to happen to him and his people. It may be his impatience with God, the God who does not seem in a hurry to break the silence and say something. And it may be his doubt toward God, the God that has commanded his devotion and worship. It is the doubt that perhaps the God who allows "our toil to bring us nought," and has "us returned [to the land of our ancestors] as worthless goods," is not the real God.

Our Tamil worker, if he entertained such doubt, did not go beyond it. He and his people remain in fear of their lives and deprived of hope for change in their fate, not able to wrestle with their God and unmask the false façade of that God. The long tradition of religious piety does not permit them to be engaged in such an impious behavior. Fear of retribution from God, deeply embedded in the religious consciousness of people for centuries, only makes them shrink back from it. This is the situation of most men and women in all times. But from time to time there are people who, no longer able to accept the situation, face their God with questions about that very God in an effort to penetrate the aura of mystery that shields that God from exposure. One such person is none other than Job of the Hebrew Scriptures, that paragon of religious devotion and piety. It is to Job that we now turn.

A Fateful Council at the Court of Heaven

After a short introduction that brings Job, the main character in the story, to the stage of this most extraordinary drama of life and faith, the author of the Book of Job turns to a bizarre scene. And what a scene unfolds itself before the eyes of the readers! There appear in the court of heaven God and Satan, an unlikely pair, deciding in earnest and with jest how to test Job's faith. But why Job? Because he is "a man of blameless and upright life... who feared God and set his face against wrongdoing" (Job 1:1). God is proud of Job and does not conceal it. "Have you considered my servant Job?" God asks Satan. "You will find no one like him on earth" (1:8). This is an ominous opening of the drama. As it will be shown shortly, this part of the Book of Job comes from a folktale. By adapting it to the main story, the storyteller, whoever the storyteller is, provides the readers with a most disturbing idea. Our ingenious playwright makes God provoke Satan! To Satan — who has been "ranging over the earth from end to end" (1:7), presumably looking for its victims — God exposes Job! God makes Job vulnerable to Satan. Is God aware of this? Does God realize that Satan will not take the provocation lightly? Does God know that God is going to be held accountable for what Job will have to go through? Taking the story of Job as a whole and trying to understand it from the popular experience of God as God of retribution, an experience legitimated and reinforced by official religion, we perceive that our playwright has cleverly paved the way for Job's revolt against that God.

Satan is quick to react to the provocation. "Has not Job good reason to be God-fearing?" Satan retorts. "Have you not hedged him round on every side with your protection, him and his family and all his possessions?" (1:9–10). Satan goes straight to the heart of the matter and points up one strong belief that motivates human religiosity — the belief that "good deeds will bring good rewards and evil will be recompensed with evil" (*shan yu shan pau, oh yu oh pau*), to use a Chinese expression. Is this not what belief in *karma* in popular Buddhism is about? Is this not what underlies the teaching of reincarnation in the caste system of Hinduism? And is this not the basis for the idea of merit and the practice of penance in some quarters of Christianity? Through the mouth of Satan our storyteller seems leading us to question whether our God is a God of retribution. Willy-nilly God is drawn into the plot laid by Satan — the plot that develops into a tragic drama in which God is unmasked as a God of retribution.

Satan now commands the initiative. The next thing we hear is Satan's challenge to God. "Stretch out your hand and touch all that he [Job] has," declares Satan, "and then he will curse you to your face" (1:11). God is trapped. God is cornered. God cannot back away from the challenge. It must have been a moment of truth for God, for at this juncture what is really at stake is not Job's faith in God but God's confidence in Job. God must prove to be God no matter what, even having to put Job in jeopardy. At last comes God's response to Satan: "So be it," God must have said pensively. The deal is struck. God hands Job over to Satan and says: "All that he has is in your hands, only Job himself you must not touch" (1:12).

Is this really what God said? We cannot but doubt our ears. But this is how the story unfolds. Still, we cannot help wondering how this God can be the God of love and justice. How could the God whom Job holds with utmost devotion hand him into the hands of the merciless Satan, that most irreverent rascal? The puzzled reader wonders. At any rate, the curtain opens and the audience is to witness a most unusual drama of life, a moving and disturbing drama.

Satan goes out from God's presence to carry out the scheme of destruction. Terrible misfortunes devastated Job and left him numb. But he stood the test well. "Throughout all this," we are told, "Job did not sin or charge God with wrong-doing" (1:22, NRSV). God is vindicated. God's confidence in Job's fidelity and loyalty to God is confirmed. A point to be noticed here is that God is in no hurry to reward Job for his steadfastness. God seems to savor the victory, leaving Job in his calamity. So the tragic drama must play itself out to the end.

As expected, Satan is not convinced and speaks up again: "Skin for skin! There is nothing the man will grudge to save himself. But stretch out your hand and touch his bone and his flesh, and see if he will not curse you to your face" (2:4–5). What a challenge! And such a sinister one at that! It discloses the true character of Satan. God must be horrified. The feeling of satisfaction is gone. Perhaps the whole thing should be called off. It is going to go too far. But what our storyteller shows us is a God who "does not stop half way once a thing is started" (*yi pu cho er pu hsiu*, in Chinese). A second deal is made. Job becomes a pawn in the deal between God and Satan for the second time. Poor Job! While this sinister deal is being negotiated between God and Satan, Job is totally unaware of it. It is being done behind his back. Is our storyteller implying that human fate is decided and controlled by the power that does not allow our say? Whether this is what is implied or not, it is a belief deeply rooted in human religious consciousness from ancient times to the present day.

Now God too seems excited. Besides excitement, there must be also curiosity. Could Job pass this second test? Could he go through it all with his trust in God unshaken? Would he still retain his faith in God at the end of it? In this second deal, as in the first, God becomes a shadow of Satan. What we see is a contrast between the aggressive Satan and the defensive God. God is being induced into doing something contrary to God's nature. Here the playwright goes a step further in laying the ground for Job later to rebel against God, to defy a false God, to fight the God who has become a mere shadow of Satan. "So be it," says God once again. "He is in your hands; but spare his flesh" (2:6). God agrees to the deal and turns Job over to Satan.

In this second act of the drama God does make sure that Job is not finished completely. Whatever Satan does to Job, Job must be spared his life. Satan is only too glad to comply. It perhaps is not in the interest of Satan to destroy Job, a mere human being. What Satan is really after must be God. Satan's purpose must be to have God discredited in people's eyes, to have God dethroned from the seat of power and authority. But there is one thing even this ruthless, cunning, and scheming Satan is not aware of, that is, this God Satan is challenging may not be God in God's own self! It does not seem to occur to Satan that the God who can enter into such a merciless pact is not the true God. Inadvertently, Satan becomes a mere instrument in the painful process of Job coming to know the real God, not the God of retribution, but the God who is in solidarity with those who suffer.

From here on the pace of the drama quickens. Satan goes out to carry out the work of destruction once again, leaving Job afflicted with "sores from head to foot," an abhorrent sight even to the members of his own family. At the height of this drama, our playwright once again demonstrates the mastery with which the folktale is adapted and steered toward development of Job's faith from faith in the God of retribution to faith in the God of suffering love. The storyteller does it both by what is said and what is not said. This second act of the drama is thus concluded with these words: "Throughout all this, Job did not utter one sinful word" (2:10). Job is vindicated. This is the basis from which Job will launch his vehement arguments with his three friends. This gives him a firm theological ground to stand on in his search for the true God. But what about the God who did a deal with Satan? That God is not heard any more. The silence about that God is as instructive as the words commending Job. The unmasking of the God of retribution has quietly begun. This is an awesome theological effort involving risk and danger. One thing that will become crystal clear to Job is that the just and loving God is not to be met in the calm splendor of rituals and rites but in the rough and tumble of this world.

Naked I Came from the Womb (Job 1:21)

Before we proceed any further to see how Job goes through his theological development in the course of his dialogue with his friends, we
need to reflect more deeply on the religious sentiment represented in the
prologue of the Book of Job (chaps. 1–2), and, we must add, also in its
epilogue (42:7–17). The prologue and the epilogue together provide a fascinating study of how God is held in the beliefs and piety of common
believers. And as we move into Job's controversies with his friends who
represented the official religious positions, we shall be amazed how the
common perception of God as the God of retribution shaped and formed
official teachings of the religious authorities.

As we have seen, the God portrayed in the prologue of the Book of
Job (chaps. 1–2) is the God in league with Satan, wreaking havoc on Job,
"a man of blameless and upright life" (2:3). It is a God who could be
"incited to ruin Job without a cause" (2:3), a man who "fears God and
sets his face against wrongdoing" (1:8). This God, and not Job himself,
is the cause of his suffering. This God, and not members of his family, is
behind all his miseries. This God, and not any other human agent, reduces
him to a pitiable sight. And it is this God whom Job and his whole family
have revered, feared, worshipped, and served with utmost devotion that
thrusts him into the abyss of despair.

And yet this same God who brought misfortunes on Job (42:11)
"blessed the end of his life more than the beginning" (42:12) when the
tragic saga concludes with an epilogue (42:7–17). Most critics of the
Book of Job tell us that the prologue-epilogue is in fact an old folktale
the storyteller used as the setting for the scenario of the drama — the un-
justified suffering of the innocent.[2] This may be so. But the old folktale
with its stress on unquestioned submission even to a tyrannical God does
not seem merely to serve as the setting for the drama. The drama itself
is so tragic in nature, so terrifying in its development, and so daring in
human defiance against God that it could not fit into a prologue and an
epilogue that smack of comedy — a comedy in which all pain and suffering come to a happy end. The tremendous human suffering between
the prologue and the epilogue would then be a sham, the tragedy that induces tears for the heroic victim would be a fake, and the outpouring of
that terribly injured soul that rends the heart of the reader would be just
play-acting.

No, the prologue-epilogue in question could not have been used by
the playwright, dramatist, or poet of the Book of Job to diminish the
seriousness of the play, to take the sting out of the drama, or to turn
its poetry into the delirium of a deranged mind. The prologue-epilogue
contains time-honored religious teachings and moral values that have en-

slaved people's minds and paralyzed their souls — teachings and values that have their most relentless advocates in Eliphaz of Teman, Bildad of Shuah, and Zophar of Naamah, the three friends who came ostensibly to console Job.

The religion of utter submission, for example, is what the traditional piety enforced on believers, including Job himself. When calamities struck out of the blue and brought ruins to his property and death to his sons and daughters, we hear from the mouth of Job those most noble words ever uttered by any human being in the grip of deep sorrow and agony:

> Naked I came from the womb,
> naked I shall return whence I came.
> The Lord gives and the Lord takes away;
> blessed be the name of the Lord.
>
> (Job 1:21)

To realize the full impact of these words, we have to see, with our mind's eye, Job in the state of extreme affliction. The noble stature of Job as a man of faith and integrity shines through them.

These are words from the heart of a sincere and devout believer totally committed to the God feared and revered in a traditional religion. It never occurs to Job to complain to God. It is beyond him to question the justice of all that he has to go through. In his utter submission to God he is not even capable of asking why all this has happened to him. He cannot charge God with wrong (1:22). How could he? That would be tantamount to blasphemy and infidelity. It would be a mortal sin. It is this Job of the prologue-epilogue that has been upheld as a model of true piety for emulation in the Christian church through the centuries. The letter attributed to James, the brother of Jesus, exhorted Christians: "You have all heard how Job stood firm" (James 5:11). Job has, for the past two thousand years, been the paragon of patience and obedience for Christian believers.

If these words illuminate the integrity of Job as a man of faith, they also heighten the danger a religion may create for individual believers and for a society. It is the danger of a religion becoming oppressive and obstructing change in history. This is the dark side of a religion of utter submission. To submit to the God of our religion without question is to submit ourselves to the status quo, to perpetuate the tradition no longer credible, and to be part of the force that seeks to stem the effort of reform. Uncritical submission to a religious belief and teaching can develop into submission in social and political matters. When this happens, there will be confusion of political authority with religious authority. Uncritical submission to the powers that be is then taken as part of submission to God.

Is this one of the reasons why a religion often becomes an accomplice of an oppressive political and social system? But after all an accomplice is an accomplice. A religion that allies itself with the political authorities that oppress people loses its integrity, credibility, and authority. It becomes dependent on secular power for its own survival and practices its loyalty more to Caesar than to God. Each and every religion has a history of practicing oppression in alliance with political powers. Christianity is no exception.

The words Job said in the midst of his suffering cannot, then, be held simply as a supreme example of faith. True, there are undeniable facts in them. Who could question the fact that Job, and for that matter all people, came from the mother's womb naked, possessing nothing? And who could deny the fact that when we return to where we came from, we do so empty-handed, bringing nothing with us. But the real question lies in the religious conclusion drawn from these natural facts, the conclusion that it is God who gives and takes away at will, that God still has to be praised and blessed in the face of the seeming injustice done to people such as Job.

Thoughts such as these do not occur to Job at this stage of his life and faith. He must have uttered those words with complete sincerity. It is beyond his dream to think that these words he has poured out from the bottom of his heart could mean something other than his unwavering trust in God. But the question is who is this God who gives and takes away? Who is this God to be praised and blessed despite all these misfortunes that struck for no reason at all? These are not questions common believers dare to raise openly, and Job at this stage is no exception. They are of course discouraged by the official religious authorities. This will become evident when Job's friends try to pressure him into confessing his sins for the tragedies that he is going through. But we are to witness a dramatic change in Job when our storyteller takes us from the prologue to the dialogue, from Job's unquestioned submission to God to his heated arguments with his friends. A different vision of God is to arise as Job moves to the next stage of the drama.

Does God Pervert Justice? (Job 8:3)

With the visit of Job's three friends — Eliphaz of Teman, Bilad of Shuah, and Zophar of Naamah — Job's *theological* transformation begins. In his dialogue with them the storyteller discloses to us Job's soul in intense struggle. It is a struggle to be liberated from the God of the traditional religion and become free for God in God's own self. This is a long, painful process that takes up almost the whole Book of Job (chaps. 3–31).

When the friends arrive at the scene, they are completely stunned by the immensity of Job's tragedy. It is far worse than they have expected. At the sight of Job in terrible suffering, their hearts must have gone out to him. "They," our storyteller tells us, "wept aloud, rent their cloaks and tossed dust into the air over their heads" (2:12) — expressions of extreme sorrow and deep mourning. "For seven days and seven nights," we are told, "they sat beside him on the ground, and none of them said a word to him; for they saw that his suffering was very great" (2:13). They are simply stunned into silence. They have come to comfort Job, but Job's suffering is so great that they are rendered speechless.

What is going on in their minds? The storyteller does not tell us. But it is perhaps not too difficult to guess. The magnitude of Job's suffering truly shocks them. They are genuinely appalled. They truly weep for their friend. They cannot find words to say to him. These three are facing Job as sympathetic friends and not as religious doctrinaires, as vulnerable fellow human beings and not as theological arbiters between God and humanity. Perhaps they should have wept their hearts out, embraced Job, and left him. Perhaps they should not have broken their silence to console him. Their tears alone would have been more than enough.

When they have recovered from their shock, however, their religious orthodoxy gets the better of them, and their "theological" sensitivity goes into action. After listening to Job's mournful litany recounting his sorrows and miseries, the first to respond is Eliphaz the Temanite. Among other things this is what he says:

> For consider, what innocent man has ever perished?
> Where have you seen the upright destroyed?
> This I know,
> that those who plough mischief and sow trouble
> reap as they have sown;
> they perish at the blast of God
> and are shrivelled by the breath of God's nostrils.
>
> (Job 4:7–9)

What an insensitive thing to say to a friend in terrible pain and suffering! And what an innuendo! Gone are the tears at the first sight of the miserable friend. What is important is correct faith, faultless theology!

These words must have first shocked Job and then angered him. He must have made up his mind at the outset of the dialogue with his friends to defend his innocence, knowing that this might lead him to oppose the traditional religion he himself espoused firmly until that moment. He is not yet defiant against God, but rather against his friends who were insinuating that he could not be suffering all this for no reason. He answers back:

> Tell me plainly, and I will listen in silence;
> show me where I have erred.
> How harsh are the words of the upright man!
> What do the arguments of the wise men prove?
> Do you mean to argue about words
> or to sift the utterance of a person past hope?
> Would you assail an orphan?
> Would you hurl yourselves on a friend?
> So now, I beg you, turn and look at me:
> am I likely to lie to your faces?
> Think again, let me have no more injustice;
> think again, for my integrity is in question.
> (Job 6:24–29)

A subtle transformation is taking place in Job. The submissive and pitiable Job asking for mercy from God and from his fellow human beings is yielding to Job who rallies around to defend his integrity as a believer and a human being.

"My integrity," says Job, "is in question." The word "integrity" put in the mouth of Job here is of great importance. It is not always a respectable word in the vocabulary of religious authorities. To assert your integrity, that is, to claim that you have done nothing wrong, is regarded as an expression of insubordination to the religious authorities and thus to God. It is pride. Is it not pride, according to the traditional interpretation, that incurred the wrath of God in the story of the Tower of Babel (Gen. 11)? Much of what is labelled "sin" amounts to a denial of integrity in believers, as if faith in God were incompatible with integrity as a human person, as if deprivation of human integrity is an essential part of faith in God. How can human beings speak of their integrity when God's image in them is said to have been totally lost — at least according to some Christian teachers and theologians?

How little Job's friends are able to understand his struggle to be freed from the God of traditional religion! They hold on to that God, defend that God, and never move from the position of self-appointed spokespersons for that God. That is why we hear the same Eliphaz the Temanite still urging Job, even after the dialogue had got well under way, to come to terms with the God of retribution. He says to Job:

> Come to terms with God and you will prosper:
> that is the way to mend your torture.
> Take instruction from God's mouth
> and store God's words in your heart.
> If you come back to the Almighty in true sincerity,
> if you banish wrongdoing from your home...

> Then, with sure trust in the Almighty,
> you will raise your face to God.... (Job 22:21–26)

What a self-serving counsel! Job's friends fail miserably to perceive the profound turmoil racing in his heart and to understand the spiritual crisis gnawing at his soul. His body may be sorely afflicted, but his spirit is defiant. His faith in the God of traditional religion that demands blind submission has already been shaken. His allegiance to the religious systems that impose slavish obedience on believers has collapsed. But his friends cannot see. They do not understand. They fail to realize that their religious clichés in defense of the traditional faith are only driving Job farther and farther away from their God.

And then there is this awe-inspiring doctrine of retribution, the doctrine that any misfortune is the divine punishment for the sin committed in public or in secret. Job of the prologue-epilogue also believes in it. It is for him, just as for all other believers, a supreme guide, an unchangeable standard, by which he judges others and also himself. This Job must have, then, been terribly shocked and completely dumbfounded when his wife, unable to endure any more all that has taken place around her, at last comes out with those shocking words: "Are you still unshaken in your integrity? Curse God and die!" (2:9). But this is Job's reply: "If we accept good from God, shall we not accept evil?" (2:10).

This is not Job in dialogue with his friends, eloquent in misery and defiant in adversity. This is the subdued Job of the folktale. Of course this Job cannot hold God responsible for his misfortunes. Should anything happen to him and his family, he would be solely accountable for it. That is why Job of the prologue-epilogue makes sure that he does everything right in religious duties. The folktale tells us that after the annual feast, most likely the feast of ingathering at the year's end,[3] Job used to "send for his children and sanctify them, rising early in the morning and sacrificing a whole-offering for each of them; for he thought that they might somehow have sinned against God and committed blasphemy in their hearts" (1:5). Job of the prologue-epilogue would not leave anything to chance when it comes to religious matters. His God is a God of retribution.

As is expected, it is this God who "restored Job's fortunes and doubled all his possessions" in the epilogue, after Job has proved to God's satisfaction his unflagging loyalty to God. For the pious and the faithful the God of retribution will reward them if they mend their ways, dutifully do their penance, and remain submissive to the end. But this Job of the prologue-epilogue is very different from the Job engaged in dialogue with his friends.

The God of Job's friends is also a God of retribution. The traditional doctrine of divine retribution is, in fact, the one single important theme on which they harp on and on, trying to force Job to submit to it. To their astonishment, however, they have discovered that Job is not remorseful. Instead of reproaching himself, he seems to be reproaching God. They actually hear him say to God: "Why hast thou made me thy butt, and why have I become thy target? Why dost thou not pardon my offense and take away my guilt?" (7:20b–21a). They must have been horrified. Only the impious could utter such words! Bildad the Shuhite does not conceal his self-righteous indignation when he at last finds words to rebut Job. He replies:

> How long will you say such things,
> the long-winded ramblings of an old man?
> Does God pervert judgment?
> Does the Almighty pervert justice?
> Your sons sinned against God,
> so God left them to be victims of their own iniquity.
> If only you will seek God betimes
> and plead for the favor of the Almighty,
> if you are innocent and upright,
> then indeed will God watch over you
> and see your just intent fulfilled.
> Then, though your beginnings were humble,
> your end will be great.
>
> (Job 8:1–7)

This is a most crude form of the doctrine of divine retribution. And it is a very universal one too. You reap what you have sown. "Planting beans," says a Chinese proverb, "you reap beans; planting melons, you reap melons" (*chung tow te tow, chung koa te koa*). This is an immutable law of religion as well as nature. How it has dominated and shaped human religious sensibility since human beings were awakened to their religious consciousness! There is no such thing as innocent suffering. Nor is there such a thing called divine injustice. Job cannot, then, be suffering without a cause.

"Does the Almighty pervert justice?" asked Bilad the Shuhite. For him and his friends this is a rhetorical question. The answer must be a categorical no. God does *not* pervert justice. This is the premise of the logic to follow. Everything depends on it. It is the criterion of religious truth. Since it is the premise, the criterion, it allows no doubting, debating, or questioning. But the trouble is that there is always perversion of justice in this world and that the victim of perverted justice does not always deserve it. From the premise, then, that God does not pervert justice, it does not follow that a person who suffers has to be "the butt and target" of divine judgment. There are social factors, political problems, or other human reasons that cause people to suffer. Even in the case of suffering caused by natural calamities such as those that struck Job, it is the height of religious perversion to link them to God's judgment on the victims because of the sins committed by them. Since this kind of perverted logic has prevailed in most religions, including Christianity, we cannot but question whether the God of retribution is God in God's own self.

As a matter of fact, the logic of divine retribution is a human logic and not God's logic. It is a logic of religion deduced from human experience in this world of give and take, reward and punishment, good and evil, and not a logic instituted by God in God's own self. As the dialogue between Job and his friends continues, we see how Job refutes that logic vehemently and brilliantly and puts his friends on the defensive. To hold on to the doctrine of divine retribution is to misrepresent God. It is a distortion of who God in God's own self is. It turns God into a monster, an executioner, an avenger. It is a false God, an idol emerged out of the depths of human consciousness. It is a God created in human image.

Jesus, as we recall, dismissed the doctrine outright when he replied to the question about the man born blind: "It is not that this man or his parents sinned" (John 9:2), causing him to be born blind. And when he was told about the Galileans, his compatriots massacred by Roman soldiers, he declared: "Do you imagine that, because these Galileans suffered this fate, they must have been greater sinners than anyone else in Galilee? I tell you they were not; but unless you repent, you will all of you come to the same end" (Luke 13:2–3). The doctrine of divine retribution deeply rooted in human religious consciousness misunderstands and distorts the moral power at work in human community. Jesus pressed his point when he said further: "Or the eighteen people who were killed when the tower fell at Siloam — do you imagine that they were more guilty than all the other people living in Jerusalem? I tell you they were not" (13:4–5). Not a few people, especially religious leaders, must have been offended by what Jesus had to tell them. What Jesus did was to refute one of the most tenacious beliefs traditionally embraced by people and firmly upheld by the religious authorities. In the eyes of the latter he was committing a heresy and undermining the very foundation of the religious community.

What Job had to cope with in his time and what Jesus had to face in his religious tradition is also what engaged Gotama the Buddha in his reflection and teaching. Here is an illuminating conversation between him and Kassapa, one of his disciples:

"Is suffering wrought by oneself, good Gotama?"
"No, Kassapa."
"Then by another?"

"No."

"Then by both oneself and another?"

"No, Kassapa."

"Well then, has the suffering that has been wrought neither by myself nor by another come to me by chance?"

"No, Kassapa."

"Then, is there not suffering?"

"No, Kassapa, it is not that there is not suffering. For there is suffering."

"Well then, the good Gotama neither knows nor sees suffering."

"It is not that I do not know suffering, do not see it. I know it, I see it."

"To all my questions, good Gotama, you have answered 'No,' and you have said that you know suffering and see it. Lord, let the Lord explain suffering to me, let him teach me suffering."

"Who says, 'Whoever does (a deed) is the one who experiences (its result),' is thereby saying that from the being's beginning suffering was wrought by (the being) himself — this amounts to the Eternity-view. Who says, 'One does (a deed), another experiences (the result),' is thereby saying that when a being is smitten by feeling the suffering was wrought by another — this amounts to the Annihilation-view."

"Avoiding both these dead-ends, Kassapa, the Tathagata teaches Dhamma by the mean: conditioned by ignorance are the karma-formations... and so on. Thus is the origin of this whole mass of suffering."[4]

Suffering is a fact of life that leads to the question about the cause of suffering. If this is true of the religious communities in ancient Israel and in Jesus' time, it is also true of the religious community in which the Buddha tried to bring about a fundamental change in people's religious consciousness and in the religion of the establishment.

This conversation between the Buddha and his disciple may strike a chord in some Christians. "Rabbi, who sinned, this man or his parents, that he was born blind?" the disciples asked Jesus (John 9:2, RSV). "Good Gotama, is suffering wrought by oneself or another?" Kassapa the disciple posed a question to Gotama the Buddha. "It is not that this man or his parents sinned," Jesus answered. Then he declared: "He was born blind so that God's power might be displayed in curing him" (John 9:3). It is unethical, Jesus seems to be saying, it is immoral to invoke the doctrine of divine retribution in the face of human suffering. The God of Jesus is not a God of retribution. Nothing would please God more than to have the blind man cured. Without further ado Jesus proceeded to restore sight to the blind man. As for Gotama, the so-called Eternity-view and Annihilation-view are both wrong. Such teaching deepens the misery of suffering and perpetuates the *karma* of suffering. That misery has to be removed. That *karma* must be broken. To break that *karma*, one has to be cured of ignorance (*avidya*) that "drives beings into the chain of transmigration" and keeps them in "darkness without illumination."[5] Gotama devoted his entire life to helping women and men to be freed from enslavement to the *karma* of suffering.

The doctrine of divine retribution, in Christian garb or in Buddhist robe, harbors a sinister deity. The tragedy is that the religious authorities and theological systems that advocate it replace the God of mercy with a God of terror. They render service to the God of injustice instead of the God of justice. Religion often makes the search for a merciful and just God necessary. This is a sad irony. Religion, in the East and in the West, needs prophets, seers, and reformers to unmask its distortion of God and to deliver innocent believers from the terrifying deity manufactured in the dark recesses of its traditions and sanctuaries. This is a formidable task. And this is what Jesus did. For this he had to pay the price with his life. The cross was Jesus' decisive struggle against the God of *karma* personified in the official religion of his day. Little did people, even his own disciples, understand the meaning of that struggle. But has the Christian church understood it better in the course of its development? The question cannot be answered with a clear yes. But more on this later.

I Am Ready to Argue with God (Job 13:3)

We must now return to Job and his friends engaged in a battle of words over the doctrine of divine retribution. It is now the turn of Zophar the Naamathite to speak. True to his theological orthodoxy like his companions, he is not about to put up with Job's vehement protest against the God of retribution. He eagerly comes to the defense of the teaching sanctioned by his religion. He must have been greatly agitated. He can hardly wait for Job to finish so that he can speak up:

> Should this spate of words not be answered?
> Must a man of ready tongue be always right?
> Is your endless talk to reduce people to silence?
> Are you to talk nonsense and no one rebuke you?
> (Job 11:2–3)

Even Zophar the Naamathite can match Job in eloquence. But his eloquence has no depth. It is eloquence of a ferocious animal ready to pounce on its prey, eloquence of one who smacks of victory over poor victims.

To be expected, Zophar the Naamathite begins to rebuke Job in earnest, his language direct and biting:

> If only you had directed your heart rightly
> and spread out your hands to pray to God!
> If you have wrongdoing in hand,
>   thrust it away;
> let no iniquity make its home with you.
> Then you could hold up your head without fault,
> a man of iron, knowing no fear.
> Then you will forget your trouble;
> you will remember it only as floodwaters
> that have passed. . . .
>
> (Job 11:13–16)

Job's utter devotion to God must have been well known, but Zophar the Naamathite speaks to Job as if he were a religious delinquent. Job's meticulous observance of religious feasts and rites must have been proverbial, and yet Zophar chides him as if he were an apostate. Job is not going to put up with all this nonsense. He is not going to wallow in self-remorse and beg for pardon and mercy either from his friends or from the God who, he believes, has dealt with him unjustly. He retorts:

> No doubt you are perfect men
> and absolute wisdom is yours!
> But I have sense as well as you;
> in nothing do I fall short of you;
> what gifts indeed have you that others have not?
> Yet I am a laughing-stock to my friends —
> a laughing-stock, though I am innocent and blameless,
> one that called upon God, and God answered.
> Prosperity and ease look down on misfortune,
> on the blow that fells the person who is already reeling,
> while the marauders' tents are left undisturbed
> and those who provoke God live safe and sound.
>
> (Job 12:2–6)

Job strikes back at his friends, asserting his innocence and dismantling the time-honored doctrine of retribution. "Those who provoke God," he must have said with bitterness, "live safe and sound." Is he alluding to his friends?

In this vein the dialogue goes on with Job growing more defiant and rebellious and with his friends more determined in their judgment of Job, not budging from their belief in the God of retribution. Eliphaz of Teman, for example, points his finger at Job and declares, perhaps with his voice quivering with anger:

> Why! you even banish the fear of God from your mind,
> usurping the sole right to speak in God's presence;
> your iniquity dictates what you say,
> and deceit is the language of your choice.
> You are condemned out of your own mouth, not by me;
> your own lips give evidence against you.
>
> (Job 15:4–6)

Job, in the eyes of his friends, is a condemned man, condemned by God and abandoned to destruction. Bilad of Shuah gives a gruesome picture of what it is like for people such as Job who have lost God's favor:

> Their memory vanishes from the face of the earth
> and they leave no name in the world.
> They are driven from light into darkness
> and banished from the land of the living.
> They leave no issue or offspring among their people,
> no survivor in their earthly home....
>
> (Job 18:17–19)

This is the fate of someone cursed by God and obliterated both in God's memory and in human memory. Leaving neither name nor offspring reduces a human person to nonexistence, to nothing.

Zophar of Naamah makes haste to chime in and speaks as if the very foundation of God's creation is built on the doctrine of retribution:

> Surely you know that this has been so since time began,
> since human beings were first set on the earth:
> the triumph of the wicked is short-lived,
> the glee of the godless lasts but a moment?
> Though they stand high as heaven
> and their head touches the clouds,
> they will be swept utterly like their own dung,
> and all that saw him will say, "Where are they?"
>
> (Job 20:4–7)

Such a wicked person, Zophar the Naamathite must have wanted to point out, is Job! "Wicked fools — like yourself," he is actually saying, "die and they are dead."[6]

These three friends have come, in this way, not to console but to judge, not to comfort but to accuse, not to help but to condemn. And their condemnation is harsh and final. Job has a formidable witness against him —

the witness of human beings who "were first set on the earth." Divine retribution is part and parcel of God's creation, for it "has been so since time began." It governs the way God rules the world and deals with humanity. The three friends take it into their hands to pronounce a death sentence on Job, sentence of an eternal death.

But Job, his sense of justice aroused and his quest for the meaning of suffering intensified, is not going to accept his friends' accusations and verdict meekly. He turns offensive and declares:

> All this I have seen with my own eyes,
> with my own ears I have heard it, and understood it.
> What you know, I also know
> in nothing do I fall short of you.
> But for my part I would speak with the Almighty
> and am ready to argue with God,
> while you like fools are smearing
>   truth with your falsehoods,
> stitching a patchwork of lies, one and all.
> Ah, if you would only be silent
> and let silence by your wisdom!
>
> (Job 13:1–5)

This is the turning point in this high drama. "I am ready to argue with God," says Job, He decides to take his case directly to God.

God May Slay Me, I'll Not Quiver! (Job 13:15)

A lesser soul than Job would tremble at these words. A weaker mortal than him would be crushed by this indictment. A formidable orthodoxy! Under its weight how many souls have cried out for mercy in terror! Under its assault how many men and women have resigned themselves to their fate! But this God of the venerable traditions, this deity of the invincible orthodoxy, is a false God.

Job's dialogue with his friends turns out to be not a dialogue at all. It becomes Job's struggle against the false God of religious traditions and theological orthodoxy. His real adversary is not his friends, but the false God they defend. To debunk that false God becomes his preoccupation. "I am ready to argue with God," says Job with determination — the God of my friends, the God of my religion, the God of my ancestors. An intense struggle of the soul for Job thus continues.

Job turns into a dauntless accuser of God. This is not Job of the folktale in the prologue-epilogue. This is a different Job, a different human being, who struggles to be free from the fetters of a legalistic religion, to break the shackles of religious conventions, and to shatter the chains that chain a human soul to the God of caprice, unreason, and oppression.

Word after word now pours out of Job's emaciated body. And what torrents of words! They are sharp, direct, and blunt. They are powerful, too. It truly is an astonishing sight. That mouth covered with sores can still speak! That body weakened by obnoxious sickness still has the strength to engage God in controversy! "I will speak in the bitterness of my soul,"[7] Job declares. His words are sharp because they are not spoken by his mouth but by his embittered soul. They are direct because they come from the spirit crying out to be vindicated. They are blunt because they well out of the depths of a person beaten and crushed for no good reason. And they have to be powerful because Job is engaging no less than the formidable God of the traditional religion in his own defense at a tribunal, at a court of law.

The consciousness of having God as his adversary makes Job a master of language. The images he employs drive his contention powerfully home to those who care to listen to him. He, for example, accuses God and says:

> Water wears away stone,
> Torrents sweep away earth's soil,
> And you destroy human hope.
> (Job 14:19)

What vivid imageries! And a perfect parallelism, too, that heightens the horror of God being the destroyer of human hope!

Stone is hard. It is solid. It is enduring. So is human hope. That is why human beings can endure from one generation to the next despite adversities. That is why they can envision life in the face of death. As to earth's soil, it is our Mother. It is the womb from which we are taken and to which we return. It hatches us, nourishes us, sustains us, in life and also in death. So also is human hope. Because of our Mother called hope, we human beings are not prisoners of the past; our time extends to eternity. On account of that hope the inner space of our spirit expands beyond the space of our physical life. Hope is then the womb in which we live, struggle, travail, dream. In it we are in touch with the source of life, in communication with all that was, is, and shall be, and in communion with that power of love called God. Hope means, then, that even though yesterday is obliterated, there is still today. It assures that should today be destroyed, there will be tomorrow. Hope is that power of continuity against the power of discontinuity. It rescues human beings from the tyranny of time. It saves us from the imprisonment of space. It frees us from enslavement of finitude. The God who saves must, then, be the God of hope. God without hope is a contradiction. It is a gross deforma-

tion of divinity. It is no longer God. It is a demon. God without hope is
demonic, not messianic.

But the God of Job, of his people, the God worshipped in his religion,
is the God who "destroys human hope." That God, just as water wears
away hard, solid, and enduring stone, wears away human hope. That God,
who like torrents sweeping away the earth's soil that bears, nourishes, and
sustains life, sweeps away Job's hope. How sadistic that God is! Job puts
his case before the imaginary jury in the court, crying out in pain and
indignation:

> God puts me in custody of the vicious,
> Tosses me into the hand of the wicked.
> I was at ease and God crushed me,
> Grabbed me by the neck and mangled me.
> God set me up as a target,
> God's archers ring me round.
> God stabs my vitals without pity,
> Pours out my guts on the ground.
> God rends me rift on rift,
> Rushes at me like a warrior.
>   (Job 16:11–14)

The hearts of the jury must have gone out to Job. If this is true, and
this must be true coming from the man in terrible spiritual anguish and
physical pain, then God is guilty, guilty, guilty! What cruelty God has
committed against this poor man, stabbing his kidneys and pouring them
out on the ground! The verdict of the jury is already clear: the God
accused by Job is a murderer! Before the court Job groans and wails:

> My spirit is broken,
> My eye is dimmed with anguish,
> My limbs are all like a shadow.
> My days are done,
> My plans shattered,
> My heart's desires.
>   (from Job 17:1–11)

The entire court must have held its breath in silent consternation. A feeling of helplessness fills the air. A sense of resignation overwhelms the
audience who hears this extraordinary witness of a man against God. It
is a hopeless case and Job knows it. He speaks for himself and for those
who suffer in body and in spirit when he says:

> Indeed this I know for the truth,
> that no one can win a case against God.

> If a person chooses to argue with God,
> God will not answer one question in a thousand.
> (Job 9:1–3)

The case against God must be closed. Human beings are no match for the God of terror. To the God of traditional piety, to the deity of religious establishment, we must concede defeat.

But Job is not a loser in his litigation against God. At one point he is able to muster his moral courage to declare: "God may slay me, I'll not quiver!" (13:15). Job puts God on the defensive. God wins the case by refusing to answer one question in a thousand! What kind of God is this? The impassioned speech Job makes at the end of the dialogue can only have come from a person who has, after many a day and night of struggle of the soul, been liberated from the God of retribution:

> Let the Almighty state the case against me!
> If my accuser had written out the indictment,
> I would not keep silence and remain indoors.
> No! I would flaunt it on my shoulder
> and wear it like a crown on my head;
> I would plead the whole record of my life
> and present that in court as my defence.
> (Job 31:35–37)

NOTES

1. The poem is by P. Mookan. See *For the Dawning of the New*, Jeffrey Abayasekera and D. Preman Niles, eds. (Singapore: Christian Conference of Asia, 1981), p. 29.

2. The Prologue of the Book of Job (chaps. 1–2) and the Epilogue (42:7–17) are regarded by most scholars "as part of an ancient folktale which the author of the Dialogue (chaps. 3–31) used as the framework and point of departure for his poetic treatment of the problem of suffering" (*Job*, introduction, translation and notes by Marvin H. Pope, Anchor Bible [New York: Doubleday, 1965], p. xxii).

3. *Job*, ibid., p. 8.

4. Majjhima-nikaya I, 49–54, in Edward Conze, ed., *The Buddhist Texts through the Ages* (New York: Harper & Row, 1964), pp. 68–69.

5. *A Dictionary of Chinese Buddhist Terms*, comp. William Edward Soothill and Lewis Hodous (Delhi: Motilal Banarsidass, 1977), p. 379b.

6. See *Peake's Commentary on the Bible*, Matthew Black and H. H. Rowley, eds. (London: Thomas Nelson, 1962), p. 599.

7. This quotation and following quotations from the Book of Job are Marvin Pope's translation in his Anchor Bible volume *Job*.

CHAPTER 3

Distance between Abba and God

There is, in fact, no winner or loser in a case like Job's. No amount of courage and passion on the part of Job can make the God of retribution speak. It is perhaps more accurate to say that however justly Job may plead and however vehemently he may protest, those who represent the theological formulation and religious interest of the traditional religion will not try to understand Job's struggle in the depth of his soul and have no sympathy for his theological questioning of the time-honored teaching on God. Perhaps their religious mind has been so framed that it is impossible for them to understand it. Such struggle is deemed a lack of faith, a sign of weak faith. Such questioning is quickly branded as heretical.

The story of Job is of course not an isolated story. It is the story of many women and men who can no longer accept the official teachings of their religion on the ground of their conscience and on the basis of their historical experience. Is this not the story of religious reformers in the history of religions? In the Book of Job we are not told that Job pressed his protest to its logical conclusion to bring about a reformation, but a profound change must have taken place in his experience of God and in his perception of the relationship between God and humanity.

An insight such as this compels us to look at the suffering and death of Jesus from a perspective different from that of the traditional church from its earliest time to the present day. I am referring to the emphasis on obedience to God as the key to understand the death of Jesus on the cross. There is, for example, a very early "christological" hymn quoted by Paul in his letter to the Philippians (2:6–8). The hymn speaks of Jesus' self-emptying, his making himself nothing. Then it goes on to extol him for accepting "in obedience" death on the cross. Jesus did empty himself to carry out God's mission among the underprivileged people. He went about his work entirely absorbed in their problems and completely identifying himself with their predicaments. Are not there, then, reasons to ask whether Jesus accepted "in obedience" death on the cross? Is there a necessary connection between Jesus' self-emptying and his obedience? Does his solidarity with people lead to his unquestioning acceptance of crucifixion in obedience to God? Would it not be conceivable that the more he strives with the poor and the marginalized, the more difficult it becomes for him to accept an untimely death as decreed by the God of love?

There are suggestions in the Gospel stories that Jesus went to his death on the cross not completely at peace with God. Of course the question is what kind of God he was not at peace with. Was he perhaps confronted with a situation similar to that in which Job and many others found themselves? This is not entirely a groundless speculation. As the writers of the Gospels tell us, Jesus' controversy with the religious authorities was ultimately related to different beliefs in God. What we see here is a conflict between two opposing perceptions of God and two different religious worlds built on them. Here, it seems, is an important factor to remember in our grappling with the problem of religious truths: human perception of God is very much shaped by social and cultural environments in which human beings live, and that perception in turn shapes their worldviews and religious beliefs. The mutual impact between our belief in God and the particular world in which we live underlies questions and conflicts related to religious truths. Does not even a quick glance at the development of Christian teachings and doctrines confirm this is the case? Later on we shall have the occasion to see how this mutual impact has affected the Christian church in its understanding of the cross.

If we follow what has been said and apply it to the life and ministry of Jesus, we may find that much more than "obedience" is involved in how Jesus confronted his own suffering and finally his death on the cross. For this reason we do not begin with "theological interpretation" of the cross. Rather we want first to look at the cross as the extreme physical suffering Jesus went through at the end of his life and see how that suffering brings into an even clearer focus the meaning of "the Word become flesh." A theological exercise such as this does not refer just to God's solo saving act; it is very much related to the experiences of us human beings — experiences of people like Job, Tamil tea plantation workers in Sri Lanka, or victims of the Nazi holocaust, in short, millions upon millions of women, men, and children in human history who suffer and die because of injustice and oppression.

My God, My God, Why Have You Abandoned Me?

The cross is an "excruciating (from the Latin for 'out of the cross') method of execution," says a report of modern medicine. There are "the shocks produced by trauma and blood loss from a severe flogging, as well as the extreme difficulty of breathing on the cross. The full weight of the body pulled down on a victim's wrists (not palms), which were nailed to the crossbar. If he tried to relieve the pressure by straightening up, his body weight pushed down on his feet, nailed to the vertical post. The painful position necessitated shallow exhalation, which led to a buildup of carbon dioxide in the blood and eventual asphyxia. Cardiac rupture could also have been involved."[1] The cross was an extreme form of inhumanity inflicted on humanity. It was an instrument of a slow torture until death. It was a cruel means of letting loose the basest human sadistic instincts on a helpless victim.

The cross, and for that matter any other form of physical torture and death, is a deep human tragedy. It is a mockery not only of the person of the victim but also of the victimizers. It is a witness to the demonic power working in the depths of humanity. The cross is also a mockery of God, the God who, according to a creation story in the Hebrew Scriptures, created human beings in God's own image (Gen. 1:26). It is the denial of the humanity of human persons and at the same time the denial of the divinity of God, the divine person. The cross testifies to how low human beings can fall. It testifies to the reality of how human beings can sin against each other and against God.

Jesus suffered that excruciating pain of the cross. He must have witnessed executions on the cross in his life. Each time he must have felt the agony of the victim in himself. The physical pain of the victim must have penetrated his whole being, making him shudder with horror. He could have cried to God on behalf of the victim whose face was contorted with pain and whose body was seized by the convulsion of death: "My God, why have you abandoned him?" But now he himself is going through that shock of pain and spasms of death.

He has fought for the dignity of human persons, but he is now himself subjected to the extreme indignity of the cross. He has practiced love, even love of enemies, but he is nailed to the cross of hatred. All his life he has struggled for justice, but now he is suffering injustice on the cross. To compound his terrible physical pain, he must have experienced an extreme form of loneliness, the kind of loneliness that makes us completely numb and demoralized. His disciples who were with him day in and day out for three years have all fled from him. Peter's words denying the knowledge of him must have pierced his heart like a two-edged sword. The men and women with whose plight he identified are not there to support him during these hours of pain and anguish. Did not some of them even shout with the crowds, "Crucify him! Crucify him!"?

Should we dismiss ideas such as these as unworthy of Jesus? Would not these ideas be entirely foreign to him who "voluntarily" went to death as the savior of the whole world? This is the theology of the traditional

Christian church. But it has done something to the cross perhaps it did not foresee or it refused to see. It removes the sting of pain and death from the cross, beautifies it, and makes an ornament of it. Even the symbolic meaning of the cross tends to get lost in Christian piety and theological exercise. What we have learned, however, is that the physical reality of the cross and its symbolic meaning are recovered only when it becomes related to people's search for the meaning of life when their lives are rendered meaningless, and to their struggle for freedom and human dignity against oppressive powers. For us to realize more deeply the physical and spiritual pain Jesus went through on the cross, it may be useful to listen to the account of someone who came out from that "death-experience" alive. This is what Dostoyevsky, that great Russian writer, tells us about the man led to the guillotine to be executed:

> ...here all final hope...is removed *for certain*; here there is a sentence, and in the very fact that there is certainly no escape from it all the horrible suffering lies, and there is no suffering on earth greater than this. Take a soldier and put him in front of a cannon in the midst of battle and shoot at him, he will still hope; but read this same soldier a death sentence which is certain, and he will lose his mind or begin to cry. Who could say that human nature can endure such a trial without slipping into madness? Why this ghastly, needless, useless outrage?[2]

This is not a literary fiction. Nor is it just a novelist's fantasy. Here Dostoyevsky is speaking out of his own experience.

When he was twenty-seven years old, Dostoyevsky was arrested for taking part in a political conspiracy and sentenced to death. He was already on the scaffold waiting for his execution when a reprieve arrived from the czar commuting his sentence to hard labor for four years in Siberia. What an immense suffering of the body, the spirit, and the mind he went through on the scaffold awaiting his *certain* death! "No suffering on earth is greater than this," he says. He knows personally what this means. This means "all final hope is gone." Out of his own experience he tells his readers that there is no greater suffering than that of losing all hope. The condemned person is reduced to a hopeless person. He becomes a mathematical point; he has become a person without space in the whole universe. He also becomes an atemporal being, a being who has lost time in the eternal flow of time. One becomes frozen at an intersection of time and space. This is the ultimate meaning of hopelessness. This is the end of everything, literally everything, even God, except that horrible abysmal unknown. One is no longer a person, not even a thing. One becomes nothingness.

To this account of ultimate hopelessness Dostoyevsky adds: "This was the agony and the horror of which Christ told, too. No, you cannot treat a man like this!" Of course not. You, the authorities of the czarist government, cannot treat me, Dostoyevsky, like this! You, you who hold power, cannot treat citizens like this! Even criminals, not to say political dissidents, cannot be treated like this! Human beings just do not have the right to treat each other like this! But the tragedy is that Dostoyevsky was treated like this. Countless men, women, and children in human history have been treated like this. Jesus too was treated like this! He too went through the experience of hope-less-ness. He too was reduced to space-less-ness and time-less-ness. He too experienced that ultimate nothingness.

Here is a deep theological perception that a writer such as Dostoyevsky is able to provide us but theologians are often incapable of or inhibited from telling us — a perception that the agony and horror of Jesus on the cross is intrinsically related to the agony and horror of men and women who face extinction at the hands of others. The Christian church and its teachers have taught as if the cross has to be absolutely unique to be the cross, as if the agony of Jesus has to be surrealistic to be of redemptive significance, and as if the horror of extinction does not belong to Jesus. There is a strong tendency in traditional theology to dwell solely on the "salvific" effect of the cross and set aside completely the real experience of the cross people have to bear in their lives and take with them to their graves. If Jesus identifies himself with people in their pain and suffering during his ministry, are there reasons to believe that he becomes dis-engaged from them at the very horrible hour of death, that somehow a divine factor is at work to make him utterly different from other human beings? Does the "Word" stop being the "flesh" it has become at that final stage of Jesus' life? Is the "incarnation," this difficult theological concept, no longer applicable to Jesus on the cross? Does Jesus become "dis-incarnate" in that extreme situation from which no human being with flesh and blood can be free?

So Dostoyevsky the writer carries on with in-carnate theology when theologians take flight into dis-incarnate theology. He continues his "worldly" theology when theologians take refuge in "other-worldly" theology. Dostoyevsky, in short, picks up the theological thread theologians leave hanging in a theological vacuum. Writers such as Dostoyevsky can do this because they, on the one hand, have no particular theological interest to protect or religious teaching to defend, and, on the other, they are in much closer touch with human realities that confront ordinary men and women in everyday life. Jesus for them can be a much more real person than for theologians.

Dostoyevsky is right. You cannot treat a person like this! This "you" for him is the czarist government. That "you" treated him like this. That is why he wants to shout at the top of his voice that the Roman colonial power, that another "you," had no right to treat Jesus like this. He must have known countless innocent men and women treated like this by those who have power over them, in Russia, his own beloved Mother Russia, and in other countries. With equal force he must have wanted to shout and protest that they cannot be treated like this either.

The problem gets very complicated when God is perceived to permit that "you" to treat Dostoyevsky and many others like this, to allow that "you" to treat even Jesus like this. If God does not permit it, at least God seems to condone it. Whether God permits it or just condones it, we find ourselves in deeply troubled theological water. This is what Job had to face in his painful debate with his three friends. This, in fact, is the most agonizing question for which most believers have no answer. This might have been Jesus' question too.

It may be that the question is implied in Jesus' outcry on the cross: "My God, my God, why have you abandoned me?" (Mark 15:34; par. Matt. 27:46). What a heart-rending cry! Is it not a cry of agony caused by unbearable physical pain? But it must have been much more than that. It must have been a cry of horror as well — the horror of being abandoned by God. That horror might have given rise to a suspicion that somehow God also has to do with it. Has God engineered it to happen? This was Job's question. Could this have been also Jesus' question? This is not an idle speculation because traditional theology does imply that God has everything to do with the cross. Of course it gives a very noble reason: God has Jesus crucified on the cross for the sake of saving sinners. A theological reason such as this has to be looked into closely. This we will do a little later. In the light of Job's contention, can we not perhaps say that there is a God of retribution behind that theological reason? Who else but the God of retribution would demand the life of a victim in order to let the culprit go free?

"My God, my God, why have you abandoned me?" Read this cry of Jesus on the cross recalling the medical report on the Roman crucifixion quoted earlier. Then it cannot be an object of calm contemplation for those who seek spiritual contentedness. Hear this cry in the echoes of the agony and horror of a condemned person such as Dostoyevsky. Then it ceases to be just a part of the lectionary reading for the Passion week in the Christian calendar that arouses no deep passion. That cry cannot be explained as a "theological trial between God and God."[3] To theologize about the cross in this way is to minimize Jesus as a *human* person, to diminish the *human* agony of the cross, to take away the *human* horror of death. Jesus was crucified as a human person, not as a divine being. The cross is an existential struggle between a human being and God. It is a painful engagement with the God of traditional religion, the God of retribution taught by the institutional church. Do we have in this cry of Jesus, then, his last struggle to be free from the shadow of that God? Is this his decisive break with that God of his religion and his church — a break that is needed to enable him to be at peace with God in God's own self, the God whose loving presence he made real to the oppressed people in place of the angry and revengeful God?

We are eternally indebted to Mark and Matthew for recording this cry of Jesus among the words he said on the cross. It discloses to us at least partially what might have been going on in Jesus' mind during those last fateful hours of his life. That is why we cannot regard it simply as a passing thought that has no deeper meaning. It in fact contains a clue to a fresh understanding of the meaning of the cross.

Why Psalm 22?

We do not know how Jesus said it. Did he just whisper it to himself? Did he say it barely loud enough for those women at the foot of the cross to hear it? Or is it a loud cry heard even by the Roman soldiers, his religious opponents, the curious onlookers? It must be the latter. This is what Mark tells us: "Some of the bystanders, on hearing this, said, 'Hark, he is calling Elijah.' A man ran and soaked a sponge in sour wine and held it to his lips on the end of a cane" (Mark 15:34–36; par. Matt. 27:46–48). Jesus' cry, "My God, my God, why have you abandoned me?," must have caused a considerable stir and excitement among those at the scene of his crucifixion. That something extraordinary might still happen appeared momentarily to be a possibility. Perhaps in the hearts of some people a hope still lingered on that the crucifixion should not be the end of Jesus.

The excitement did not last long, however. Jesus did not respond to the sour wine held to his lips on the end of a cane. No Elijah came to rescue him from the cross. Nothing extraordinary happened. As it turned out, the cry was, according to Mark's account, one of the very last things Jesus said before he died. Except for his religious opponents, people must have been disappointed. Again Jesus seemed to have betrayed their expectation.

The Vine and Its Branches

These words on the lips of the dying Jesus come, of course, from Psalm 22 in the Hebrew Scriptures. Why this particular psalm? What was in Jesus' mind when he uttered them? There are many psalms to quote from. Jesus must have been familiar with them also. He could, for example, have recalled those trusting words of Psalm 31:

> With thee, O Lord, I have sought shelter,
>   let me never be put to shame.
> Deliver me in thy righteousness;
>   bow down and hear me,
>   come quickly to my rescue;
> be thou my rock of refuge,
>   a stronghold to keep me safe.
>   (Ps. 31:1–2)

This psalm, like Psalm 22, is also a psalm of lamentation and thanks-giving of someone "who, suffering from illness for many years, calum-niated and persecuted by haughty adversaries, shunned by friends, seeks refuge in God in the face of the threat of a violent death."[4] This prayer would have been worthy of a man who demonstrated in words and in ac-tion complete trust in God for good or for ill. Did not Jesus say to his care-worn listeners: "Set your mind on God's reign and God's justice be-fore everything else, and all the rest will come to you as well" (Matt. 6:33)? Did he not also say: "Come to me, all whose work is hard, whose load is heavy; and I will give you relief" (Matt. 11:28)? These words must have come from his deep awareness of his relationship to God. God was his comfort in time of difficulty. God was his assurance when he was torn between the mission of God's reign and the mission of liberation from the Roman colonial rule. God was his relief and refuge when he faced danger. Should he not, then, have said on the cross: "My God, my God, be thou my rock of refuge, a stronghold to keep me"?

There are also those moving "farewell discourses" Jesus is reported to have given to his disciples (John 14–17). The picture of Jesus that emerges from these discourses is that of trust, confidence, and assurance. "Set your hearts at rest," he exhorted his disciples. "Trust in God always; trust also in me" (John 14:1). Trust is the basis of sound and healthy human relationships. Without it human relationships will be vitiated by intrigues and destroyed by conflicts of interests. This is also the case with the relationship between God and human beings. It is even more so in the latter case. Jesus was able to rekindle that trust in God in people, espe-cially those women and men excluded from the religious establishment and deemed as lost to God. What a formidable task for Jesus to restore their trust in God! But this is precisely what Jesus was able to do with so-cial and religious outcasts. God once again becomes trustworthy to them and they to God.

This undoubtedly is the heart of Jesus' ministry. Jesus sums up this relationship of trust when he says: "I am in my Father, and you in me and I in you" (John 14:20). This is a radically new and fresh insight into the relationship that involves God, Jesus, and other people. This is the relationship of inter-penetration. God is God because of it. Jesus is what he is because of it. And people are also what they are because of it. God alone is not God. God detached from humanity, being in God's own isolated splendor, is not God. And people experience God within them. God-consciousness in them makes them what they are as human beings. No deprivation of any kind, be it power, wealth, prestige, even human rights, can reduce a human person to a nonperson as long as that God-consciousness remains. Once that God-consciousness is removed, a human person becomes a nonperson, nonhuman. There must, then, be something frightful about being abandoned by God, about losing that "God-in-me" awareness.

As if to drive this point deeply into his disciples' minds and hearts, Jesus uses the metaphor of the vine and its branches. "I am the vine," he says, "and you the branches. He who dwells in me, as I dwell in him, bears much fruit; for apart from me you can do nothing" (John 15:5). God is not mentioned here, but God is implied. The relationship of Jesus and the disciples as that of the vine and its branches is the extension of the relationship between God and Jesus. God, Jesus, and the disciples, and by inference human beings, are bound together in a vital relationship, vital in the sense of having to do with life. Once this vital relationship is broken, life ebbs away and death sets in, just as the branches wither and die when they are separated from the vine. It is utterly inconceivable that Jesus on the cross would be deprived of this vital relationship because God had abandoned him. And God without it would be less than God too.

This is the faith of Jesus. It is deeply rooted in the consciousness of being in vital relationships with God and his fellow human beings. It must be this faith that enables him to be firm in the conviction that the final victory is his. This faith is so strong that he could envision a new future beyond desertion by his disciples and death on the cross. No wonder he brings his discourses to a note of triumph when he says: "Look, the hour is coming, has indeed already come, when you are all to be scattered...leaving me alone. Yet I am not alone, because the Father is with me. I have told you all this so that in me you may find peace. In the world you will have trouble. But courage! The victory is mine; I have conquered the world" (John 16:32–33). This was Jesus before his final showdown with the religious and political authorities. It makes us wonder all the more why it is Psalm 22, and not psalms such as Psalm 31, that was on his lips in his last moments on the cross.

The Shepherd and the Sheep

Or there is Psalm 23, made immortal by its exquisite language and vivid imagery, its profound faith and its unwavering trust in God. It is "the mature fruit of a heart which, having passed through many bitter experiences and having fought many battles, had been allowed to find at the decline of life in its intimate communion with God the serenity of a contented spirit — peace of mind and in all dangers, strength."[5] In those moments of extreme pain and agony Jesus might not have been able to recite the whole of this marvelous psalm that sums up the beauty and power of faith — a faith he himself practiced and tried to inculcate in people, but at least he could have died with those words of the ancient poet:

> Even though I walk through the valley
>   of the shadow of death,
> I fear no evil;
> for thou art with me;
>   thy rod and thy staff,
>   they comfort me.
>
>   (Ps. 23:4, RSV)

It is not these trusting words of Psalm 23, but the bitter words of Psalm 22 that Jesus uttered. It is not the tranquility of the soul that has overcome the world expressed in Psalm 23, but the agitation of the spirit in the face of struggle against violence and injustice in Psalm 22 that seem to have taken hold of Jesus.

Psalm 23 begins with the imagery of shepherd, an imagery very close to Jesus' heart. "The Lord is my shepherd," says the psalmist. It is this imagery of shepherd and that of sheep that Jesus uses again and again to drive home to people the loving relationship between them and God. The bond between the shepherd and the sheep is natural and instinctive. It is forged not on the basis of social demands, religious requirements, or even moral imperatives, but out of mutual affection and trust. Jesus himself must have been familiar with all this. John the Evangelist reports him to have said: "The man who enters by the door is the shepherd in charge of the sheep. The door-keeper admits him and the sheep hear his voice; he calls his own sheep by name, and leads them out. When he has brought them all out, he goes ahead and the sheep follow, because they know his voice" (John 10:2–4). The shepherd knows each and every sheep of his flock *by name* and his sheep know *his voice*. What binds them together is the life they share, the kinship that has developed between them. Jesus firmly believes that such kinship of affection and trust exists between God and people.

Psalm 23 is a truly great psalm. It is great not only because of its poetic beauty and literary masterliness, but because of its spiritual depth. It must have come from someone who had gone through the turbulent storm of life, undergone great pain and suffering, and experienced the horror of deathly power in and around him or her. To come out of all this with one's spirit unbroken and with one's faith in God strengthened is the triumph both of God and humanity. This experience of triumph turns, for our psalmist, not into self-glorification, but into a confession of faith. "For thou art with me," says the poet, "thy rod and thy staff they comfort me."

This must have been Jesus' confession too when he is confronted with danger and threatened by his opponents with death during his ministry. He is able to exhort his followers saying: "Do not fear those who kill the body and after that have nothing more they can do" (Luke 12:4). This is not human courage before the power of death, but faith in the power of God to overcome it. That faith is the real source and origin of fearlessness.

For our psalmist the confession of faith becomes a confession of wonder in God's saving activity. The psalm is brought to the height of peace and confidence with these words:

> Thou preparest a table before me in the presence of my enemies;
> thou anointest my head with oil, my cup overflows.
>
> (Ps. 23:3)

In the valley of the shadow of death and in the presence of one's enemies — this is the reality the psalmist had to face. It is also the situation in which Jesus found himself. The oil with which Jesus is to be anointed is blood, his own blood. This is the time when he ought to have been able to say that his cup overflows, that it overflows with his faith in God's unfailing love, the love that will never abandon him.

But Why Psalm 22?

It is, however, not the trusting words of Psalm 31 but the bitter words of Psalm 22 that Jesus on the cross uttered. It is not the tranquility of the soul that had overcome the fear of death in Psalm 23 but the turmoil of the spirit in deep stress and agony expressed in Psalm 22 that seems to have taken hold him. Abandoned by his fellow human beings and also by God, Jesus seems left alone to engage himself in his last futile struggle against violence and injustice.

There must be something in Psalm 22 that links Jesus with the ancient psalmist. "My God, my God, why have you abandoned me?" In these words of the psalmist Jesus must have heard the echoes deep in his heart. Absorbed in his work among underprivileged people, intensely engaged in his controversy with the religious leaders, unafraid in his challenge to the Roman colonial authorities, Jesus has to be conscious of God's power. He cannot afford to indulge himself in doubt about God's presence with him. Each and every moment of his intense engagement with people is at the same time his intense engagement with God. If he had even the slightest question about God, it is so deeply tucked away in the depths of his mind that he is scarcely aware of it. But as these moments of intensely active engagement with his most extraordinary ministry are over and when the moments of the excruciating pain and loneliness on the cross set in, that question about God long forgotten must have come out of its hiding and tormented him, even just for a few fleeting moments. Maybe, and I must stress the word "maybe," it is in these few moments that Jesus, in spite of himself, finds himself uttering those words in Psalm 22. And this gives us a rare glimpse into Jesus' theological mind, into the depths of his spirit in communion with God.

It is necessary, then, to reflect on the situation in which believing men and women, such as the psalmist of Psalm 22, are prompted to ask, "My God, my God, why have you abandoned me?" This is a devastating question. They must have been in deep agony of the soul to come out with such a question. They must have been beset with the troubles that turned their lives into chaos and made them utterly helpless. All this must have tormented them with religious doubts.[6] Like Job they must have done all they could to live a life worthy of the God of their religion. Theirs is a demanding God. They must have made every effort to please their God with strict observance of the laws and rituals prescribed by their religion. Their faith is not merely a matter of external formality but a matter of the heart. It may well be that they have done much to extend their love for God to the love for their neighbors and that they are able to say as Job:

> If I have withheld their needs from the poor
> or let the widow's eye grow dim with tears,
> if I have eaten my crust alone,
> and the orphan has not shared it with me . . .
> if I have seen anyone perish for lack of clothing,
> or a poor man with nothing to cover him,
> if his body had no cause to bless me,
> because he was not kept warm with a fleece from my flock,
> if I have raised my hand against the innocent,
> knowing that people would side with me in court,
> then may my shoulder-blade be torn from my shoulder,
> my arm wrenched out of its socket!
>
> (Job 31:16–22)

But the reward for all this is "abuse, scorn and jeering by people" (Ps. 22:6). Persons like the psalmist find themselves "laid low in the dust of death" (Ps. 22:15), "telling a tale of misery" (Ps. 22:17).

How could they, then, not have been assailed by doubt about their God? Is my God a caring God? Why does God leave me in such a desperate state? Is the God of my religion really the God who saves? If God did rescue my ancestors from slavery, why does this same God show not the slightest sign of rescuing me from my misery? Why does God leave me alone to fight my adverse fate? Is this God of my faith, my people, my religion, a God of love and justice? Or is this God as capricious, insensitive, terrifying as other gods?

These are all *human* questions of course, but what else could they be? Religious questions have to be human questions, questions raised by human beings about themselves, about the world in which they live, about the cosmos mysterious to them, and about the God who is out of their sight. In theology and in matters of faith we must learn to ask questions on our own behalf and not on behalf of God. Christian theology has for too long presumed to speak on behalf of God. The result is that it has put God in an impossible position. Christian theologians are often just like Job's friends who try to play God to the poor Job. Their God is a moral God who does not do immoral things such as afflicting the innocent and destroying the helpless. That is why they have almost forced Job to admit that he has sinned, that he has blasphemed God, that he deserves all these miseries. Theirs is an insensitive theology and their God is a vindictive God.

But this kind of theology has not been able to help and comfort the human souls crying out in agony. This kind of God cannot silence them and command their obedience. It is right that Job rebelled against his friends' theology and questioned the justice of their God. It is not strange that more and more men and women today, like that victim of racial hatred in Sri Lanka, are no longer convinced by this kind of theology and refuse to take for granted a God who is indifferent to their plight and misery. Here is the beginning of a theology that takes human beings seriously. It is this kind of serious theology that we find in Psalm 22. And it is not an accident that Jesus, that very human person of human persons, cries out in pain and agony to God on the cross, not using the words of Psalm 31 or Psalm 23, but of Psalm 22. On the cross Jesus is engaged in a theology that shatters the rules and wisdom of traditional religion.

"My God, my God, why have you abandoned me?" We have to agree that this is "the most staggering sentence in the gospel record."[7] Uttered by the psalmist these words are staggering enough, because they defy commonplace religious wisdom. Said by people like Job, they contain a deep feeling of resentment and defiance. Coming from millions and millions of persons suffering hunger, poverty, or oppression, they expose the impotence of the God worshipped in church and temple and taught by erudite religious teachers. But uttered by Jesus, these words are not only staggering but *most* staggering. On his lips as he hangs on the cross, they are not only most staggering, but most agonizing. Coming from the dying Jesus, they are not only most agonizing, but most horrifying. The moments when God must be nearest to him, the hours when God must be closest to him, the time when God must be fully and completely with him and in him, God abandons him!

Abandonment by God in the depth of suffering is the greatest of all sufferings. Absence of God at the height of human agony is the most cruel of all cruelties. Forsakenness by God in the abyss of death is the most hopeless of all hopelessness. Stripped of our belongings, our relatives and friends, our dignity and humanity, we experience excruciating suffering. Still, we are not yet finished. But stripped of God, we have lost all defense, all meaning, all hope, and all reason to live. Such must be Jesus' suffering on the cross. In that depth of suffering Jesus must have met that psalmist whose words he particularly remembered. He must have also heard echoes of Job's cry. He must have found himself in the company of millions upon millions of people, past and present, dying with a horrible thought of God's abandonment in their hearts.

In that abyss of pain Jesus is most fully human. There is no divinity to separate him from other human beings. There is no "very God" to shield him from the "very man" and to make his suffering a sham. There is not any theo-logical justification to turn his suffering into the design of God to save sinful human beings from their sin. The equation of suffering and sin in the theology of Job's friends and in some of traditional Christian theology is simply outrageous. This is an inhuman theology. It is a logic conceived in the minds of armchair theologians. It is a caricature of the true loving God. In that depth and abyss of suffering one has to rebel against that God of religious orthodoxy, to challenge that God, and to *abandon* that God.

Distance between Abba and God

It has been pointed out that "nowhere else in the gospels does Jesus address God as God," and that "elsewhere, in the supreme agony even in the garden, it is his Father to whom he appeals, with all the boundless wealth of affection that lies in the infant name 'Abba.' "[8] This is an extremely important observation. Between Abba and God there is a great distance, the distance created by the cross. The "Abba" of the prayer with which Jesus taught his disciples to pray has vanished. On the cross where he needs "Abba," Jesus addresses God as God and not as "Abba." What are we to make of this?

It has been stressed that Jesus' use of the word *Abba* in addressing God is unparalleled in the whole of Jewish literature. "*Abba* (as *jaba* is still used today in Arabic) was the word used by a young child to its father; it was an everyday family word, which no one had ventured to use in addressing God. Jesus did. He spoke to his heavenly Father in as child-like, trustful and intimate a way as a little child to its father."[9] Very few in Jesus' time dared to address God as "Abba," or "Father." To Jesus, however, God is "Abba," or "Papa," from whom he can ask for daily bread and for forgiveness of sins (Luke 11:2–4; par. Matt. 6:9–13), like a child from its parents. The bond of love between him and Abba-God is very deep. His trust in Abba-God is unshakable. He spent his life reactivating this bond of love and trust in people — the men, women, and children to whom God is not "Abba" but a stern Judge, a vindictive Deity, a remote and hidden God. The parental bond of love and trust between them and God is broken. They fear and tremble before the God enthroned in the holy of holies inaccessible to them. This God is not the Abba-God of people, but the God of church authorities, the God secluded in the fortress of unintelligible doctrines and defended and protected by religious taboos and rituals. This is a God of retribution.

Jesus breaks away from that God. For him God is "Abba-God" and not Judge-God. "Is there a man among you," he asked those men and women around him, "who will offer his son a stone when he asks for bread, or a snake when he asks for fish?" The mothers and fathers in his audience must have responded to Jesus with a strong no. No mother, no father, would do such a thing! A parent who would do such a thing must be a child abuser. That parent must have a sick mind. But why does Jesus have to say such an obvious thing? Why does he have to ask such an obvious question?

This is just the point. The experience everyone has and knows does not lead to the obvious experience and knowledge of God. Somehow it has been decided that there is no direct relationship between the two. Jesus is anxious that the people reconnect their experience as human beings with their knowledge of God. And how best could he accomplish this except to appeal to their parent-instinct, the instinct that is the most basic, spontaneous, natural, of all human instincts, the instinct that is translated into one of the deepest kinds of love, the love that goes beyond logic, transcends conditions, and expresses itself in self-giving and self-sacrifice? Jesus continues: "If you, then, bad as you are, know how to give your children what is good for them, how much more will your heavenly father [Abba] give good things to those who ask him!" (Matt. 7:9–11; par. Luke 11:11–13). The connection between human experience and the knowledge of God is at once established. If a parent were to give a stone to his or her children instead of the fish they ask for, that parent would cease at once to be a parent: he would no longer be "papa" to them and she not "mama" to them any more. He betrays his fatherhood and she her motherhood. It must be the same with God. The God who ceases to be "Abba" to human beings betrays Godhood. The God who is no "Papa" or "Mama" to men, women, and children who struggle to live in the face of adversities of life, who try to make sense of this senseless world, is no longer God. But Jesus must have driven home to them a further point: God is not just like a father or a mother; God *is* Abba (Father or Mother)! It is in this Abba-God that all our human loves have their origin, especially the love of parents for their children.

How did Jesus himself come to experience and know God as Abba? Was it forged by the love of his parents? Did it come from his strong reaction to the rigid and autocratic concept of God upheld by the orthodox religion? Did it develop out of his deep empathy with the people ostracized by the official religious community? We can only guess. The Gospels are not illuminating when it comes to the question of how Jesus' faith was shaped and developed. But the fact is that God was "Abba" to Jesus throughout his life and during those evening hours he had spent in the Garden of Gethsemane before he was arrested. "Abba, Father," he said, "all things are possible to thee; take this cup away from me. Yet not what I will, but what thou wilt" (Mark 14:36; pars. Matt. 26:42, Luke 22:42). Indeed, "only one who had all his life found God the most real of all the facts of experience could, in the face of the overwhelming wave of spiritual anguish, have said" this.[10] In that critical hour of his life Jesus was in deep communion with God, not with an "almighty" God, but with a "trusted 'Abba.' " When a momentous happening was about to take place, he was in earnest consultation not with an "omniscient" God, but with a loving Father. As he was besieged with the conspiracy of the religious authorities to do him in, he ardently sought the counsel of God, not God the law-giver but God the caring Parent.

"Abba, Father, all things are possible to thee," Jesus prayed. All the simplicity, all the expectation, all the anticipation of a trusting child are contained in those words. Jesus at that hour in the garden is not praying to the all-powerful God for whom nothing in heaven and on earth is impossible. No, he is a human child clinging to its Abba-God for strength, for protection, for deliverance. Against the background of ominous darkness, bleak loneliness, a sublimely beautiful picture of union and communion of a trusting child and a loving Abba is illuminated. It is a picture of Jesus addressing his Abba in prayer when his "heart is ready to break with grief" (Mark 14:34). The struggle of a human soul could not have been more intense. The agony of the human spirit could not have been deeper. It is in intense struggle such as this, in deep agony such as this, and in desperate awareness of human impotence, that we are driven to the loving and saving God.

But Jesus did not address God as "Abba" on the cross. He did not say: "My Abba, my Abba, why have you abandoned me?" His "Abba" could not have abandoned him. The God he trusted all his life as Abba like a child could not have forsaken him. For the first time and also the last time in the Gospel records he cried to God not as Abba but as God. This is a great puzzle. It is a mystery almost incomprehensible. But there is more than a puzzle and a mystery involved here. Jesus' cry to God raises a grave theological question: Who is this God to whom Jesus directed his agonizing cry?

Many biblical scholars and Christian theologians through the ages have sought to solve this theological question. Here is a typical explanation by an exegete:

> With his dying powers he [Jesus] cries to God and now no longer sees in him the Father, for a wall of separation has risen between the Father and the Son, namely the world's sin and its curse as they now lie upon the Son. Jesus thirsts for God, but God has removed himself. It is not the Son that has left the Father, but the Father the Son. The Son cries for God, and God makes no reply to him.[11]

Human sin! This is the culprit. It separates what is not separable — the relationship between God the Father and Jesus the Son. The sin of disobeying God's command committed in another garden when Adam and Eve ate the forbidden fruit (Gen. 3) tears asunder that which cannot be torn asunder — the bond of love between Abba and Jesus.

Sin as a theological concept has dominated the way in which the Christian church has understood the relationship between God and humanity. This we already pointed out when we discussed sin in relation to the power of destructiveness that human beings inflict on one another. Even sin such as this is not so powerful as to destroy the parental love of God for humanity. To think otherwise is to underestimate the power of God's love. It is really a mystery why the Christian church constantly underestimates the power of God's love. And when it identifies sin as disobedience to God, it concedes to sin the power it does not have, that is, the power to alienate God from humanity. True, human beings may alienate themselves from God on account of the crimes they commit against one another. They pretend not to hear God. They refuse God a place in their lives. They even proclaim that God does not exist.

But this is a one-sided action on the part of human beings. They may estrange themselves from God, but God does not estrange God's own self from them. They may pretend not to hear God, but God does not cease to speak to them on that account. They may refuse God a place in their hearts, but God does not give up making inroads into them. And they may declare that God no longer exists, but God does exist, is really real, in the world. No matter how sin is understood — as the power of human destructiveness or even as disobedience to God, it is theologically not correct to say that "Jesus thirsts for God, but God has removed himself. It is not the Son that has left the Father, but the Father the Son. The Son cries for God, and God makes no reply to him." It has to be pointed out that the God in this biblical exegesis and theological statement who turned away, who made no reply to Jesus and left him, is *not* the Abba-God for whom Jesus thirsted and cried.

It is evident that there is something fundamentally amiss in the teaching of the church and in the theologizing of its teachers. We are again told:

> The nearest we can hope to come toward penetrating this mystery is to think of Jesus as being covered with the world's sin and curse and that, when God saw Jesus thus, he turned away from him.... That is why Jesus cried, "my God, my God," and not, "my Father."[12]

God turning away from Jesus on the cross covered with human sin? Is this what the cross actually means? We have to come back to this question later. Let us for the time being assume Jesus is covered with human sin. Does the God Jesus experienced as Abba turn away from him because of this? Is there not much evidence in Jesus' own words and deeds suggesting that Abba-God would do just the opposite, that is, that Abba-God would turn toward Jesus who is allegedly covered with all human sins and going through extreme physical and spiritual pain and suffering?

Again two things get confused here: the God of theologians and the Abba-God of Jesus. The God of theologians is understood on the premise that "Jesus is covered with the world's sin and curse." And there is another premise derived from the first: this God who hates the world's sin and curse is the God of vengeance. This is the God portrayed in the story of the flood in the Hebrew Scriptures (Gen. 6:9–9:19). "Now God saw that the whole world was corrupt and full of violence," so goes the story. The upshot of it all was God's resolve to destroy the world. How an ancient story such as this has affected the Christian understanding of God! How it has shaped the church's doctrine of God! And how it has exerted far-reaching influence on the Christian theology that developed the meaning of the cross!

But is it not obvious that such understanding of God in relation to humanity and particularly in relation to Jesus on the cross runs counter to Jesus' experience of God as Abba? His parable of "the father's love" (Luke 15:11–32) at once comes to mind. In the parable Jesus portrays the father with deepest affection and profound sensitivity. We can almost see in front of our eyes the father in terrible anguish. Here is his younger son demanding "not only the possession" of his property, "but also the right of disposal," and wanting an immediate "settlement because he proposes to lead an independent life."[13] This is outrageous, to say the least. The son, in the first place, is acting against the laws of inheritance in force at that time. According to those laws, there were two ways in which property might pass from father to son — by a will, or by a gift during the father's lifetime. In the latter case, the rule was that the beneficiary obtained possession of the capital only after his father's death.[14] Whether by a will or by a gift, then, the younger son had no legal right "to turn the whole of his share [of the property] into cash" (see Luke 15:13) under the very eyes of his *living* father. The action of the younger son must have shocked his father and plunged him into deep grief. Here is his son, his own flesh and blood, who can hardly wait for his death, the son he has brought up with all his love, on whom he has lavished all his care, the son for whom he would not spare anything good, however high the cost. But this very son of his is now giving him an ultimatum, wishing him dead rather than alive.

The incredible thing in Jesus' parable, however, is that the father's heart goes out to this unfilial son day in and day out. And here is the genius of Jesus' storytelling. He does not spare a word at all on how the father waits for his prodigal son to return. None at all! But Jesus says it all — the waiting father's anguish, pain, grief — by telling his audience how the father receives back his wayward son. The son is moving slowly, pensively, and shame-facedly toward his father's house, after having made a fool of himself, turned himself into a religious outcast, reduced to an emaciated body in rags. Then come these words from Jesus, the master storyteller: "But while he was still a long way off his father saw him, and his heart went out to him. He ran to meet him, flung his arms round him, and kissed him" (Luke 15:20). What a masterful portrayal of the father and his boundless love for his son who has grievously sinned against him! The word "love" is not mentioned. But that marvel of all marvels — love — fills the canvas and saturates it. Love is not a word; it is an action. It is not rhetoric; it is acceptance. The word "forgiveness" is not used. But how real and how spontaneous the father's forgiveness for his son is! And how unconditional too! These few quick crisp words from Jesus tell what love is, what forgiveness means. Even if a human parent could be like this, how much more God as our Abba!

Jesus' theology of God's boundless love expressed completely in these spontaneous actions taken by the father must have confronted the official theology of his day and provoked a deep sense of amazement both in his followers and in his critics. They were all part of an Oriental culture in which for a father "to run to his son in this way is not only extremely unusual but considered undignified."[15] The power of love breaks the power of custom. It nullifies the dictates of etiquette. It defies religious sanctions. And it touches and changes the heart even as hard as stone. Such love is beyond the human sense of respectability. It is beyond religious orthodoxy. Love liberates that father from his social restrictions and theological inhibitions. And the love of God must be a thousand times, a million times, infinite times more than the love of that father. The liberating power of God's love must, then, be a thousand times, a million times, no, infinite times greater than that of the father who, casting aside all his Oriental manners and religious discretion, runs to his wayward son, embraces him, and kisses him.

This is the God of Jesus. And Jesus is intent to "incarnate," to "make flesh," this God of his in his life and work. Far from turning away from "sinners," he mixes with them. When questioned by the religious authorities, he has his answer ready. "It is not the healthy that need a doctor, but the sick," he says matter-of-factly. This is common sense. Everybody knows that. Even his fiercest opponents practice it. But the irony is that what is common, sensible, right, proper, and indispensable in daily life becomes uncommon, insensible, wrong, improper, and dispensable in religious life. How sad and how insane! Jesus restores sanity to religion. He injects common sense into faith. He instills humanity into theology. Hence his marvelous theological one-liner: "I did not come to call the righteous, but sinners" (Mark 2:17, RSV; pars. Matt. 9:13, Luke 5:32). The God of Jesus eats and drinks with sinners, but the God of his religion eats and drinks only with "the righteous." The God of Jesus runs to sinners, flings arms round them and kisses them, but the God of the religious authorities keeps aloof from them, despises them, and excommunicates them. The God of Jesus forgives "seventy times seven" (Matt. 18:22), but the God of official theologians condemns and punishes. The God of Jesus is Abba, the parent who creates life, renews it, and fulfills it.

What happened, then, on the cross when Jesus cried, "My God, my God, why have you abandoned me?" Suppose the traditional teaching of the church is right: the sin and curse of the whole world lies on Jesus. Paul in his letter to the Corinthians says: "For our sake God made him [Jesus] to be sin who knew no sin" (2 Cor. 5:21, RSV). According to this theological logic Jesus, though himself sinless, bears our sin on the cross. The fact, then, is that he is made a sinner, an outcast. In him God should have seen all sinners of the world. In him God should have been confronted with all the outcasts. All "prodigal" sons and daughters are to be identified in Jesus. Is this, then, not the time when the logic of God's boundless love that Jesus so strongly stressed in his parable must be working with full force? If God is like the father in his parable, instead of turning away from Jesus on the cross, should not Abba-God be "running to Jesus, putting arms round him, kissing him?"

But this is not what we are told by traditional theology from that of Paul onward. A contradiction in the mind of the Christian church is most striking here. There is, on the one hand, the enormous sin committed by human beings against God — the sin of disobeying God. Jesus went to the cross because of it. There is, on the other, the unconditional love of

God that Jesus taught and practiced. The cross, instead of dissolving the contradiction, enhances it. What is the problem that lies behind this contradiction in the teaching of the church at this very heart of the Christian faith? The God of retribution! This is the problem. The God of the church and its theology is basically the God of retribution. On the cross it is this God who wins victory over the God of love. Jesus who bears the sins of the world must die for human beings to be forgiven and for the God of retribution to be vindicated. That is why when Jesus was going through the pangs of death God "removed himself," according to the interpretation quoted earlier, "left the Son and made no reply to him."

Theology such as this, although having dominated the thinking of the church and Christians for centuries, has failed to grasp the meaning of the incarnation and do justice to the deep theological insight contained in the phrase "the Word become flesh." It is the theological experiences of more and more Christians in the Third World under different historical settings in recent years that have made them realize serious defects in the traditional theology of the cross. It is necessary for us, then, to grapple once again with the cross, especially with what is known as the scandal of the cross, not as an abstract theological concept but as a historical reality related to the life of Jesus and to the lives of men, women, and children in the past and today.

NOTES

1. See *Science Digest*, vol. 94, no. 8 (August 1986), p. 14.

2. Fyodor Dostoyevsky, *The Idiot*, trans. Henry and Olga Carlisle (New York: New American Library, 1969), p. 44.

3. This is Jürgen Moltmann's theological understanding of the cross. See his *The Crucified God*, trans. R. A. Wilson and John Bowden (New York: Harper & Row, 1974), pp. 151–152.

4. Arthur Weiser, *The Psalms*, trans. Herbert Hartwell (London: SCM Press, 1962), p. 275.

5. Ibid., p. 227.

6. Ibid., p. 220.

7. William Barclay, *The Gospel of Matthew, chs. 11–28* (Edinburgh: Saint Andrew Press, 1957), p. 406.

8. Theodore H. Robinson, *The Gospel of Matthew*, Moffat New Testament Commentary (London: Hodder & Stoughton, 1928), p. 232.

9. Joachim Jeremias, *The Parables of Jesus*, trans. S. H. Hooke (New York: Charles Scribner's Sons, 1955).

10. Robinson, *The Gospel of Matthew*, p. 219.

11. R. C. H. Lenski, *The Interpretation of St. Matthew's Gospel* (Minneapolis: Augsburg, 1943), p. 1119.

12. Ibid.

13. Joachim Jeremias, *Discovering the Parables* (New York: Charles Scribner's Sons, 1966), p. 101.

14. Ibid.

15. Robert H. Stein, *An Introduction to the Parables of Jesus* (Philadelphia: Westminster Press, 1981), p. 121.

CHAPTER 4

The Scandal of the Cross

The Apostle Paul, writing to the Christians at Corinth, says that Christ nailed to the cross is a "stumbling-block" to Jews (1 Cor. 1:23). The word "stumbling-block" is the English rendering of the Greek word *skandalon*. This is a correct translation true to its original meaning. This is what Paul meant when he said that Christ, the messiah, crucified on the cross was a stumbling-block, an obstacle, to Jews in their expectation of God's intervention in the history of their nation. Of course they did not have to wait until the crucifixion to brand Jesus as a *skandalon*, a stumbling-block to their national aspiration. Jesus, in the eyes of the Jewish religious authorities, was already a *skandalon*, an obstacle, to the religion of their nation through what he said and did. How much Paul wished to remove Jesus and his death on the cross as a *skandalon* for his fellow Jews! And how hard he tried to tell them the cross is "the power of God and the wisdom of God" (1 Cor. 1:24) to those "on the way of salvation" (1 Cor. 1:18).

This Greek word, taken over by Paul with its literal meaning, became a key word in his missionary approach to his fellow Jews. His all-out effort to convert the Gentiles to Christ did not dampen his zeal for them. In that great discourse with the Christians in Rome he was moved to say: "I am a missionary to the Gentiles, and as such I give all honor to that ministry when I try to stir emulation in those of my own race. For if their rejection has meant the reconciliation of the world, what will their acceptance mean? Nothing less than life from the dead!" (Rom. 11:13–15). These were Paul's words from his "lung and bowels" (*fei fu chi yen* in Chinese), from the bottom of his heart. To remove the cross of Christ as a *skandalon* to Jews was as important to Paul as to reach the Gentiles with the gospel of salvation in and through Christ.

The Christian church has inherited Paul's missionary zeal for Jews, complete with the Greek word *skandalon* meaning stumbling-block, or obstacle. It has taken upon itself the task of removing that *skandalon* and engaged itself in Christian mission to the Jews over the centuries. Although the word *skandalon* can be religiously and politically misused, resulting in horrendous atrocities such as the holocaust of Nazi Germany, the effort to convert Jews to the Christian faith dies hard still today in some Christian quarters. Time is overdue for Christian theology fundamentally to revise its biblical and theological teaching on the relationship between the Hebrew Scriptures and the New Testament, above all, on the meaning of Jewish history in direct relation to God's salvation and *not* by way of Christianity.

But it is to the people outside the "Christian" West that the Christian church has directed the full force of the meaning of the Greek word *skandalon*.

In Asia and in Africa Christianity encountered the *skandalon* of *skandalons* in what it regarded as paganism, not only in its religious manifestations but in its cultural expressions. Militant missiology and missionary practices were developed to remove paganism as a *skandalon*, as a stumbling-block and an obstacle to Christianity. Here a subtle shift took place, a shift that has until now eluded Christians and theologians: the word *skandalon* is detached from the cross and then attached to so-called paganism. Paganism, then, becomes the target of the Christian missionary campaign just as the cross, in Paul's view, was the object of Jewish derision in his days. In reconstructing a theology of Christian mission today, we have to pay serious attention to this shift and treat it with theological deftness.

What has been said above leads to some questions related to our main concern here. Granted that Paul used the meaning of the Greek word *skandalon* to say what the cross was to his fellow Jews, is it really what the cross is? Has not this contextual use of the word by Paul — contextual because Paul was addressing the Jewish attitude toward the cross — misled the Christian church in its understanding of the cross? Has it not given rise to some far-fetched theological speculations about what God tried to do through the cross? We shall presently discuss some of these speculations in the theological traditions of the church.

To come to grips with the cross, to penetrate its meaning deeply, it is essential, I believe, to relate the word *skandalon* to the cross, not in its meaning in the original Greek, but in the meaning of the English word scandal, derived from the Greek word *skandalon* but given a new, though related, connotation. Scandal, according to the dictionary definition, is "any act, person, or thing that offends or shocks moral feelings of the community and leads to disgrace." It is, further, "a reaction of shame, disgrace, outrage, etc. caused by such an act, person, or thing."[1] The cross as a scandal, not in the Pauline and the traditional theological sense, but in the sense used in the English language, discloses what the cross must have been: an act of shame, disgrace, and outrage committed by human beings, an act that offends and shocks the moral feelings of the human community and the heart of God, who loves Jesus and other human beings as Abba, as Parent. The cross of Jesus, in other words, is a scandal to Abba-God as well as to humanity, perhaps more to the former than to the latter. In what follows we want to explore further the meaning of the cross as a scandal to the Abba-God of Jesus.

Scandal to God

It was a great scandal, this innocent man Jesus hanging on the cross. Even Pontius Pilate, the Roman governor who tried Jesus must have known that there was no ground to accuse Jesus of treason against the Roman power. To the religious leaders intent on Jesus' death and to the people incited to demand his blood, Pilate, out of a shrewd political calculation that will be discussed later, said: "You brought this man before me on a charge of subversion. But, as you see, I have myself examined him in your presence and found nothing in him to support your charges. . . . No more did Herod, for he has referred him back to us. Clearly he has done nothing to deserve death. I therefore propose to let him off with a flogging" (Luke 23:13–16). In the eyes of the Roman law *clearly* Jesus committed no crime. This must have been evident even to ruthless colonial rulers such as Herod and Pilate. *Clearly* he did nothing to deserve death. This was Pilate's verdict. Still, he sentenced Jesus to die on the cross. Is this not a great scandal, an outrageous act?

It was an unbelievable scandal, this just man dying on the cross like a criminal. Who could believe it except the religious authorities that engineered all this? With extreme cunning Caiaphas the high priest confided to the chief priests and the Pharisees meeting in the Council: "You know nothing whatever; you do not use your judgement; it is more to your interest that one man should die for the people, than that the whole nation should be destroyed" (John 11:50). Coming from political power-holders these words would have sounded horrible. Uttered by the spiritual leaders whose sole business was the welfare of the people on earth and in heaven, the statement sounded even more horrible. They were fearful of Roman reprisal against them, should that Jesus movement lead to a popular uprising. Jesus must die, Caiaphas shrewdly reasoned, so that they would be spared by the Romans. And having him removed, the threat he was posing to the religious status quo would be removed too. To the great majority of people, however, who had no part in such dark thoughts, the cross for Jesus must have been utterly unbelievable. Yet Jesus had to carry the cross to his execution. Is this not an unbelievable scandal — a scandal unthinkable to the loving God?

It was a shameful scandal, that compassionate man crying out to God in the throes of death on the cross. Jesus was all compassion to women, men, and children who had crossed his path. Children had no status in the structure of the religious establishment, but Jesus accepted them fully into fellowship with him. To the disciples who tried to stop children from getting near him Jesus said: "Let the children come to me; do not stop them; for the kingdom of God belongs to such as these." And he showed what he meant when "he put his arms round them, laid his hands upon them, and blessed them" (Mark 10:13–16; pars. Matt. 19:13–15, Luke 18:15–17). There was also the woman nearly stoned to death under "the Law of Moses" for her sexual misconduct. But this is what Jesus said to her: "Nor do I condemn you. You may go; do not sin again" (John 7:11). The whole world must have been gripped with shame when this compassionate Jesus was condemned to die on the cross. It was a scandal shamelessly committed by humanity.

And the cross was a scandal of a divine magnitude. From the start Jesus proved to be extraordinary in every way. The Spirit, it was remembered, descended on him when he was baptized by John the Baptist in the Jordan (Mark 1:9–11; pars. Matt. 3:13–17, Luke 3:21–22). That Spirit empowered him to become completely free for God and for all sorts of people, especially for the sick, for the poor, for those marginalized by society and religion. He was dauntless before the religious authorities who had the power over believers' lives. He argued with them, contradicted them, rebuked them, exposed their hypocrisies and showed how vulnerable they were before the loving God and the suffering people. He was equally blunt with the Roman colonial rulers. When he was warned about an attempt on his life by Herod, he declared openly: "Go and tell that fox, 'Listen: today and tomorrow I shall be casting out devils and working cures; on the third day I reach my goal' " (Luke 13:32).

But that freedom to move on earth, freedom to be with the wretched of the earth, freedom to defy powers and authorities of this world, and freedom to be with God and to be filled with God, was gone when Jesus was nailed to the cross. He was reduced to a pitiable sight deprived of that marvelous freedom, the freedom that made him profoundly different from ordinary human beings, freedom that enabled him to be completely identified with people in their sorrows and woes. Emptied of the power of the Spirit, he hung on the cross, helpless, pitiful, with signs of life ebbing slowly away from him. He was no longer in command of his own life. He even lost the freedom of life. The crucifixion deprived him of the freedom to be free. And he was not able to free himself from the cross. That is why he became an easy target of abuse and jeer. "Come down from the cross and save yourself," said some. "He saved others, but he cannot save himself," taunted the others (Mark 15:29–32; pars. Matt. 27:39–43, Luke

84   THE SCANDAL OF THE CROSS

23:35–37). And they were right. No miraculous rescue took place and Jesus died on the cross. Was not the cross a divine catastrophe as well as a human tragedy? It was a scandal of a divine magnitude. The God of Jesus must have been scandalized by it. It was a scandal to God.

Yes, the cross is a scandal to the Abba-God of Jesus. Surely this God, and not the God of the traditional belief and the official religion that abandoned Jesus, did not want it to happen. The God of Jesus is not a murderous God, creating religious victims out of believers. A murderous God is a God who demands blood from the devotees to satisfy its pleasures, commands sacrifice from them according to its whims, and confronts them with fear and punishment when they fail to conform to strict religious observances. To conclude that Jesus' death on the cross was planned in advance by God in order to save the world from its sin is to turn his God of love into a God who is no different from the God of his own religion, whom he vigorously refuted, and from the gods of most religious traditions.

It has to be pointed out, then, that to the very end Jesus did not seek martyrdom. Unlike many a martyr in the history of Christianity who courted death as a way of salvation, Jesus did not rush into it. Just before his arrest he was still praying to God: "Abba, Father, all things are possible to thee; take this cup away from me. Yet not what I will, but what thou wilt" (Mark 14:36; par. Luke 22:42). What a heart-rending prayer! It gives us a glimpse of the very humanness of Jesus — Jesus as a thoroughly, completely, and supremely human person. This is not a prayer of one deity to another deity, of the second person to the first person in the Godhead. It is a prayer of a very human person facing the last critical decision in life and involving God in this final hour of decision-making.

This short and passionate prayer reveals the faith of Jesus who calls God "Abba" like a child. "All things are possible to thee," prays Jesus to his Abba-God. Is this not what children think of their parent — father or mother — especially when they are small? To children parents are big and dependable. Parents provide everything for them, from food to toys, and seem to know everything they want to know and do everything they want to do but cannot do. Parents seem capable of all things. If children have such absolute trust in the parents, why do we, who are God's children, not have such trust in God our Abba? Perhaps this is what Jesus tried to drive home to his disciples when he talked to them about faith: "If you have faith no bigger than a mustard-seed, you will say to this mountain, 'move from here to there!,' and it will move; nothing will prove impossible for you" (Matt. 17:20; par. Luke 17:6). Of course Jesus was not asking his disciples to take his words literally and expect that faith has to be accompanied with a show of supernatural physical power. Jesus was no literalist. Nor did he try to make his disciples literalists. He wanted to stress that simple but deep trust in God as Abba is the very foundation of faith. Without such trust faith becomes a calculated risk, something to be bargained, negotiated, and rationalized. This is no longer faith but a business deal. Jesus retained such childlike faith in the garden of Gethsemane when he was aware of imminent danger before him.

But the childlike faith of Jesus in God as Abba has to be different from children's instinctive trust in their parents. In his prayer in the garden Jesus also said: "Yet not what I will but what thou wilt." Are we to understand this to mean that Jesus offered to be part of God's plan of salvation decided by God long in advance? This is what the Christian church understands Jesus to mean. Or do we agree with the earliest Christian community when it confessed that Jesus "in obedience accepted even death — death on a cross" (Phil. 2:8)? Yes, we do, provided that the obedience of Jesus is not a passive obedience, not an obedience to a wrathful God, but to the loving God as Abba.

There seems, however, something else in Jesus' prayer in Gethsemane. What is involved here, contrary to the tradition of the Christian church, is not the conflict between Jesus' own will and God's will, a conflict that led Jesus to submit his will to God's will. How could there be such a conflict while throughout his life and ministry Jesus said and did nothing but what he understood to be God's will? What made Jesus different, qualitatively different, from other human beings, was his being able to know what God's will was and acting on it regardless of consequences. This ability of Jesus to discern God's will clearly and without fail must have come from his deep awareness of God's presence in him, an awareness that perhaps no other human being is able to have so deeply as Jesus, neither in the past, nor in the present or future. And his capacity to say it aloud in public and practice it despite the threat and opposition of his enemies must have come from the power that the presence of God in him generated. There is, therefore, no reason to think that when confronted with the greatest crisis of his life he began to be tormented with the conflict between his own will and God's will.

There must be some other explanation of Jesus' deep agony in the garden of Gethsemane. It must be this: although Jesus did not court death on the cross, he must have realized that it was bound to come because of the enmity he had aroused in the religious authorities. And now the inevitable seems to have arrived. He must have shuddered at the thought of the extreme pain of the cross. If this is what he has to face, if this is the cup he has to drink, he cannot do it alone. His prayer, then, must be a prayer of his determination to carry to the end what he set out to do three years before, what he believed to be God's will. He could have been assailed with doubts at times. He might have been tempted to take a different path to fulfill God's will. But each time he was able to have his commitment to God's will rekindled and reaffirmed. Now the last struggle with the powers of this world had begun. His prayer in the garden of Gethsemane must have been, then, a prayer of his re-dedication to do the will of his Abba-God. It must have also been the prayer of invocation, asking God to be with him in the ordeal he was about to enter. And as we will discuss later, Jesus died on the cross, though abandoned by the God of the religious authorities, finding peace in the loving Abba-God he had come to share with suffering men and women.

Legendary Jesus

This portrayal of Jesus is quite different from the one to which most of us are accustomed. What has been portrayed almost exclusively in the Christian tradition, whether in the West or in the East, is Jesus who works wonders, who performs miracles, and who is more of a divine being than a human being. Is this perhaps partly why he was remembered to have done so much healing of the sick? It was even reported that he made Lazarus, dead and buried, come out alive from his tomb (John 11:1–44). He was known to have raised the daughter of Jairus, president of the synagogue, back to life (Mark 5:21–43; pars. Matt. 9:18–26, Luke 8:40–56). There was also a story about his walking on the sea of Galilee (Mark 6:45–52; pars. Matt. 14:22–23, Luke 6:16–21). For Jesus to be our savior, he must be endowed with superhuman power not shared by us mortal human beings. This seems plausible enough to Christian piety. But upon deeper reflection, does it not contradict the central tenet of the Christian faith expressed in "the Word become flesh"? Does it not elevate, or perhaps degrade, Jesus to the rank of a legendary being we find in popular beliefs?

Little wonder that soon after his death legends began to grow about him and his person. The first to come to be surrounded with legendary character is his birth. His has to be a birth different from the births of ordinary human beings. He has to be "unique," that is, a category all by himself and with no comparison to others, from the very beginning of his life, even at his conception. We are indebted to Matthew and Luke for giving us two accounts of Jesus' birth — the accounts, though varied in content and "contrary to each other in a number of details,"[2] still "could be made the vehicle of the message that Jesus was the Son of God acting for the salvation of humankind."[3]

How they told the story of Jesus' birth with a profound sense of wonder and awe! "Now the birth of Jesus Christ took place in this way" (Matt. 1:18, RSV). Matthew begins as if he were telling the story before an audience ready to devour every word from his mouth. He then continues:

When his mother Mary had been betrothed to Joseph, before they came together she was found to be with child of the Holy Spirit; and her husband Joseph, being a just man and unwilling to put her to shame, resolved to divorce her quietly. But as he considered this, behold, an angel of the Lord appeared to him in a dream, saying, "Joseph, son of David, do not fear to take Mary your wife, for that which is conceived in her is of the Holy Spirit; she will bear a son, and you shall call his name Jesus, for he will save his people from their sins." All this took place to fulfill what the Lord had spoken by the prophet:

> Behold, a virgin shall conceive
> and bear a son,
> and his name shall be called
> Emmanu-el

(which means, God with us). When Joseph woke from sleep, he did as the angel of the Lord commanded him; he took his wife, but knew her not until she had borne a son; and he called his name Jesus. (Matt. 1:18–25, RSV)

The story must have fascinated the audience. It discloses to them who Jesus must have really been.

We took him, people must have said to themselves, for the carpenter Joseph's son (Matt. 13:55 and Luke 4:22), but he in fact is not like us, born of our human parents; he is of divine origin. Perhaps this is what the Gospel writers wanted to communicate to people, and they succeeded. That Jesus is totally and categorically different from us human beings is supremely important to them. The disciples were disappointed in him and deserted him at the cross. But their experience of Jesus as the risen Christ dramatically changed all this. They now perceive Jesus as "the Son of God." This is the heart of "the Christ of their faith" in contrast to the Jesus they knew in the flesh, as a person of flesh and blood with whom they had lived and worked for three years.

How could Jesus, then, have been conceived in wedlock? How could he have come into being through an ordinary biological process? It has to be a conception with no human father. It has to be a birth that has no parallel in human experience. This of course reflected the utter devotion of the earliest Christian community to him. This is how the followers of Jesus in that community came to know Jesus. Perhaps the story of Jesus' birth in the Gospels of Matthew and Luke tells us more about the way in which the faith of the earliest Christian community developed than about the person of Jesus himself.

In retrospect, however, a perception of Jesus in this way poses a serious problem to the solidarity of Jesus with human beings. To say that Jesus was conceived and born in a manner utterly different from that of us human beings is to say that he is *not* like us, that he is *not* one of us. His flesh is not quite our flesh. Even his emotion and will are not the same as ours. Jesus, in short, is *by nature* different from us. It is evident that this contradicts the heart of what is theologically known as the "incarnation," the Word become flesh, the theological insight that Jesus is one and the same as us human beings in every way from birth to death. The credibility of his solidarity with us and the integrity of his identification with humanity are derived from the fact that Jesus is not just *like* us but the same as us, that he does not only *share* humanity with us but *is* part of that humanity.

To divinize Jesus as the Son of God and to regard his humanity as less than real and authentic in Christian piety led the story of Jesus' conception and birth to take on a legendary character. Hence, the annunciation of the angel Gabriel to Mary, the mother-to-be of Jesus (Luke 1:26–38), the idyllic scene of the angels announcing the birth to the shepherds in the field (Luke 2:8–20), the visit of the three astrologers from the East (Matt. 2:1–12), and so on. In this way the story of Jesus' conception and birth came to share legendary characteristics of many other stories told about great religious personalities, heroes, and kings.

To make the life of a great religious founder into a legend may be motivated by deep devotion and sincere piety, and we should not minimize what it seeks to symbolize and what message it wants to convey. After all, legends, along with myths and fairy tales, can be a profound symbolic language seeking to uncover mysteries deeply embedded in God's creation. They tell us the meaning of life and the world in a way our daily language is not adequate to convey. Because of this, we should not take a legend for the message itself, nor the idealized being for a real person. Nor should we allow fascination with otherworldly appearances to be confused with meeting demands and responsibilities of daily life.

The fantastic legend about the birth of the founder of Buddhism is a case in point here. Buddha was a historical person born in Lumbini, near the Nepal-Indian border, to a Kshatriya family that belonged to the Sakya (Sakiya) clan, the date of his birth variously reckoned to be 624 B.C.E., 567 B.C.E., and 466 B.C.E.[4] But in due time his birth came to have a legendary character told, for example, in the *Buddha-Karita of Asvaghosa* as follows:

> Then falling from the host of beings in the Tushita heaven, and illuminating the three worlds, the most excellent of Bodhisattvas suddenly entered at a thought into her [Maya, Buddha's mother], like the Nâga-king entering the cave of Nânda.

Assuming the form of a huge elephant white like Himalaya, armed with six tusks, with his face perfumed with flowing ichor, he entered the womb of the queen of king Suddhodana, to destroy the evils of the world.

The guardians of the world hastened from heaven to mount watch over the world's one true ruler; thus the moonbeams, though they shine everywhere, are especially bright on Mount Kailasa.

Maya also, holding him in her womb, like a line of clouds holding a lightning-flash, relieved the people around her from the sufferings of poverty by raining showers of gifts.

Then one day by the king's permission the queen, having a great longing in her mind, went with the inmates of the gynaeceum into the garden Lumbini.

As the queen supported herself by a bough which hung laden with a weight of flowers, the Bodhisattva suddenly came forth, cleaving open her womb.

At that time the constellation Pushya was auspicious, and from the side of the queen, who was purified by her vow, her son was born for the welfare of the world, without pain and without illness.

...As was Aurva's birth from the thigh, and Prithu's from the hand, and Mandhatri's who was like Indra himself, from the forehead, and Kakshi's from the upper end of the arm — thus too was his birth (miraculous).[5]

The single most important word in this legend is perhaps the word "miraculous." The Buddha, who made such an impact on so many women and men of his time and who inaugurated a new era of human search for salvation, must be different from all other mortal human beings. He was an avatar, Bodhisattva incarnate, to save the living multitudes from the suffering of this world. His birth has got to be miraculous!

This legend of the Buddha's birth is quoted not to compare it with the story of Jesus' birth.[6] Nor is the purpose to highlight how the Christian story is distinct from the Buddhist story. Each story has its own peculiarities shaped by the history, culture, and ethos to which it belongs. Each story in turn shapes the popular piety of believers and their life and worldviews. But there is a universal theme in most of such birth stories: veneration of the religious personality concerned as divine, in special relationship with God and endowed with a particular gift (charisma) to lead men and women to God. It is this earnest longing for salvation that expresses itself in the supernatural character attributed to the life of a religious founder.

But the Holy Spirit!

What draws our attention in particular in the biblical story of Jesus' conception and birth is the mentioning of the Holy Spirit. Matthew refers to it first in passing as part of his story and then directly in the angel's announcement to Joseph in his dream. "Before they [Mary and Joseph] came together," reports Matthew, "she [Mary] was found to be with child of the Holy Spirit." This is followed by an angel saying to the troubled Joseph in a dream: "Do not fear to take Mary your wife, for that which is conceived in her is of the Holy Spirit." Luke's version of the annunciation is even more direct. The angel Gabriel assured the frightened Mary and said: "The Holy Spirit will come upon you, and the power of the Most High will overshadow you" (Luke 1:35).

Whether it is Joseph or Mary, they are both deeply troubled, though for different reasons. Seeing the very unusual circumstance in which the conception of the child takes place, who would not be troubled? Not only Mary and Joseph, the principal characters in this drama, are troubled, the earliest Christian community must also have been troubled by it. Does the reference to the Holy Spirit in the story have something to do with this? The important thing to realize here is "the fact that the child was conceived through the Holy Spirit is not part of the narrative flow."[7] In other words, the Holy Spirit is not the original part of the story of the virgin birth told and retold in the Christian circles. It must have been Matthew and Luke who introduced the Holy Spirit into the story.

If this is the case, then what we have here is a flash of theological insight on the part of these two Gospel writers. For one thing, the focus of the story is shifted from the virgin birth to the part the Holy Spirit plays in the conception of Jesus. Is the shift intended by Matthew and Luke? We do not know. But this should not obscure its deep theological implications for the life and work of Jesus among the men and women poor and oppressed in their society at large and in their religious community in particular.

What has to be pointed out, in the first place, is that the Spirit is present with Jesus from the outset of his life, even at his conception. He does not have to wait until his baptism in the Jordan by John the Baptist to be endowed with it (see Mark 1:9–11; pars. Matt. 3:13–17, Luke 3:21–22). His baptism is a confirmation of what God already did to him at the inception of his life and at the same time it marks his dedication to the ministry to which he was called. Thanks, then, to the reference to the Holy Spirit in the Nativity story, the focus shifts from the legendary character of the conception and birth of Jesus and comes to be linked with his call to live and practice God's will among his people, especially among the people who have no privilege and status in society and in the eyes of the religious authorities.

That Jesus was conceived by the Holy Spirit implies, further, that Jesus' conception and birth cannot be explained in a purely biological way. It has to do with the life-giving power of God. Does this not at once remind us of the story of how God "breathed into *Adam's* nostrils the breath of life" and made human beings "living creatures" (Gen. 2:7)? Human life has much in common with nature; it was formed "from the dust of the ground (*adamah*)," but nature alone does not explain it. Human life is not just a natural thing with a beginning and an end confined to a limited span of time and space. It begins before its physical space-time and continues after it. We know neither what that life before life nor that life after life is like, but we do know that life as well as this life here and now is a life in the Spirit of God, a life "inspired" by it. Human beings, then, are spiritual by nature. We are spiritual beings. Spirituality is not something added to us. Of course we more often than not forget this spiritual nature of our biological existence, yielding to the dictate of the animal instinct for destructiveness. Even this does not alter the fact that in and through the Spirit we are related to God in a special way.

Does not the conception of Jesus through the Holy Spirit point up this essential fact concerning humanity? This leads to an important theological observation: because of the Spirit present in Jesus and in us all, Jesus is not a stranger to us human beings, past, present, or future, East or West, North or South; neither are we human beings strangers to one another. The bond of relationships here is strong and nothing, even sins and crimes we human beings commit against one another, can destroy it because it is part of God's creation.

This leads to our affirmation that Jesus, instead of being radically different from us human beings through "virgin birth," is radically related to us because of the Spirit powerfully present at his conception. In the Gospels we see how Jesus expresses this radical relationship between himself and other human beings in what he says and does. He extends God's saving love for *all* people — children, women as well as men. He expands that love to *all* humanity — Jews and those outside the Jewish community. On the basis of this bond of love between God and human beings, he goes on to recast humanity not in terms of wealth, power, or social status but in terms of the innate goodness given by God, even though that goodness may be marred and lost. And how he goes about mending that goodness that is marred and recovering that goodness that is lost, risking the wrath of the religious authorities! This means nothing less than the "re-definition" of what it means to be human, what it means to be religious, and ultimately what it means to be saved. And for us today this should of course lead to the "re-definition" of how we are related to the people who are our neighbors but outside the Christian church, how we regard their relationship to God, and what it means for us all — us Christians and those who are not Christians — to be saved.

These questions will occupy us later when we concern ourselves with "the reign of God" in the second volume. What I want to stress here is the far-reaching significance of the Holy Spirit in the conception of Jesus, the significance perhaps not realized and anticipated by Matthew and Luke when they referred to the Holy Spirit in their account of Jesus' conception. The Holy Spirit, that presence of the saving power of God, is the meaning of the life and ministry of Jesus. And it is this same Spirit who relates Jesus to all other humanity through the centuries and across geographical boundaries. He is related to us, his fellow human beings, in the power of the Spirit, inspiring us when we are dispirited, giving us moral power to live when we are de-moralized, showing us solidarity in our suffering and pain, and rekindling zeal for the present life and hope for life eternal. The Spirit present at Jesus' conception is that Spirit of God present at the beginning of the creation, now in this world of ours with its conflicts and fears, and in the time to come when the old heaven and earth are transformed into new heavens and a new earth.

It is the vision of God's salvation for all creation and all humanity, in which the Holy Spirit "overshadows" the conception of Jesus and his entire life and ministry, that must have also inspired Paul, the Apostle to the Gentiles, to write to the Christians in Rome saying: "For all who are moved by the Spirit of God are sons [and daughters] of God. The Spirit you have received is not a spirit of slavery leading you back into a life of fear, but a Spirit that makes us sons [and daughters], enabling us to cry 'Abba! Father!' In that cry the Spirit of God joins with our spirit in testifying that we are God's children; and if children, then heirs. We are God's heirs and Christ's fellow-heirs, if we share his sufferings now in order to share his splendor hereafter" (Rom. 8:14–17).

Paul was writing to the mixed Christian congregation of Jews and Gentiles in Rome. His spirit must have soared as he envisioned the Spirit of God at work both in that congregation and beyond it, confessing God as "Abba! Father!" Here Paul was the true heir of the religious reorientation Jesus brought about during his ministry, disclosing God as Abba to people and opening their eyes to God's solidarity with suffering men, women, and children in the world. Is it not this same Holy Spirit who "overshadowed" Mary, mother of Jesus, and Paul, the Apostle to the Gentiles, that is now "overshadowing" more and more women and men today, among them Christians, to strive for peace and justice in human community and within God's entire creation? This is a long way both in terms of time and distance from that city of Nazareth where Mary became aware of being "overshadowed" by the Spirit of God in her conception of a baby to be born as Jesus. But in terms of God's time and distance, is it not no time and no distance at all? Did not a psalmist in ancient Israel say to God: "For a thousand years in thy sight are but as yesterday when it is past, or as a watch in the night" (Ps. 90:4)? We Christians should learn to understand God's purpose for all humanity and creation in relation to God's own time and distance and not on the basis of our own "Christian time and distance." Only insofar as we make ourselves available for the impact of God's Spirit on our lives can we perceive the extraordinary things God has been doing in the world of cultures and histories outside Christianity as well as inside it, just as Mary and Joseph became committed in faith to the out-of-the-ordinary conception that had taken place within Mary.

Mouse-trap with a Bait

In the popular piety of Christians and in the official teaching of the Christian church on the birth of Jesus, however, the importance of the Holy Spirit has not been duly appreciated. Instead, the cult of the Virgin Mary developed on the basis of the stories of Jesus' conception and birth and shaped Christian spirituality. Christian theology too, Orthodox, Roman Catholic, or Protestant, has on the whole emphasized the virgin birth at the expense of the Holy Spirit.

However, it is important to bear in mind that the stories of Jesus' conception and birth with legendary character should not distort and obscure the message of God's salvation in the world. This is not what happened to the Gospels in the New Testament. "The Gospel [of Matthew] proper," it is pointed out, "never refers back to the special information supplied by the infancy narrative, e.g., to a birth in Bethlehem, to a major stir caused by the birth when the Magi came to Jerusalem, or even to the virginal conception."[8] As to the Gospel according to Luke, "none of the Lukan infancy narrative has had major influence on the body of the Gospel, so that if the first chapters had been lost, we would never have suspected their existence."[9] And it is well known that Paul never referred to the stories of Jesus' birth in his letters, although he must have been aware of them. What he did, as we have just seen, was to understand the life and work of Jesus in relation to the Spirit of God. From there he developed a high christology of Jesus dying for the sins of the world and rising from death for its salvation, a christology that was to shape the christology of the Christian church from the early Christian community onward to the present day. But that is another story.

Perhaps this is just as well. If the story of Jesus' conception and birth with its supernatural trappings had pervaded and shaped the entire Gospels, the scandal of the cross could have been de-scandalized by their

authors themselves. In their accounts of the Passion, Jesus would perhaps
not have cried, "My God, my God, why have you abandoned me?" Instead, there would have been angels from heaven tending Jesus with all
care and love, as they did when Jesus came out exhausted from his temptation in Matthew's account (Matt. 4:11). The cross would have become
"legendarized" with all its sting removed from it. And this is what often
happened in the history of Christianity. Did not a legend soon grow saying that it was that hapless Simon of Cyrene, forced to carry the cross
for Jesus to the place of execution (Mark 15:21; pars. Matt. 27:32, Luke
23:26), who was actually crucified, and not Jesus?

Paul, in his defense of the cross, said bluntly that the cross was a
"*skandalon* [in the sense of 'stumbling block' and not 'scandal' discussed
earlier] to the Jews" (1 Cor. 1:23). The cross was a stumbling-block to
them because they, in their faith and theology, just could not accept a suffering messiah. To many Christians, among them some illustrious thinkers
and leaders, is not the cross also a stumbling-block because Jesus born
the Son of God just could not undergo such an indignity as death on the
cross? How could Jesus the Son of God die just as other mortal human
beings?

Various theological explanations are, then, devised to justify the reason why the crucifixion had to take place. One of the most popular
explanations is to regard the cross as a price God had to pay to the devil
in the transaction to reclaim the human soul fallen victim to sin. It was
Origen, that great theologian and philosopher of the school in Alexandria
(c. 185–c. 254), who said:

> If then we were "bought with a price," as also Paul asserts, we
> were doubtless bought from one whose servants we were, who also
> named what price he would for releasing those whom he held from
> his power. Now it was the devil that held us, to whose side we had
> been drawn away by our sins. He asked, therefore, as our price the
> blood of Christ.[10]

Deep devotion to the God of Jesus vibrates in these words. Profound
faith in the God of love to save human beings from their sin at any cost
ennobles the language.

Still, the cross as a price paid to the devil removes the scandal and the
tragedy of a just and loving person such as Jesus suffering an ignominious
death. The cross is reduced to a business transaction between God and
the devil. It is the term demanded by the devil to settle the transaction
and God agrees to it. Does this not remind us of the deal between God
and Satan in the prologue of the Book of Job that was the subject of our
discussion earlier? Could it be that early Christian theologians such as

Origen took the story of Job in the prologue and literally applied it to their "theology of the cross"? This is not an entirely far-fetched idea.

The fact of the matter is that theology such as this seems to be haunted by the shadow of the God of retribution. It has to be said that throughout its history Christian theology has not been able to come out of that shadow as it tries to fathom the meaning of the cross. Even to this day when the myth of Satan and God dealing with each other to decide the fate of human persons is already exposed as myth not to be taken literally, it continues to dictate the ways in which most Christians think of the cross. And it is this crude form of a "theology of the cross" that has exerted enormous influence on Christians in Asia in their piety toward the cross and in their evangelical zeal.

A variation of the theme of transaction is the imagery of hook and deception, a favorite imagery for early Greek theologians. Gregory of Nyssa (c. 330–c. 395), for example, wrote:

> ... he [the devil] who practiced deception receives in turn that very treatment the seeds of which he himself had sown of his own free will. He who first deceived man by the bait of sensual pleasure is himself deceived by the presentation of the human form... whereas he, the enemy, effected his deception for the ruin of our nature, He who is at once the just, and good, and wise one, used His device, in which there was deception, for the salvation of him who had perished, and thus not only conferred benefit on the lost one, but on him too who had wrought our ruin.[11]

So the cross is a tit-for-tat business. This is the crudest form of theological reasoning at best. The cross becomes a bait to deceive the devil into letting its prisoners off its hook. It is something God devised to beat the devil at the devil's own game.

Even Augustine (354–430), that great theologian and church leader, was not free from indulging in such a "theological game." The imagery he used was that of mouse-trap — very strange indeed! This is how he put it:

> As our price He [God] held out His cross to him [the devil] like a mouse-trap, and as bait set upon it his own blood.[12]

This is a theological imagination run wild. Such theological ingenuity may be a good pastime for theologians, but it caricatures God, making light of the burden of the cross and what it stands for — a tremendous suffering both for God and for Jesus. And of course the cross as a shameful scandal committed by human beings is completely lost sight of. How Augustine, among the most astute theologians the Christian church has produced in its long history, would come up with "theology" such as this is a mystery. Fortunately, this kind of "theological" justification for the cross did not become an obsession, at least not for Augustine.

Christus Victor?

The cross is not a myth; it was a historical happening. The cross is not a legend; it did take place one sad day in the ancient city of Jerusalem before eyewitnesses. And it is quite probable that one of the last things Jesus said before he died was those devastating words from Psalm 22: "My God, my God, why have you abandoned me?" These words ought to have put an end to speculation about the "nature" of Jesus. Theological reflection on Jesus, what is called christology, ought to begin with these words of Jesus, and not with the story of his conception and birth. Nor should it begin with Jesus' resurrection. It is true that the authors of the Gospels wrote their accounts of Jesus from beyond the grave of Jesus. Their resurrection experience, that is, their awakening to faith in Christ, became the beginning of their Jesus stories. They were reflecting on Jesus backwards, from the end to the beginning, from the risen Christ to the historical Jesus, from the empty tomb to the cross, from Easter Sunday to Good Friday. That is why Friday, the day Jesus was crucified — a really bad day, a terrible day, a miserable day, an outrageous day — came to be called "Good" Friday.

But the amazing thing is that so much of Jesus in the flesh and blood, Jesus the son of Mary and Joseph the carpenter, Jesus a rabbi, still remains in those stories. Perhaps the writers of the Gospels were more concerned about that Jesus — the Jesus the disciples touched, the Jesus they heard, the Jesus they admired, the Jesus in whom they had staked their national hope, and the Jesus they finally deserted to die on the cross. It was that Jesus, and not the Jesus the Magi had come from the East to worship, not the Jesus to whom the shepherds hastened from the field to do obeisance, that preoccupied them. Their Jesus was the Jesus with whom they shared the despairs and hopes of daily life, the Jesus with whom they spent the last agonizing hours on earth, that they wrote about in great length, and not the Jesus whose body somehow had disappeared from the grave, not the Jesus who appeared to them as the risen Christ. Mark's Gospel, for example, the shortest of the three Synoptic Gospels, is primarily a story of Jesus' passion (suffering).

This is the main difference between the authors of the Gospels and Paul. In his letters Paul is full of Christ risen from the dead. Perhaps Jesus' resurrection is more important to him than Jesus' cross. Did he not say to the Christians in Corinth: "If there be no resurrection, then Christ was not raised; if Christ was not raised, then our gospel is null and void, and so is your faith; and we turn out to be lying witnesses" (1 Cor.

15:14–15)? Yes, he did emphasize that he proclaimed "Christ crucified," that this Christ crucified was "the power of God and the wisdom of God" (1 Cor. 1:23–25). But could he have said the same thing about the cross as he did about the resurrection? Christian theology, particularly christology, developed by Christian theologians during the last two thousand years, has largely been the elaboration of Paul's theology of the risen Christ.

The whole thing is so logical — this christology of the Christian church from the days of the early church to the present day. It is a theology of "Christus Victor," to use the title of the book by Gustaf Aulen, a Swedish theologian.[13] It is a theology of victory — victory of God over evil powers through Christ, then through the Christian church. It then becomes a theology of the victory of Christianity over "pagan" religions after the nineteenth century when the Western church began to expand to Africa, Asia, and other parts of the world. But, we now know this missionary expansion of the church in the West is not without its problems.

What kind of victory has the Christian church won — a victory of God or a victory of the church? A victory of Jesus or a victory of the powers and principalities of the West? It is a very complex problem. We can no longer accept without question a theological statement such as this made by the author of Christus Victor: "Christ — Christus Victor — fights against and triumphs over the evil powers of the world, the 'tyrants' under which humankind is in bondage and suffering, and in Him God reconciles the world to Himself."[14]

Yes, the evil powers of this world are real. They were real before the time of Jesus. They were real in his time. They were of course real after him and are very, very real today. Soon after the publication of Christus Victor, Europe and the whole world were to become the battleground of human atrocities and destruction. Is this not ironical? This is a tragic irony, for it was in the "Christianized" West as well as in the "pagan" East that the satanic power of destruction went about devastating human lives, bringing untold miseries to millions upon millions of men, women, and children. Of course the world was at the same time involved in life-and-death "fights against the evil powers of this world," but how the world triumphed over them is another story. And we all know that victory was won with an enormous cost of human lives.

Evil powers are no abstraction. They are very real, and they seem to get more and more real as human beings become ever more ingenious in the invention and manufacture of the technology of destruction. Jesus in his days had to fight them, but did he triumph over them? And how are we in our time to overcome them? We must "keep steadily in view the reality of evil in the world," but does not the theological advice to "go and meet the devil with a battle-song of triumph"[15] sound too unreal, even too facile, in view of the terrible reality of evil? How could Christians give such advice to the women and men who struggle as they live in dire poverty, who suffer under political and social oppression, who are victims of human greed and inhumanity? And how does it fit into the extreme pain and agony of the death Jesus suffered on the cross?

The Cross Is Human Violence

Traditional Christian theology has spoken about evil powers mostly outside the context of the brutal realities of suffering and death human beings have to undergo at the hands of one another. It tends to dwell on the "nonphysical" aspect of the work of evil powers, relating it to the struggle of human souls that for some reason feel separated and abandoned by God. Jesus himself, as we have seen, went through that agonizing experience of abandonment by God on the cross, but he, like Job long before him, must have realized that the God who abandoned him was not his own Abba-God but the God of the religious authorities and the traditional beliefs. In contrast, traditional Christian theology has not been critical of the premise that God is a God of retribution. It has also tended to spiritualize and personalize evil powers said to result from the sin of disobedience that human beings commit against the God of retribution. It is no wonder that the Christian church makes little impact today when it sermonizes about sin and evil as part of saving individual souls, ignoring the fact that often the church and its members are part of the oppressive social, political, and economic systems and structures. Without facing this reality, the Christian church cannot reclaim its integrity nor can its theology regain its credibility, especially in the eyes of people outside Christianity in the Third World. This is a critical question for Christianity, particularly in parts of the world such as Asia dominated by other religions.

Human suffering raises questions about the meaning of life. But in its deepest dimension it also raises questions about God, the God of an organized religion and a religious hierarchy. That God can be a strange God estranged from the lives of people and alienated from their human longings and experiences. During his ministry Jesus brought a familiar God to people instead of a strange God, a loving God and not a judging God, a warm-hearted God in the place of a cold-hearted God. But this was to transgress a religious taboo. He was abandoned to death both by the religious authorities and their God.

It may be that Jesus on the cross had to fight that God of official religion for the last time. The cross is *not*, as some theologians would have us think, Jesus-God tearing away from God, the Son-God going through the pain of separation from the Father-God. The cross is not such a "theo"-logical thing. It is not "the Second Person" of the Trinity forsaken by "the First Person" of the Trinity. Nor is it "the Second Person" of the Trinity left in the lurch by "the Third Person" of the Trinity. Such "trinitarian" language makes little sense of the cross on which Jesus died. Highly abstract theological language such as this almost suggests a mutiny within God.

What, then, is the cross of Jesus? What does it mean? What does it disclose? What does it symbolize? What reality does it represent? The cross is the suffering of Jesus of Nazareth and it is the suffering of humanity. The cross means human beings rejecting human beings. It is human beings abandoning human beings. It shows how human beings, in the grips of demonic powers, are inflicting injustice on each other, tearing each other apart, destroying each other. The cross is the plot of an organized religion blinded by its own power and orthodoxy and unable to tolerate those deeply and sincerely religious persons eager to restore faith in the God of love and mercy. And the cross discloses the complicity of sociopolitical powers ready to defend their self-interest at any cost, even at the expense of the law, even at the cost of the lives of those God-inspired persons faithful to the truth and devoted to love for others.

This is what the cross of Jesus means and symbolizes. It was not planned by his Abba-God, but by human beings. It was not instituted in the name of Abba-God, but in the name of the God imprisoned by an organized religion and its power-holders. It was not conspired by Jesus' Abba-God, but by the God invented by the religious authorities. The cross was not carried out by the Abba-God of the crucified Jesus in a clandestine deal with the devil that had "sinful" human beings under its power, but by the political authorities that regarded political expediency far more important than respect for human rights. Nor did the cross reveal the Abba-God not to be Abba-God, consenting to the death of the innocent Jesus in order to "save" human beings from their "sins."

The cross, in reality, is the height of human defiance against that Abba-God. It is a violence committed not by that Abba-God but by self-serving humanity. It discloses the depth of human sin. It is a triumph of demonolatry and a defeat of a God domesticated by an organized religion. But of course a domesticated God is not the true God. The cross reveals the impotence *not* of the God of Jesus but the God of those who conspired to put Jesus to death, the God who had to acquiesce in the evil plans hatched in the inmost part of the religion that held that God captive. The cross, in short, is human violence and not divine violence. And the story of the cross continues. It will perhaps be repeated over and over again until the end of time.

NOTES

1. See the entry "scandal" in Webster's *New World Dictionary*, 2d college ed. (New York: World Publishing Company, 1970).

2. Raymond E. Brown, *The Birth of the Messiah: A Commentary on the Infancy Narrative in Matthew and Luke* (New York: Doubleday, 1977), p. 32.

3. Ibid., p. 29.

4. See Joseph M. Kitagawa, *Religions of the East* (Philadelphia: Westminster Press, 1968), p. 156.

5. From the *Buddha-Karita*, Book I, 19–29, in F. Max Müller, ed., *Sacred Books of the East*, vol. 49 (London: Clarendon Press, 1894). Quoted by Thomas Boslooper in *The Virgin Birth* (Philadelphia: Westminster Press, 1962), pp. 139–140.

6. Boslooper, who refers to the Buddhist legend, is sympathetic in his treatment of other religious traditions, but his purpose is to stress the "uniqueness" of the biblical story of Jesus' birth.

7. Brown, *The Birth of the Messiah*, p. 124.

8. Ibid., p. 49.

9. Ibid., p. 240.

10. Quoted by L. W. Grensted, *A Short History of the Doctrine of the Atonement* (Manchester: Manchester University Press, 1920), p. 37.

11. Ibid., p. 40.

12. Ibid.

13. Gustaf Aulen, *Christus Victor*, trans. A. G. Herbert (London: SPCK, 1931), p. 20.

14. Ibid., p. 176.

15. Ibid.

CHAPTER 5

Karuna of God

It is evident — is it not? — that in the cross we have to deal with us human beings. It raises questions about humanity. Human beings who are capable of the cross — what are they? Human beings who inflict torture and pain on defenseless persons like Jesus — what kind of creatures are they? Human beings who conspire to put innocent people such as Jesus to death — is there anything they are not capable of? And human beings who build institutions, religious as well as social, political, and economic, to commit organized crimes against the powerless — what does one make of them?

But this is one side, and one side only, of the cross. If in the cross we have to deal squarely with human beings, we must also probe deeply how God, the Abba-God of Jesus, is involved in it. The cross is not a cunning device of God to deceive the devil into releasing its victims. It is not a bargain God struck with the devil to let its captives go free. Jesus is neither a pawn nor a ransom that God paid to the devil for human beings to be delivered from its clutches. If the cross discloses what we human beings are, it also reveals what God must be. If it demonstrates what we human beings are capable of, it also reveals what God must be capable of. And the cross, instead of a transaction between God and the devil with Jesus as victim, is the reality and symbol of how God, Jesus, and humanity are engaged with each other in struggle for peace, justice, and life. In what follows we want to explore how God, not the God of retribution, but the Abba-God of Jesus, is related to Jesus on the cross and to suffering humanity. Can we tentatively, very tentatively, call this a history of God, even a biography of God, in light of the cross and in relation to human suffering?

A Biography of God

Before speaking of a biography of God, I must point out that we human beings do not have an autobiography of God, that is, an account of God written by God. But the problem is that some Christians, particularly some evangelists and theologians, speak as if they have read God's autobiography, know God's will inside out, and can speak on God's behalf with absolute certainty. This often results in religious authoritarianism, dictating the life and faith of believers with creeds, doctrines, and laws. But God is neither the sum total of Christian teachings nor the *magnum opus* of erudite theologians.

What we have are biographies of God. A biography is an account about someone written by someone else. It is a second-hand account of the subject of study and portrayal. It may tell us a great deal about it, but it is never the subject itself. It may disclose the life and thought of the person concerned, but only partially, never totally. And the biographer may try to be as objective as possible, letting the subject speak for himself or herself. Actually, this is what makes a biography a good biography. If a biography is full of the biographer's own ideas and biases, it is a bad biography. One reads in it not so much about the subject of the biography but about the biographer. In Chinese this is called *hsuan pin to chu*, which literally means "a talkative guest usurping the place of the host," that is, to dominate the show on an occasion when one is supposed to be only a spectator. A biography, then, becomes a kind of autobiography of the biographer. This is the worst kind of biography. It is in fact no biography at all.

Christian theology, in a sense, is a biography of God from the perspective of the Christian faith. It is an effort to give an account of God against the background of the Christian traditions. It is an attempt to let God speak for God's own self on the basis of what Christians perceive to be signs of God's activity in human community. This is both the agony and joy of doing theology — agony because one is dealing with a subject that is beyond human grasp, and joy because somehow God may communicate to us through the realities of life and world. It is when theology recognizes its limitations as a biography of God that it is freed from the dogmatism that takes a second-hand account of God for a first-hand account of God by God's own self. The margin of error in "the science of God" (theo-logy) is so great that it is the height of *hubris* to claim definitiveness for a particular system of beliefs and a particular school of theological thought. I am not advocating relativism. Even Paul, that most astute theologian, had to say, faced with God's mystery: "For now we see in a mirror dimly" (1 Cor. 13:12, RSV). This is the basic premise of Paul's faith and theology. Because of it Paul was able to tell us a great deal about God. He was a superb biographer of God.

If theology is a biography of God, there must be as many theologies as biographies of God. This is one of the most exciting discoveries of our day. While the domination of the West lasted, the world was made to believe that there was only one biography of God and thus only one kind of theology, that is, the biography of God and theology based on the experiences of Christians within Western culture. The same logic applied to what is called "christology," the understanding of who Jesus is in himself and of what he had to go through, especially his death on the cross. But this is no longer the case. We have come to realize that human beings have, since the very remote past, been engaged with biographies of God. And we also know that Jesus has become the subject of devotion and controversy, love and hate, for people, regardless of whether they are Christian or not. It is natural that, just as there is more than one biography of God and theology, so there is more than one biography of Jesus and christology.

Would it not, then, be important to attempt a biography of God in relation to how God is perceived by women and men in different contexts of life? Would this not illumine the ways in which God is related to the cross of Jesus and to the life of people who suffer injustices in the world and who grope in the dark for the ultimate meaning of life? And would not all this in turn disclose to us all the more clearly how the Abba-God of Jesus is different from the God of the religious tradition into which he was born? Theo-logy must be informed by christo-logy set in a wider and deeper context of the realities with which people have to cope in their daily lives.

The Speaking God

What stands out most prominently in most biographies of God is the fact that God is perceived to be a speaking God. If this is true of the religious experience of humankind, it is also true of the experience of God in the Bible of Christianity, both the Hebrew Scriptures and the New Testament. God did speak a lot in the Bible. In fact the Bible begins with God's speech. It tells us how God fills the creation with commands at the beginning of time. "God said, 'Let there be light,' and there was light" (Gen. 1:3). In this fashion, every time God enunciated a command, something came into being. Even human beings are the results of God's words: "Let us make the human being in our image and likeness" (Gen. 1:26). God's voice must have created a resounding echo in the creation that had just come into existence.

The God who created heaven and earth and all things is a speaking

God. Faced with chaos God just could not keep silent. Confronted with darkness, God could not remain quiet. And when God saw the world lying at the mercy of the abysmal formlessness, God could not remain speech-less. To be God is to speak, and God does speak. To be God is to be able to communicate, and God does communicate in a variety of ways, above all in speech. To be God is to be heard, and God does make God's own self heard in human language. Did not the prophets in ancient Israel often begin addressing people by declaring, "Thus says the Lord!"?

God, however, does not speak casually. When God speaks, something comes into existence. God does not speak at random. God's speech is premeditated, bringing order into the universe. Is this not how God, so reasoned the writers of the first creation story (Gen. 1:1–2:4a), "let the waters under heaven be gathered into one place, so that the dry land may appear," calling "the dry land earth and the gathering of the waters seas" (Gen. 1:9–10)? With uncanny theological insight John the Evangelist shares his vision of a speaking God when he says: "In the beginning was the Word, and the Word was with God, and the Word was God" (John 1:1). God and the Word! Can we not also say, putting God before the Word: "In the beginning was God, and God was with the Word, and God was the Word"?

God speaks! This is the hope of creation. Because God speaks, life becomes possible and history real. And God's speech anticipates the future, prepares and empowers human beings for it. To put it differently, "the stories of the creation of the world and humanity are not the result of an intellectual inquiry into the origin of the here and now. They stem from a concern for security in the face of the existing situations. The importance of the intellectual inquiry about the origins should not be disputed; but it is something which has been added later. The question of existence itself takes precedence."[1] God and our existence. Mediating between the two is God's Word. That God speaks is essential to us human beings and to the whole of creation.

God does not speak in a vacuum. In fact, there is no vacuum in God's creation. It is filled with God's words become trees, birds, sun, moon, stars, and of course human beings. Further, God does not speak only in the beginning of time; God speaks at all times. God's speech does not grow old. It is heard as new speech each time it is heard. Nor does God speak in abstraction. God speaks about our existence and into our existence. Our existence concerns how we live and what we do. It consists of our hopes and fears, our life and death. God's speech, then, has to be the living speech addressed to our concrete situations. God's words are active words. It is this speech and these words of God that were heard when God created heaven and earth. And it is this speech and these words that peoples and nations have heard and continue to hear in their stories of the beginning of the world.

There is, for example, this story of creation from Boshongo, a central Bantu tribe of the Lunda Cluster, Africa:

> In the beginning, in the dark, there was nothing but water. And Bumba was alone.
>
> One day Bumba was in terrible pain. Bumba stretched and strained and vomited up the sun. After that light spread over everything. . . . Bumba vomited up the moon and then the stars, and after that the night and its light also. . . . Still Bumba was in pain. Bumba strained again and nine living creatures came forth. . . . Last of all came forth human beings. . . .
>
> When at last the work of creation was finished, Bumba walked through the peaceful villages and said to the people, "Behold those wonders. They belong to you." Thus from Bumba, the Creator, the First Ancestor, came forth all the wonders that we see and hold and use, and all the brotherhood and sisterhood of beasts and human beings.[2]

What a vivid and impressive creation story! This is a supreme example of how powerful the simplicity of human language can be.

Bumba the creator is in pain! Creation is something like childbirth. Bumba, the First Ancestor, is in the pangs of birth! Pain is of course a kind of language. It is the body language. It is the soul language. It is the spirit language. It is the language of the whole person. It is spoken with the totality of one's being. For pain involves the whole of the person, not just a part of it. Words can be spoken from the mouth but not from the heart. These are lying words. But pain, real pain, cannot be spoken just with one's mouth. There is no lying pain. Pain has to do with the entire self.

Words, however, can betray the speaker's soul and corrupt his or her heart. They can also betray and corrupt the listener's heart and soul. This is the demonic side of human language. This kind of language is expressed in many different ways. There are flattering words, for example, spoken with mixed motivation often out of self-interest. This is the language used by those who serve the power above them. There are slandering words used by those who seek the downfall of their opponents. There are also treacherous words in disguise to catch unsuspecting friends off guard, bringing them disgrace. This is, to use a Chinese expression, *hsiao li ch'ang tau*, that is, to conceal a dagger behind a smile.

But pain! How can it betray the person who suffers it and those who witness it? It does not flatter anyone. It does not slander in order to bring disgrace to anyone. Pain is not capable of language such as this, especially when it is the language of childbirth. The picture of a mother going through the pain of bringing a child into the world is a sober picture. It is a picture of a mother engaged in the most noble and at the same time most painful act of life. Childbirth is a participation in God's act of creation, in God's pangs that bring into being all created things including human beings.

So Bumba the creator was in terrible pain. And that pain gave birth to the sun, the moon, and the stars. It also gave birth to living creatures, human beings among them. Pain is the language of Bumba's creation. But pain is not the last word. At most it is the last but one word. There is no way to get round pain, neither for God nor for humanity. But there is language beyond the language of pain and there are words after the words of pain. That is why Bumba, after the terrible pain was over and after the work of creation was finished, said to the people, "Behold those wonders. They belong to you."

Bumba speaks! Bumba spoke in pain, now Bumba speaks in joy. Bumba was in terrible agony, but now Bumba comes to people with words of wonders. Bumba's own pain turns into people's well-being. Bumba knows that now is the time for people to hear those words that say why Bumba was in pain. Bumba cannot let them keep wondering in fear of what is going to happen. And it is those marvelous words that they are to hear from Bumba, their great Ancestor: All these wonders belong to you! To the people Bumba is the speaking First Ancestor, a speaking God.

How brilliantly this simple creation story from Africa portrays the deepest mystery of God's creation in relation to the human experience of the mystery of life born out of pain! This creation story should be read with the creation story in the first chapter of the Book of Genesis. Do we not, then, realize that the words God spoke in the beginning were also words of pain? God's speech that gave birth to all things in creation, above all to human creatures, was the speech uttered in the midst of God's birthpangs. It is those painful words, that speech of birthpangs, that God continues to speak in the life and history of Israel and the Christian church, and also in the life and history of peoples and nations.

But God does not leave us in doubt wondering whether these words of pain are God's last words. The fact is that they are not. That is why each act of creation is followed by the words of affirmation: "and God saw that it was good." And when at last the grand finale comes, the sense of wonder and joy can not be suppressed. "God saw all that he had made, and it was very good" (Gen. 1:31). Good for whom? For God? Yes. But this is not all. The creation itself is good. And it is particularly good for the human beings whom God has created in God's own image. The similarity between the biblical story of creation and that African story of creation is unmistakable. The remarkable thing is that in both stories God the creator

is perceived as a God who speaks, a God who is on speaking terms with
human beings.

And how much God spoke to the people of Israel! God could not help
it. God had to "vomit" words of pain and love for them. Prophets in ancient Israel heard those words. Very often they heard them as words of
God's anger. They were really terrible words. Isaiah the prophet heard,
for example, such terrible words aimed at Judah:

> O sinful nation, people loaded with iniquity,
> race of evil doers, wanton destructive children
> who have deserted the Lord,
> spurned the Holy One of Israel
> and turned your backs on God.
> Where can you still be struck
> if you will be disloyal still?
> Your head is covered with sores,
> your body diseased;
> from head to foot there is not a sound spot in you —
> nothing but bruises and weals and raw wounds
> which have not felt compress or bandage
> or soothing oil.
>
> (Isa. 1:4–6)

God speaks in anger! These words are directed against Judah. They are
also directed against Israel and against the nations. That same prophet
heard how these angry words became punishing words on the day of
the Lord:

> The Day of the Lord is coming indeed,
> that cruel day of wrath and fury,
> to make the land a desolation
> and exterminate its wicked people.
> The stars of heaven in their constellation shall give no light,
> the sun shall be darkened at its rising,
> and the moon refuse to shine.
> I will bring disaster upon the world
> and their due punishment upon the wicked.
>
> (Isa. 13:9–11a)

These are horrible words. The anger of God is going to undo the whole of
creation!

If these words of God's anger are dangerous to the world, they are
dangerous to God as well. How could God destroy the world God created? How could God allow darkness to return to devour light? How
could God let hate rule over love? It would mean God's birthpangs had

been in vain. It would mean God was allowing the destruction of the
"children" conceived in God's own womb. Ultimately, this would mean
God denying God's own self, God rejecting God's own self, and God
destroying God's own self. Anger is, then, contrary to God's nature. It
cannot be a permanent characteristic of God. It cannot define what God
is. It cannot determine God's nature. Otherwise, God would have to be
other than God.

The Listening God

But God could not be other than God. This must be the conclusion the
prophets had to reach about God after those horrible words of anger and
destruction. They are led to perceive something other than anger that is
fundamental to God, something that makes God truly God. In the message
sent to his fellow Jews exiled in Babylon the prophet Jeremiah gives us a
glimpse of this God disclosing God's own true self. "These are the words
of the Lord," said Jeremiah:

> Cease your loud weeping,
> shed no more tears;
> for there shall be a reward for your toil,
> they shall return from the land of the enemy.

> I listened; Ephraim was rocking in his grief:
> "Thou hast trained me to the yoke like an unbroken calf,
> and now I am trained;
> restore me, let me return,
> for thou, Lord, art my God.
> Though I broke loose I have repented:
> now that I am tamed I beat my breast;
> in shame and remorse
> I reproach myself for the sins of my youth."
> Is Ephraim still my dear son,
> a child in whom I delight?
> As often as I turn my back on him
> I still remember him;
> and so my heart yearns for him,
> I am filled with tenderness for him,
> This is the very word of the Lord.

> (Jer. 31:16–20)

The speaking God is the listening God! The God who speaks is the God
who listens! We cannot be more thankful to the prophets such as Jeremiah
who tell us that this is what God is.

"I listened." God has the time to stop and listen. God is capable of listening. God is willing to listen. This is why we can pray and must pray. Just as we cannot talk to a person who refuses to listen, so we cannot pray to a God who does not listen. The God who turns deaf ears to our prayers does not deserve our worship. Of course we cannot take advantage of the God who listens and weary God with our petty thoughts and selfish ideas. That is perhaps why Jesus said to his disciples when he was teaching them about praying to Abba-God: "In your prayers do not go babbling on like the heathen, who imagine that the more they say the more likely they are to be heard. Do not imitate them" (Matt. 6:5).

I do not think Jesus is unduly concerned about the length of a prayer. The length is not the problem, but "babbling" is. A babbling prayer, even if it is extremely short, is extremely long, while a sincere prayer, a prayer that wells out of our heart, that cries out of the depth of our agony and suffering, cannot be measured in terms of its length. Think of persons bedridden for many years with a serious illness. Theirs is a long prayer. Imagine those women and men in concentration camps. Theirs is one long prayer, as long as their incarceration lasts. And think of those people suffering from hunger for days, months, and even years. Again their misery is one unending prayer.

Often such prayers turn into pleas, spoken or unspoken, to God for explanation and intervention. And surely they can be very long. Here is, for example, a "Prayer in Jakarta," that capital city of Indonesia in which, like in many other cities in the world today, the poor and the underprivileged struggle to live against all odds:

> Oh, One God,
> how tense we become
> to see life pawned,
> thoughts produced in factories
> and a society raised like cattle.
>
> Night falls on a dirty atmosphere.
> Upon what can hope be founded
> when deceit has become the art of life?
> revenge is sharpened in damp dark shelters
> ready to be swept up by a wave of insanity.
> Fights in everyday life
> have become something natural.
> Proverbs and maxims
> will not solve the problems
> of a life that is dull,
> imprisoned, with no windows.

All understanding God,
how irrational the gap is,
the gap
equal to forty years of a worker's wages,
that separates
a landscaped garden courtyard
from houses without wells or WCs.
Human hearts have turned to steel.
Like a disinterested dash board,
arrogant panzer tanks,
revengeful tractors.

All-compassionate God,
when tears become valueless,
and words become mud,
I look to north and south —
Where are you?

Where are the ceramic pots for the coins?
Where are the shopping diaries?
Where is civilization?

God of judgment,
empty hopes, futile optimism,
Only common sense and life's energy
are realities that I can grasp.[3]

This is a very long prayer, as long as the suffering of the person praying to God, as long as the human malaise created by human insensitivity and cruelty toward human beings and nature. It is also as long as the human civilization which, along with the glories it has achieved, has succumbed to corruption and decay.

God is God because God is patient enough to listen to such a long prayer. The question is how we know God listens. "I look to north and south," says the "Prayer in Jakarta." Then comes the agonizing question: "Where are you, all-compassionate God?" In this question we are back to the most primordial question of human beings in search of the merciful God.

The Remembering God

For the prophets of ancient Israel the answer to the question is to be found in God's memory. God remembers us! "I still remember Ephraim," Jeremiah perceived God to be saying. And how wonderful God's memory of us is! God continues to say through Jeremiah: "And so my heart yearns for him [Ephraim], I am filled with tenderness for him." God's memory is the hope of humanity. It is the hope of all creation.

The memory of God is not the memory of hate but the memory of love. Hate has no place in God's memory. Nor is it a memory of anger. Anger has to be transient. It comes and goes. We cannot be angry forever. The life filled with perpetual anger would be a most miserable kind of life. The life consumed by anger is a self-destructive life. For anger destroys relationships. It makes a person closed and hard. Paul is absolutely right when he exhorts Christians at Ephesus: "If you are angry, do not let anger lead you into sin; do not let sunset find you still nursing it; leave no loophole for the devil" (Eph.4:26).

We cannot even be angry righteously forever. There is certainly a place for righteous anger in human community. We have to get angry at injustice, corruption, and lawlessness in society. But then righteous anger is more love in agony and action than anger seeking the punishment and destruction of one's enemies. When this is not the case, righteous anger easily gets turned into self-righteous arrogance that tolerates no difference of opinion and opposition.

God's memory is filled with love for Ephraim and for humankind. "Is Ephraim still my dear child, a child in whom I delight?" Of course Ephraim was, is, and will be God's child. Nothing under heaven can alter this "blood kinship" between God and Ephraim. For the sake of us human beings it is crucial that God remember Ephraim. Because of God's memory, God's "heart yearns for Ephraim." In these few words Jeremiah enables us to see the extremely tender and loving heart of God, the heart that yearns for human beings just as parents yearn for their children. Remove this yearning from God, then God is no longer God. Short of such yearning, God cannot remember us human beings anymore. And God without a memory of us in love would be a fearful and destructive God. God without memory of us is a God who offers us no hope. This, of course, is not the Abba-God of Jesus but the God of a religious establishment that controls the life of people with fear and intimidation.

The Mute God

But this speaking God, this God who has been speaking almost without stop, this God who has been speaking loudly, suddenly falls silent. This God, who has been listening with all empathy, seems not to listen anymore. And this God who remembered human persons as God's children and yearned for them seems neither to remember nor to yearn for them anymore. What a terrible vacuum is created here! That vacuum is a vacuum of silence. And the cross of Jesus is that vacuum of silence. The cross seems to mark a turning point in the biography of God. After the cross do we now have to deal with a mute God instead of a speaking, listening, and remembering God? A mute God may be the God of the religious hierarchy, but is the Abba-God of Jesus also a mute God?

If God spoke so much in the past, should not the cross be the occasion for God to speak even more? Is it not the time for God to be heard ever more loudly and clearly? Is this not the crisis that requires God's powerful words? An inhuman thing such as the cross, an outrageous crime of crucifying the eternally just and infinitely compassionate Jesus — should not this provoke God not just to speak out but to cry out, not merely to listen but to act, not only to remember but to come to the rescue? But the God who has been speaking incessantly since the beginning of creation has, all of a sudden, stopped speaking. All that can be heard is the weeping of Mary, the victim's mother, and a handful of his followers, mostly women. And mingled with the weeping of the sorrow-stricken women is the heartless jeering of some of Jesus' opponents.

Surely this mute God is not the God Jesus used to know. In his pain and agony on the cross he must have felt it difficult to be reconciled with that God. It is reported, for example, that after his baptism by John the Baptist he heard a voice addressed to him from heaven saying: "Thou art my Son, my beloved; on thee my favor rests" (Mark 1:11; pars. Matt. 3:17, Luke 3:22). Jesus must have heard these words deep in his heart. That voice and those words marked the beginning of his ministry. They assured him that the cause he was about to take up was God's cause, the path he was about to pursue was God's path, and the goal he wanted to reach was God's goal. These were solemn words, words of confirmation, words of promise, and words of acceptance from God.

And Jesus heard that voice from heaven again and again in the course of his life and ministry. That voice came back to him in different forms and on different occasions. There was that temptation to which he was submitted at the outset of his mission and throughout his ministry — the temptation of the idolatry of power, even God's power, and the temptation of the powers of this world (Luke 4:1–13; par. Matt. 4:1–11). It must have been that voice he had heard at his baptism that enabled him to overcome those temptations. And perhaps it was this voice in his heart that finally enabled him to reject the pressures of becoming a political messiah. The temptation must have been great. How could he have withstood it without that inner voice of God?

That voice returned to him again and again. He must have lived with it constantly. That voice was heard, the story of the Transfiguration tells us, when he was in deep communion with God. This time it was heard by some of his disciples. "This is my Son, my beloved," said that voice, "listen to him" (Mark 9:7; pars. Matt. 17:5, Luke 9:35). It must have been with this voice in his heart that Jesus did what he did and said what he said. That voice made him free from the traditions and laws of his religion and enabled him to experience God's saving presence among the men, women, and children rejected by the religious authorities.

His prayers are responses to that voice. Jesus must have prayed a lot. He fasted, according to Matthew's Gospel (4:2) forty days and forty nights in the wilderness to prepare for his work. These must have been days of prayers — prayers in response to that formidable voice from heaven: "Thou art my Son!" What could that voice mean? What is demanded of me? Jesus must have prayed and prayed to have an answer. What are the implications of this awesome responsibility to be the son of God, to enter into a special relation with God, and to be entrusted with a ministry that has no precedent in his time?

It was a turbulent ministry he was thrust into. He found himself mobbed by the sick, the dispossessed, the poor. He took the religious leaders to task. He showed courage and wisdom in dealing with the Roman authorities. That voice he heard at his baptism must have come back to him again and again to strengthen him, to renew him, to guide him. "Very early next morning," it is reported, "he got up and went out. He went away to a lonely spot and remained there in prayer" (Mark 1:35; par. Luke 4:42). This must have been his usual practice. It had to be. The speaking God expected the speaking Jesus. The speaking Jesus needed the speaking God.

In this communion of prayers Jesus must have grown more and more certain that his was to do the will of God. It was out of that firm conviction that he taught his disciples to pray to God: "Thy will be done on earth as in heaven" (Matt. 6:10). This was his own prayer. He lived that prayer. His whole life was filled with it. And his ministry was that prayer in practice. He carried it all the way to the garden of Gethsemane where he wrestled, for the last time, with God's will for his destiny. "Abba, Father," he prayed, "Not what I will, but what thou wilt" (Mark 14:36; pars. Matt. 26:39, Luke 22:42). God's voice and Jesus' voice must have become interwoven in Jesus' prayer. They must have echoed deeply in the heart of Jesus and in the dark night of the garden. And of course the God whose voice accompanied Jesus throughout his ministry up to the moment of the final decision in Gethsemane was the God Jesus was able to call Abba, and not the God of the tradition dominated by the religious authorities.

But even that Abba-God's voice ceased after Jesus' last prayer in the garden — the voice that resonated in his heart for the past three years. The creation that used to be filled with the words of that God is now filled with human words — words of unbelief. The world inspired by that God's speech becomes now confused with human speech — speech of accusation. Jesus, full of the Spirit of that God, is now dispirited on the cross with death staring in his eyes. And there is no voice from heaven that responds to the prayer Jesus mustered his last breath to say: "My God, my God, why have you abandoned me?" There is only silence, dead silence. Even his Abba-God is silent.

Traditional theology has not understood this silence of Jesus' Abba-God at his crucifixion. It is puzzled by that silence. It has sought, then, to explain it by theories of atonement, some of them very ingenious, as we have seen. But those theological explanations have only made that silence even more silent. For the God who could turn away from Jesus in the throes of death must have not been different from that God in the prologue to the Book of Job who struck a bargain with Satan to test Job's faithfulness. The God who could regard Jesus' suffering on the cross as a punishment for sins, even if not his sins but sins of the world, would be no better than the God of retribution, the God of karma from whom even the Buddha sought to liberate himself and others. And the God who could allow Jesus to go through the shame, pain, and death of the cross as a bait to trap the devil that had human beings in its clutches would be a grotesque God not worthy of respect. The cross is caricatured when it is seen as a trick devised by God to deceive the devil. The cross would be a supreme injustice committed by God against Jesus to satisfy God's glory supposedly tarnished by human sins. The fact, however, is that this God could not be the Abba-God of Jesus. Traditional Christian theology failed to distinguish the Abba-God of Jesus from the God of retribution who demanded blood and death as a price for the forgiveness of sins.

But why was Jesus' God silent? Why did not his Abba-God respond to his last cry for help? This is an eternal mystery. We can only hazard a guess. Perhaps the God of Jesus was shocked into silence! The cross was such a scandal to God that even God was reduced to silence. That the forces of this world, especially the forces of religion in league with the forces of politics, would inflict such cruelty on an innocent and just man must have shocked God into silence. Silence of horror! Horror can render us into speechlessness. It can make God speechless too. Confronted with horror, words flee and speech stops. It chokes us. It plunges us back into the confusion before creation, before words were spoken by God to bring creation into existence. Horror thrusts us back into the formless darkness that prevailed before the beginning of time, the time created by God to bring form to the universe.

The cross is that primordial chaos, that hostile darkness, that form-less-ness in the beginning when God created heaven and earth. The cross is the return of that power of the deep, that monster that frightened the minds of our ancestors in those ancient days and haunts our minds to-day. The cross undermines God's creation. It once again challenges God's power. It stands for the work of the devil rising from the depths of creation to assert itself once more. And it represents the power of Satan in us human beings over against the God of retribution, putting that God on the defensive. We already saw in the prologue of the Book of Job how that God succumbed to Satan's challenge. It provoked a vehement protest from Job, the victim of that test. But is God going to succumb to the test once again, provoking Jesus' protest? "My God, my God, why have you abandoned me?" — could this cry be Jesus' protest against that God who would deal with Satan and leave him to suffer all alone?

The Abba-God of Jesus cannot be like the God of Job's friends or the God of hierarchical religion who keeps believers at arm's length. But then why was Abba-God silent? The silence of Jesus' God must have been the silence of grief. God was grieved into silence. It must have been a deep grief. When grief is shallow, silence does not follow. On the contrary, shallow grief gives rise to many words. We want to explain in so many words what the grief is about. We try to reason on and on how it happened. Shallow grief can make us talkative; we want to tell people — friends, relatives, even passersby, what we grieve about. But deep grief renders us silent. It deprives us of the power of speech. We sink into the depths of our soul and immerse ourselves in agony beyond speech. There that grief does not take form in words. There grief does not proclaim itself in utterance. There that deep grief overwhelms our entire body and spirit, mind and soul. We become a bundle of grief. No word is heard, yet grief becomes word itself. No sound is made, yet grief fills the space with sound. No utterance is formed, yet grief exudes utterance. No shout is heard, yet grief turns into a shout that deafens our ears. At the sight of the cross perhaps God retreats into this kind of silence, sinking into this kind of speechlessness.

And that silence of God could be a silence of protest. After so much horror and grief protest is not easy. This is our experience. Horror renders you numb, and grief sucks out your life force. There is precious little left to do anything else. You continue stupefied and your grief seems to have no end. To protest injustice, we have to have moral courage. To protest brutality we have to have spiritual power. To protest inhumanity we have to have what Gandhi called *satyagraha*, soul-force or truth-force. And on top of all these we have to have the physical strength to protest injustice, brutality, and inhumanity. Job still had that physical strength that enabled him to protest against his friends who defended the God of retribution for what had happened to him. But there must be millions and millions of men, women, and children who have lost the spiritual power and the physical strength to protect their humanity, to struggle for justice and freedom.

Protest does not have to be done with words and actions, however. There are situations in which protest has to be done in silence. Then that silence becomes powerful silence, ominous silence, frightening silence. That is why the secret police in the service of a dictatorial regime try to break that silence with torture. They will do everything in their power to make their victim speak and sign the confession of the crime against the state they themselves have prepared in advance, the crime that their poor victim never committed.

Something like this also happened to Jesus. Jesus spoke a lot, really a lot, during his ministry. He told many stories about his Abba-God. He made people think with his parables. He challenged them with his message of God's reign. And how he engaged in controversy with religious leaders and theologians of his day! He was a master of words. He was a genius of a storyteller. He was a superb polemicist, too. What a rich and colorful three years! No wonder John, the author of the Gospel that bears his name, concluded his account of Jesus with these words: "There is much else that Jesus did. If it were all to be recorded in detail, I suppose the whole world could not hold the books that would be written" (John 21:25). Numerous theological libraries in the world today bear testimony to this exclamation of John.

But the strange thing is that Jesus, who had spoken so much, who had done so much, kept almost completely silent before the religious authorities and before the Roman court. When the high priest asked him whether he had answers to the accusations made against him, "he kept silent; he made no reply" (Mark 14:61; par. Matt. 26:63). Later, when Pontius Pilate, the Roman governor, asked him whether he had anything to say in his own defense, Jesus astonished him by making no reply (Mark 15:4–5; par. Matt. 27:13–14). Jesus' silence was of course not his acquiescence to the charges brought against him. Nor was it his resignation to the inevitable fate of death at the hands of his enemies. That silence of Jesus could have been a silence of protest. It was a powerful protest against the enslavement of the human spirit by the traditions of the prevailing religion, an uncompromising protest against dehumanization of people through injustice committed by those in power.

The silent protest of Abba-God reinforced Jesus' protest. That God must have been fully present with Jesus in deep agony. That God did not respond to Jesus' cry, not because God had abandoned him, but because God's horror and grief must have turned into silent protest. "Look!" God must have been filling the air with silent grief and protest saying, "What have you human beings done to Jesus, 'my beloved son'? You have driven him to the point where even he, the one so close to me, so devoted to me, feels he is abandoned by me. What a scandal you have committed against him! What disgrace you have done to your own humanity!" The scandal of the cross is the scandal of humanity. That scandal is too much even for God. In that deep silence God must be protesting the scandal human beings committed against God's "beloved son." In silence God is in profound agony with Jesus and through Jesus with victims of human atrocity.

Karuna of God

And that silence of Abba-God must be a silence filled with pity. God seems to be saying in silence: "What have you done to that man of compassion Jesus? What have you done to yourself, to your humanity?" The cross is not so much a crime committed against God as a crime against humanity — humanity endowed with that which makes human beings human, that is, the Spirit of God. That denial of the Spirit of God does not make God less God. It does not reduce God's glory. What it does is to deny human beings their humanity. It makes them less human. By crucifying Jesus, human beings have abdicated their privilege as God's "beloved children." They have yielded to their demonic instinct. The cross of Jesus is a sad testimony to the fact that there can be no complacency about human nature, that human beings are capable of becoming inhuman.

Is this not what history tells us? That crime against humanity is committed again and again throughout human history, perhaps much more in our so-called civilized world than in the "primitive" world of our ancient ancestors. We human beings are born with the demon of inhumanity in the unconscious realm of our being. And from time to time that demon leaps out of the depths of that unconscious realm to dominate human actions and smear history with blood and death. Where does that demon come from? The biblical story of the garden of Eden ascribes that demon to the snake that seduced Adam and Eve to eat the forbidden fruit. But then where did that snake come from? We are in a vicious circle here. It could not have come from God. Perhaps all we can say is that human beings can, in a fit of anger, in the grip of insanity, under the spell of selfish greed, lose their humanity and become subhuman. Loss of humanity is the greatest crisis of humanity. It turns human beings to cold-blooded murderers. It destroys human community and demolishes human culture. It even threatens the power and integrity of God.

A Buddhist parable called "The Parable of Me and Mine" is an allusion to the fact that human beings, if not born with that demon of inhumanity, are under its power from an early age. "Some children were playing beside a river," so begins the parable:

> They made castles of sand, and each child defended his castle and said, "This one is mine." They kept their castles separate and would not allow any mistakes about which was whose. When the castles were all finished, one child kicked over someone else's castle and

completely destroyed it. The owner of the castle flew into a rage, pulled the other child's hair, struck him with his fist and bawled out, "He has spoilt my castle! Come along all of you and help me to punish him as he deserves." The others all came to his help. They beat the child with a stick and then stamped on him as he lay on the ground.... They then went on playing in their sand-castles, each saying, "This is mine; no one else may have it. Keep away! Don't touch my castle." But evening came; it was getting dark and they all thought they ought to be going home. No one now cared what became of his castle. One stamped on his, another pushed his over with both his hands. Then they turned away and went back, each to his home.[4]

This is a parable of human history, a history full of animosity, greed, and destructive power.

But is not there something else that prevents human community from succumbing completely to the dictate of that demon of destruction? This is the question to which religious seekers want to find an answer, among them Gotama the Buddha. For him compassion is the answer — compassion for all creation from the smallest insects to human beings. This is what is known as "compassion of Bodhisattvas," in the Buddhist tradition. There is, for instance, a hymn of adoration offered to Avalokitesvara, the Bodhisattva of compassion. It should move not only Buddhist hearts but also Christian hearts:

> O you, whose eyes are clear, whose eyes are friendly,
> Whose eyes betray distinguished wisdom-knowledge;
> Whose eyes are pitiful, whose eyes are pure,
> O you, so lovable, with beautiful face, with beautiful eyes!...
>
> Eminent in your pity, friendly in your words,
> One great mass of fine virtues and friendly thoughts,
> You appease the fire of the defilements which burns beings,
> And you rain down the rain of the deathless Dharma.
>
> In quarrels, disputes and in strife,
> In the battles of human beings, and in any great danger,
> To recollect the name of Avalokitesvara
> Will appease the troops of evil foes....[5]

Pity (*karuna*) is the heart of Buddhist spirituality. It is not just pity for some. It is "infinite pity for all" (*pei wu liang hsin*); and it develops into "the great pitying vow of Buddhas and Bodhisattvas to save all beings" (*pei yun*).[6]

This pity (*karuna*) is not just sympathy for those who suffer. Nor is it merely a deep feeling for helplessness of life. In some Buddhist sects pity (*karuna*) is related to "the womb treasury (*garbhadhatu*, or *garbhakosa-dhatu*), the universal source from which all things are produced; the matrix, the embryo; likened to a womb in which all of a child is conceived.... It is container and content; it covers and nourishes; and is the source of all supply."[7] What a profound word "pity" (*karuna*) is in the Buddhist faith!

Pity (*karuna*) is like a womb in which a life is created, nourished, and empowered. Pity is that womb. Womb is that pity itself, that power of life. What reigns in the womb is silence. It is a very dense silence. It is a silence that does not leave a vacancy. The womb is filled with silence and silence fills every part of the womb. It is a silence of pity (*karuna*) that is engaged in the nourishment of the life in embryo. The silence that fills the womb embraces that life, gives it protection, empowers it, and enables it to grow. In that silence the rhythms of that life reverberates, filling the mother with pity (*karuna*) for it. That silence will be broken when the womb completes its task, when the womb ejects that life out into the world. The cry of a new life that has struggled out of its mother's womb declares that the profound silence in the womb is over, that pity (*karuna*) has fulfilled itself.

God's silence at the cross of Jesus may be this kind of silence. It may be a silence of pity (*karuna*). It is not just anger. It is not simply grief. It is not merely protest. It, above all, must be pity, *karuna*, the matrix, the womb, engaged in the creation of life and nourishment of it. In that silence of the womb, pity (*karuna*) struggles to empower the embryo of life for the day of fulfillment. That silence of God is like a womb enveloping Jesus on the cross, empowering him during the last moments of his life and nourishing him for the resurrection of a new life from the tomb.

This at last may be the secret of the silence of Jesus' Abba-God as he called out in despair, "My God, my God, why have you abandoned me?" The God of the religious authorities may have abandoned Jesus, but his Abba-God has not abandoned him. On the contrary, his God must be creating a womb of silence for Jesus to grow into a new life. No, God is not creating it. God's own self is that womb. God once again has taken Jesus into God's own self — the most secure, loving, powerful womb. No language is necessary, for that womb of God is God's language. No words are required because that womb of God is more powerful than words. No response in audible form is needed. Who could fail to feel the warmth of that womb, to experience its love, to regain the vitality of life — life force — from the creating power of God's womb? Surely Jesus could not have.

Is it because of this that Jesus' cry of God's forsakenness is not his last cry on the cross? That is his second to last cry — not a decisive cry that renders other cries unnecessary, not a final cry that ends all cries, not an ultimate cry that makes all other cries superfluous. In actual fact, the decisive, final and ultimate cry is still to come. Mark and Matthew tell us Jesus made that cry before his death (Mark 15:37; Matt. 27:50), but they do not tell us what that cry was. It is Luke who tells us what Jesus said in that decisive, final, and ultimate cry: "Father, into thy hands I commit my spirit" (Luke 23:46).[8]

In his cry of dereliction Jesus addressed God as God — that God revered but feared, worshipped but remote, divine but impersonal. But in his last cry, Jesus cried to God as "Father" — that intimate, caring, loving, and personal Abba-God, that "Papa" to whom Jesus used to address in his prayers like a child would its father, that "Papa" whom Jesus taught his disciples to pray. In that final cry, the distance between Jesus and God is dramatically shortened. In that decisive cry, "unprecedented simplicity and directness of approach to God"[9] is restored. In that ultimate cry the child and the parent find themselves again in the embrace of *karuna*. In those agonizing moments Jesus must have heard God's silence — the silence of pity (*karuna*). Jesus, just before he resigned himself to the abyss of nothingness, to the darkness of death, must have realized he was in "that source, matrix, in which a child is conceived and nourished, from which all things are produced." Finding himself in God's womb of life and love, Jesus was already on his way to resurrection. As a matter of fact, his resurrection had already begun on the cross.

And it was a *loud* cry, too, that decisive final cry. All three Synoptic Gospel writers, Mark, Matthew, and Luke, testify to this. "Father, into thy hands I commit my spirit!" The cry was so loud it must have filled the universe with its echoes — long echoes that resound farther and farther into the infinite space. The cry was so loud that the womb of God in the deep silence of *karuna* must have contracted with boundless compassion. And that cry of Jesus was so loud that it must have penetrated the wall of silence created by the religious authorities between Jesus on the cross and the onlookers and passersby. Penetrated by that loud cry of Jesus, a Roman soldier, of all people, could not help but say: "Truly this man was a son of God" (Mark 15:39; pars. Matt. 27:54, Luke 23:47). Can we venture a guess here that Jesus still hanging on the cross was already the risen Christ to that Roman soldier even before those women close to him and his disciples had the experience of the resurrection?

The Cross of God

It has been a long week, this Passion week. In chronological time it is just a few days, but in salvation time it is years, ages. History, since its inception, has been one Passion week after another. And it is going to be one Passion week after another until the end of time. The cross of Jesus discloses human history as one long week of Passion. It is written with the blood of those fallen victim to the inhumanity committed by human beings themselves. It is told in tears by countless women, men, and children oppressed and crushed by the demonic power turned loose by the brutal forces of inhumanity. History consists of heart-breaking stories of people without power and protection living in the world of injustice. From within that history, from the depths of that history, cries rise to accuse the inhumanity of human beings, to protest the injustices of the world, and to plead with the God of *karuna*.

In Jesus' cry of dereliction on the cross we hear cries of dereliction from all parts of God's creation. Jesus' cry is reinforced by all these cries. It begins with a whisper, but it turns into a loud voice. It starts as a moan, but now it becomes a shout. It is nothing but a murmur at the outset, but now it becomes a mighty chorus moving the heavens and shaking the earth. It is first a lament, but it is transformed into a battle cry, sending fear into those who inflict inhumanity on their fellow human beings. Is this not how different histories are written — histories of oppressed people? Is this not how different stories are told — stories of the powerless women, men, and children? Is this not why the book of human history is an unfinished book — a book with new paragraphs and new chapters to be crafted by the masses with their tears, sweat, and blood?

The cry of people is so timid at first that it is thought to be unheard. It is so weak that it is deemed to be drowned in the sea of noises. It is so small that it is taken to be not serious. And it is so remote that it is regarded as hardly possible that it will reach the center of power. But this is to underestimate that timid, weak, small, and remote cry. For, again like Jesus' cry of dereliction, whenever and wherever each of those cries is raised, all other cries rush to it to strengthen it, to expand it, to magnify it, with of course Jesus' cry of dereliction among them. A universe of cries is created in and around each and every little cry of dereliction. These universes of cries touch each other, intersect with each other, intermingle with each other, filling God's creation with mighty cries of dereliction.

How can the God of the complacent religious authorities not be affected by it? How can the God protected by the official teaching of retribution not be exposed by it? And how can the God used by those who hold religious and political powers to intimidate poor men, women, and children not be dethroned from the seat of power and authority when that cry grows into a mighty shout of people? It is with excitement and awe that we observe today the collapse one after another of dictatorial political regimes. It is also with deep pathos that we see how religious authorities deprived of protection from political powers are forced to begin all over again to be part of the people of God.

The Abba-God of Jesus, the God of *Karuna*, breaks silence. That God has spoken. But how does God speak? Where is God to be heard? The answer is not to be found ready-made in catechisms, in theological textbooks, in the confessions and creeds recited in church on Sunday. God's voice does not come from heaven but from the earth. It is not communicated by angels in the sky but by people in the streets and in factories.

This is why the voice of Jesus on the cross is the voice of God. And that voice tells us a secret, an important message, about the whereabouts of God: Jesus on the cross is where God is — his Abba-God and our God of *Karuna*. Jesus in the depths of suffering — this is where God is to be found. Jesus crying out in pain — this is where God is to be heard. Does this not give us a clue as to where we can find God and hear God in the world today? Does this not compel us to look for the traces of God and to train our ears for the voice of God in this mundane world of conflicts, suffering, and death?

The cross of Jesus is the cross of God. The cross people have to bear is the cross of God too. The cross of Jesus and the cross of suffering women, men, and children are linked in God and disclose the heart of the suffering God. The God who bears that cross with Jesus and with people throughout the ages is not the God who negotiated with Satan to inflict suffering on Job. Job had to fight that God. We all have to fight that God, too, the God of legalism, the God of religious absolutism, the God of theological dogmatism. That is an imposter God. Job had to defy that imposter God. Jesus had to unmask that imposter God. And people must be freed from that imposter God. The Abba-God of Jesus, the God of *karuna*, too must fight that imposter God, not by cunning, not by brutal power, but by bearing the cross with people who suffer. From that cross of God unfolds the stories of God's reign on earth.

NOTES

1. Claus Westermann, *Genesis 1–11: A Commentary*, trans. John J. Scullion, S.J. (Minneapolis: Augsburg, 1984), p. 24.

2. From Mavina Leach, *The Beginning* (New York, 1965), pp. 145–146. See Mircea Eliade, *From Primitives to Zen: A Thematic Sourcebook of the History of Religions* (New York: Harper & Row, 1967), pp. 91– 92.

3. See *Your Will Be Done* (Singapore: CCA-Youth, 1984), p. 60. The poem is by W. S. Rendra from Indonesia.

4. *Yogacara Bhumi*; *Sutra*, chap. IV, translated in 284 C.E., Takakusu XV, 211. See Edward Conze ed., *Buddhist Texts through the Ages* (Oxford: B. Cassirer, 1954), p. 275f.

5. *Saddharmapundrika* XXIV. See Conze, *Buddhist Texts through the Ages*, p. 197.

6. *A Dictionary of Chinese Buddhist Terms*, p. 371b.

7. Ibid., p. 312a–b.

8. This is Psalm 31:5 with one word added, the word "Father." That verse is the prayer that every Jewish mother taught her child to say as the last thing at night (see William Barclay, *The Gospel of Luke* [Philadelphia: Westminster Press, 1956], p. 30).

9. *The Interpreter's Dictionary of the Bible* (New York/Nashville: Abingdon, 1956), vol. 1, p. 433a.

CHAPTER 6

An Interrupted Life

Christians and theologians in Asia and in other parts of the Third World have learned since the end of World War II to take history seriously, history not in general but in relation to the political changes that have taken place both internationally and domestically. The history of our nations has, in most cases, been the history of Western colonialism. Under the domination of colonial powers we were not free to govern for ourselves and to represent and speak for ourselves in the international community. The destiny of our nations was not decided by ourselves in Delhi, Manila, Singapore, or Jakarta, but in London, Washington, or Amsterdam. We were alienated from our own history and lost control of it. We had only a subordinate role to play in shaping our own lives and developing our own careers.

This has all changed. With the demise of colonialism people in the Third World got back their history. We regained our historical consciousness. I believe this is one of the most significant things that has happened in the Third World in the twentieth century. We are no longer slaves who have no history except that of our masters. We are not colonial subjects any more for whom history is made elsewhere. Even the rise of dictatorships that replaced colonialism in many Third World countries is not able to abort the resurrection of historical consciousness. People have learned to struggle against dictatorship and in our struggle we have become aware of the role we are playing in the building of nations with justice, freedom, and democracy.

This being the case, how could Christians be indifferent to the call to be part of the history-building of our nations? How could we remain contented with a faith that cannot interact with our society historically? The impact of the movement of history on thinking Christians compels us to question the a-historical nature of our faith, the faith that came to us in a set of ready-made formulas with no historical roots in our societies. We have realized that this is a self-contradiction on the part of the

Christian church in the West. Traditional Christian theologians are untiring in their emphasis on Christianity as a historical religion in contrast to other religions such as Hinduism, Buddhism, or primal religions as a-historical religions. But they do not realize, on the one hand, that their verdict is based on their misconception of these other religions and, on the other, that Christianity transplanted in the soil outside the West has become largely an a-historical religion.

The point I want to make is that Christianity in Asia, for instance, an offshoot of that "historical" religion, became largely an "a-historical" religion with an almost exclusive stress on the salvation of individual souls, leaving the world around it to fight for its salvation. This was the case of Christianity in China during the civil war before 1949 when the Nationalist and Communist forces were fighting to the last drop of each other's blood for the domination of their country. After the war was over and the dust of the bloody struggle finally settled, Christians and churches in China had a lot of repenting to do. Christianity in other parts of Asia is of course no exception. This is the experience of most Christians and churches in the Third World. We only hope that this history will not repeat itself. There are some encouraging signs and also some worrying signs. Once again Christianity in China, for example, having gone through those sobering experiences, is today finding itself in an old dispute between conservatism and liberalism. This is a kind of luxury Christians in today's world can ill afford, not least the Christians in China. We cannot but lament how deeply the a-historical Christian faith from missionary Christianity became rooted in the minds of Third World Christian believers.

What has just been said has some important implications for our effort to explore ways in which Jesus, that extraordinary religious personality in Palestine a long time ago and the center of Christian faith for almost two thousand years, is related to men and women throughout the world and through the ages. Jesus, in my view, has to be delivered from the age-long theological bondage and allowed to enter into human situations, not as a theological formula but as a historical person. The meaning of Jesus as the Christ, as someone who is entrusted with the divine mission to bring about justice, love, and peace in human community, gets illumined in his historical solidarity with those men and women who strive and suffer for the same cause for which he had to suffer and die. The theological uniqueness imputed to him by the Christian church has to yield to his solidarity with people in their struggles in particular historical situations. Is not Jesus the Christ precisely because he did not count such theological uniqueness a thing to be grasped, but emptied himself to find common cause with women, men, and children in suffering and pain, to paraphrase a hymn of the early Christian community in Paul's letter to the Philippians? In the interrupted lives of millions and millions of people fallen victim to violent powers, therefore, we may find how Jesus and other human beings are related in an uninterrupted life in the saving love of God. This is the theme that will further occupy our reflection and discussion here. We will deal with it against the background of the historical and existential experiences of people in Asia who have been, through much tribulation and travail, fighting for their right to be free and human.

Case of Rumor

On August 13, 1982, the Cochin edition of the *Indian Express* carried this news item:

> An orphan youth was starved for two days, then yoked to a bullock-cart and forced to run with it, being beaten all the while till he dropped dead, after covering four kilometers. His "relatives," one of them a local landlord for whom he worked, went to the police to record his "accidental" death! ... He was suspected of having stolen the landlord's wrist watch.[1]

This news report has all the elements of a tragic drama — a drama repeated again and again not only in India, but in other parts of the world, not only in the second half of the twentieth century but in all centuries. And this drama bears some resemblance, though faint, to that greatest of all tragic dramas, which brought the Passion story of Jesus to its painful end.

To begin with, there was a false accusation against the young man. He was accused of stealing the landlord's wrist watch. At most there was a suspicion that the youth was to blame for the theft. But it was only a suspicion. Whether false accusation or suspicion, it makes no difference for those who have the power of life and death over their poor victims. A mere suspicion without hard evidence is enough, more than enough, for the powerful to pronounce a judgment and carry out a sentence. The poor youth must have been a victim of a society that serves the needs of the privileged class at the expense of the outcast people.

Did not something like this also happen to Jesus when he was arrested? It was reported in those days that "the chief priests and the whole council sought testimony against Jesus to put him to death" (Mark 14:55, RSV; par. Matt. 26:59). Those in higher authorities who had masterminded Jesus' arrest did get some persons to "bear false witness against Jesus" (Mark 14:56–57, RSV; par. Matt. 26:60), saying: "We heard him say, 'I will pull down this Temple, made with human hands, and in three days I will build another, not made with human hands' " (Mark 14:58; par. Matt.

26:61). And when Jesus was brought to Pontius Pilate, the Roman governor, for trial, it was the whole council that accused him of "subverting our nation, opposing the payment of taxes to Caesar, and claiming to be messiah, a king" (Luke 23:2). The religious case now became a political case. Jesus the religious offender now turned into Jesus a political offender. A religious offense compounded with a political offense would ensure his death penalty. Jesus was trapped and there was no way out of it.

The case against the Indian orphan youth is, of course, infinitesimal in comparison with the case against Jesus. It was a case of a simple theft, allegedly involving a wrist watch of the landlord. But behind this seemingly simple case is a caste system deeply rooted in the Hindu culture that justifies the oppression of the outcasts. Aided by this religious caste structure of society is the political system that gives those in the upper caste absolute power over the outcast people. Show of power in that caste society is almost part of religious duty, and abuse of power is taken for granted in that political culture. What we have here, then, is not a simple case of theft. It has to do with the total religious and political culture of a society in which power and privilege are protected as a matter of religious obligation at the expense of the poor and the powerless.

The case against Jesus is of a totally different magnitude in terms of its implications for the entire human community. Still, it has something in common with the case of the Indian youth at the deepest religious level. It involved a religion that shaped and conditioned the entire life of a people, though not on the basis of castes, in relation to a hierarchical structure built on religious laws, ethnic identity, and even profession. And it also concerned a powerful empire that had colonized the Jewish nation and built the *pax Romana* in the Mediterranean world with military might and brutality. From the beginning the trial of Jesus was not going to be a simple case. The highest religious and political elites of the time racked their brains to undo a person who had done nothing of what he was accused of. The outcome was predictable. Jesus, like that Indian youth, died a violent death.

It had, then, to be a formidable case. For awhile Jerusalem, the entire city, must have been filled with talk about it. It must have made the headline news for the people of the town. That is why two followers of Jesus on their way to Emmaus after Jesus' execution said to the stranger, who had joined them in their journey, half in astonishment and half in reproach: "Are you the only person staying in Jerusalem not to know what had happened there in the last few days?" (Luke 24:18) The whole incident must have left a deep impression on people, whether town-dwellers or visitors.

It was, of course, a very unusual case, surrounding a man called Jesus. It must have developed into a public concern for all people to ponder and talk about in the marketplace, at cafes and restaurants, and at home. But they had to be careful what they said about it. After all, the verdict on the man was official. To contradict it would bring upon them reprisals from the political and especially from the religious authorities that had engineered it. But what about the unofficial verdict of the people who had followed the case closely? After the excitement and frenzy that had taken hold of them subsided, they must have come to the conclusion that the man was innocent. To them the whole event must have been like a nightmare. Some of them must have deeply regretted having been instigated to witness against Jesus.

This is an unofficial verdict. But in a repressive social, political, and religious atmosphere prevailing in a society, a verdict, though unofficial, is often a correct verdict, while a verdict, even though official, is a wrong verdict — not only wrong, but outrageous. That unofficial verdict that Jesus was innocent, that he was a victim of religious oppression and political expediency, must have, then, circulated underground, been whispered behind the closed doors, and tormented the hearts of many a man and woman.

This unofficial version of Jesus' suffering and death "must have been handed down secretly to his early followers" in a type of tradition known as "rumor."[2] Rumor is not just gossip spoken behind someone's back. It is not merely talk exchanged between idlers. Nor is it babble of someone who has nothing better to say. "Rumor" can be a very serious matter. It, among other things,

> *originates* from the effort to disclose the truth of an event which is closely connected to the fate of that group. Rumor is, however, put into circulation by two different classes: the assaulting-class and the victim-class. The assaulting class, who wants to carry out an unfair act or an illegal policy, also spreads a rumor in order to prejudice the judgement of the victims and to mislead them. On the other hand the victims, realizing that an important event which they experienced is in danger of being distorted through the manipulation of the assaulting class, spread a rumor in a collective effort to disclose the true facts. So, a rumor takes on the nature of witness. A rumor is not an objective description of facts, but it contains a trustworthy historical core.[3]

Struggles in human society, be they political or religious, are struggles between official rumors and unofficial rumors. Conflicts in human community, be they religious or political, are conflicts between the rumors of the ruling class and the rumors of the oppressed class. The tensions that threaten the sanity of women and men are the tensions between false rumors and true rumors. This is especially true in a society in which people are deprived of their freedom of thought, speech, and action.

Groundless Rumors

One of the masters of rumors is Kim Chi Ha of Korea, whom I quoted in the Prologue. His work "Groundless Rumors," published in 1972, is a most penetrating parable of how rumor can become a powerful force that shakes a society under autocratic rulers. It begins with "origin of a sound":

> Since not too long ago in the town of Seoul
> A strange sound repeating itself incessantly has been heard,
> A strange weird sound.
> There are some people who, each time they hear the sound, shake
> Like an aspen leaf and shed cold sweat.
> It is even more strange because these people are money bags
> Who can shit giant turds.
> Kung...
> That's it... Kung
> What's that sound...

That strange sound, it turns out, comes from a man named An-Do languishing in prison.

He was a innocent man, unemployed, poor, starved, and sick. In desperation he cried out: "What a bitch this world is!" Those words proved fatal to An-Do, although said in innocence and desperation. He was arrested, taken to court, and declared guilty for

> thinking up groundless rumors which would mislead innocent people, the crime of intending to voice the same rumors... the crime of disrespecting the fatherland... the crime of promoting social disorder and creating social unrest, the crime of agitating the mind of the people, the crime of growing weary of life... the crime of possibly helping the enemy, the crime of entertaining anti-establishment thought... the crime of anti-government riot conspiracy...

An-Do was tortured, mutilated, and thrown into prison. He moaned in anguish and groaned in pain:

> No, no, no, no. What has been done to me?
> I was clad in rags and starved, worked,
> Beaten and oppressed, but did not utter a word of protest.
> I didn't rest, didn't lie down, didn't even sleep,
> And yet what have they done to me?

What devilish crime did I commit to bring upon me a punishment so
   severe?
You wild geese flying up in the sky, do you know how I feel?
Can you tell me whether my mother is standing on the new road
   near our shack
Waiting for my return?
Is she weeping soundlessly, looking in the direction of Seoul,
   wearing her out-of-season clothes?
Wild geese, tell my mother
I will return even if I am dead — Even if my body is torn into one
   thousand or ten thousand pieces.
I will break out through the walls of this jail, I'll leap over the fence
Even if I have to sell my soul to the devil.
I will return, mother, whatever happens, I will return.

And then An-Do wanted to sing, but he had no head.
He wanted to cry, but he had no eyes.
He wanted to shout, but he had no voice.
With neither voice nor tears, he cried soundlessly day after day,
   night after night, shedding blood-red tears,
Crying soundlessly in the depths of his soul, crying no, no, no.

An-Do is of course not an isolated case. How many innocent men and
women suffered such brutality and torture in the state prison built by the
authoritarian rulers to silence complaints, grievances, and opposition of
the people!
   What can An-Do do, his body badly mutilated, his spirit crushed, unable to see and speak? There is one last thing he can still do and must
do. He must use what still remains of him to create a rumor that tells his
plight, voices his suffering, and protests injustice done to him, and let it
get out of his prison walls to make those in power shake with fear and to
move the hearts of his fellow citizens. He proceeds to make what is left
of his body — his torso — tell that rumor as loudly as possible. So,

Roll,
Roll your trunk.
An-Do rolled over and over,
Back and forth from wall to wall, Kung, back and forth from wall to
   wall, continuously, Kung
And one more time Kung and again
Kung
Kung
Kung

And there were powerful people who had money and who could shit
  giant turds who trembled each time they heard that sound;
Who could not fall asleep each time they heard that sound, over-
  come by a terrible fear.
They gave the order to execute An-Do at once.
But the sound persisted,
Kung.

A strange and mysterious thing, that Kung sound is driving some
  people mad; it never stops.
Yes, it is strange indeed.
It is heard even now, day and night.
Some people say it is the work of a ghost,
Others that it is An-Do who did not die but is still alive, somewhere,
  rolling his trunk from wall to wall . . .
The latter, as they whisper this story in the streets of Seoul, have a
  strange fire in their eyes.[4]

What powerful rumors! And tragic too! These are stories of the oppressed
people of Korea. But those who held power branded them as "groundless" rumors. For his "Groundless Rumors" Kim Chi Ha, the originator
of the rumors, "was arrested and sent to a sanatorium in Masan. He was
forbidden to meet with the foreign press under threats of further penal-
ties being applied to his family and friends and was eventually charged
on May 31 [1972] with 'having made remarks slandering the incumbent
government.' "[5]

Rumor or not, the fact is that the Indian youth did not steal the landlord's wrist watch; still he was beaten to death. It was a case of murder
brutally committed by the heartless landlord in broad daylight. That Korean prisoner of conscience did not slander the government. All he did
was to tell what it is really like to live in a society under the strict control of an autocratic regime. He was brave enough, or perhaps innocent
enough, to speak up about what people did not dare to say out of fear. For
this he had to suffer torture and imprisonment. It was a case of political
violence committed by the ruling power.

This turns our thoughts to Jesus, that man from Nazareth two thousand
years ago. He did not blaspheme God. He did not attempt to overthrow
Roman colonial rule. What he did was to tell people what God is really
like, what has to be done to restore integrity to human persons, and what
a religious community should be like to be an instrument of God's love,
justice, and reconciliation in the world. But he was put to death, falsely
convicted of high treason against both God and Caesar. It was a case of
"killing one's enemy by another's hands" (chieh-tao sha-jen), as the Chinese saying puts it, a case of religious murder carried out with the help

of political authorities. It was also a case of political murder that took advantage of the intrigue within the religious authorities.

Death Is a Public Event

The story of An-Do, the victim of a ruthless political power, in "Groundless Rumors" does not end with his death. He lives in the memory of the people and inspires them to keep his story alive. They cannot tell it in the open; they can only whisper it to each other in a clandestine manner. But "as they whisper this story in the streets of Seoul, they have a strange fire in their eyes." This is a magnificent ending to a tragic drama of life, an ending that inspires the people to envision the arrival of a new dawn in their continuing struggle for freedom and justice.

This must be the meaning, or perhaps the redemptive meaning, of the death of the innocent — death that inspires people to tell about it "with a strange fire in their eyes." Was this not perhaps also the case of the untimely death of the Indian orphan youth at the hand of the merciless landlord? It was just a local story. It did not develop into an earth-shaking story for all the world to know. It was quickly dismissed by the police as an "accidental" death. To the local bullies whose job was to do the bidding of the landlord it was merely a pastime in their harassment of helpless people. But for the frightened outcast men and women forced to hear the painful cry of the youth being tortured to death the story was something else. It could be their own story. The tragic fate of the youth could be their own fate. They must have felt tension arising in their bodies and a chill in their hearts. Their faces must have been pale with anguish. They were unwilling witnesses to the execution of the hapless orphan.

But they are more than just witnesses. The cry of the youth is their cry. His struggle to live is their struggle. His pain is their pain. His death is theirs also. In short, in the execution of that defenseless poor orphan youth they were watching their own execution. As they recalled the story later and recounted it to others, they must have had "a strange fire in their eyes." It was that same strange fire in the eyes of the people in Korea when they told the story of An-Do. The eyes of Kim Chi Ha himself, a political dissident in the state prison, must have glowed with that strange fire when he wrote that story. And how that strange fire in the eyes of the people changed the history of Korea from dictatorship to democracy! It must be that same fire that has inspired the outcast people in India to stand up and fight for their rights as human beings.

And it could have been that strange fire in the eyes of those women who watched Jesus' crucifixion that made them the first witnesses of his resurrection. Even his disciples, who deserted him, must have had that strange fire in their eyes when they began to tell the story of the life and death of their master later. It must have been that strange fire in the eyes that inspired them to become bold witnesses to his message of God's reign. That strange fire in the eyes of the people is the fire of courage, hope, and life. It must be the fire of redemption from God to purge human corruptions, purify human sins, and rekindle human hope for a better world here and now and for an eternal life in God.

In some sense this has to do with the public nature of death, that is, of each and every death. Death is a public affair that evokes deepest pathos from the very depths of humanity. It is a sad affair and as such cannot be beautified, idealized, or idolized. And how public death is as a sad happening! It is heard in the crying of the bereaved ones. It is seen in the solemn funeral procession. It shakes the souls of the living by a requiem that fills the air with tremors of sorrow and pain. And the poet sings, for instance, in tune with the heart devastated by death in a war:

> A woman shrieking
> in the city
> in the night
> in the dust
> in the hospital
> now a strand of hair hanging at bayonet point.

> The land still grows
> but men are drained of passion
> why is poetry today
> so sad
> like a prayer?

> On the deserted rockland
> above the layer of prehistoric soil
> bleached-white bones
> facing time
> cause in those coming after
> a twinge of sorrow.[6]

In this poem grown out of the destruction of war, death not only evokes sorrow but becomes a public protest. A woman shrieking at the sudden approach of death! That shrieking is heard near and far. No one can pretend not to hear it. The world public must know what the shrieking of that woman means. When the shrieking subsides, the world is to see "a strand of hair hanging at bayonet point." Death as a protest is as eloquent as a strand of hair hanging at bayonet point. Death as sorrow, sadness, and protest in public display reveals human futility at its deepest. Sorrow over death is contagious. Sadness decreed by it induces public emotion. Death brings time to a temporary halt. It fills space with a vacuum. And death as protest turns that sorrow, sadness, and despair to a call for an end to destruction of lives before their fulfillment. It transforms sorrow, sadness, and despair into a redemptive power that brings healing to human persons and their community. Is this also the meaning Jesus attributed to his death when he, according to John's Gospel, said: "A grain of wheat remains a solitary grain unless it falls into the ground and dies; but if it dies, it bears a rich harvest" (John 12:24)?

How Did It Happen to Jesus?

The death of that Indian youth was the result of the evil forces that have corrupted human beings and their community. He was one of the countless number of men, women, and children who become victims of those who hold power and use it demonically. What, then, about Jesus? How did the ordeal of the cross happen to him? How did it take place? Did it occur by accident? Did it happen because Jesus wanted it? Or was it predetermined by God for the salvation of the world as traditional Christian theology has us believe?

Jesus did not die an accidental death. Nor did he seek death. His death was premeditated and predetermined not by God but by human beings. In life Jesus identified himself with the poor and the oppressed. He made a common cause with them. Also in death he shared the same injustice, intrigue, and oppression that were their lot. It was, in the first place, the religious authorities challenged by Jesus that carried out the plans to do away with him (Mark 5:1–6; pars. Matt. 12:9–14, Luke 6:6–11). The conflict between Jesus and the religious leaders came to a head when Jesus, in an outburst of great passion, "drove out those who bought and sold in the Temple [of Jerusalem], upset the tables of the money-changers and the seats of the dealers in pigeons," pointing his finger at them and declaring, "You have made it [the Temple] a robbers' cave" (Mark 11:17; pars. Matt. 21:12–13, Luke 19:45–46). This was a declaration of war against the powerful religious establishment. Jesus could not possibly get away unharmed. Sure enough, "the chief priests and the scribes heard it and sought to destroy him" (Mark 11:18a, RSV; par. Luke 19:47a).

A tense atmosphere must have developed and become intensified in Jerusalem, not because of the impending great feast of Passover, but because of the inevitable showdown between Jesus and his religious opponents. Passover is a solemn feast, "a sacred commemoration of God's redemption" in times past, "a celebration of the great acts of God in Israel." It is also a pilgrim festival. It was estimated that "as many as a hundred thousand pilgrims may have come to Jerusalem annually for the feast from all lands of the Diaspora." The entire event, including the daily afternoon sacrifice at the Temple should have fully preoccupied the religious authorities with "all twenty-four divisions of priests in attendance" instead of only one at normal times.[7] But the presence of Jesus in the city turned their minds to something else. "The chief priests and the doctors of the law," we are told, "were trying to devise some cunning plan to seize Jesus and have him put to death. 'It must not be during the festival,' they said, 'or we should have rioting among the people'" (Mark 14:1–2; pars. Matt. 26:3–5, Luke 22:2).

This is the immediate background of the events surrounding Jesus' last few days in Jerusalem. It reveals the ruthless nature of the hostility caused by religious conflicts. The minds of his opponents are already set on the plans to do away with him. It is not a question of right or wrong, not even the question of whether it is justifiable morally and religiously. It is the question of how they can carry out their plans so as to bring about the least repercussions. When the whole city is getting ready for the solemn commemoration of God's saving acts, when all the faithful from near and far are gathering to offer their deep devotion to the God of salvation, the chief priests and company are plotting the death of one who sought to restore love and justice to the religion that had fallen far short of the God of that justice and love. The death of Jesus was in this way premeditated and predetermined in the inmost recesses of a religion hidden from the eyes and minds of the pilgrims and devotees who had come to celebrate the great saving acts of their God.

But implicated in the death of Jesus were not the religious authorities only. The Roman colonial power too was involved. The Roman rulers must have watched the conflict between Jesus and the Jewish authorities with interest and concern. Of course they were not interested in religious issues surrounding the conflict, but in the political implications of the conflict: the more intensely the Jews become preoccupied with internal conflicts, the more difficult it will be for diverse groups among them to organize a united front against the foreign colonial rule. This would be an ideal case of "divide and rule," the political craft skillfully employed by colonial rulers and dictatorial powers not only in ancient times but throughout history in the East and in the West.

For the Roman colonizers of Palestine in Jesus' day, however, there must have been a cause for concern. Jesus was gaining more and more popularity among the people. The crowds that followed him grew larger and larger as time went on and their fascination with him could not remain purely religious. The line between religious fervor and political zeal is very thin and given timely provocation the former would boil over into the latter. This is true in a nation ruled by a foreign power. How could not this be the case with the Jews who believed in theocracy? For them God is not only the God of their religious life but also the God of their political life. The presence of foreign rulers in their theocratic nation betrays

their faith and pollutes their life, including their political life. The Roman
colonial authorities must have watched Jesus' rise to fame and popularity
with increasing concern and even alarm.

Their concern and alarm were not entirely unfounded. On a number
of occasions Jesus said things in the hearing of the masses of people that
could sound sharp and provocative to Roman ears. There is, for example, the bloody incident in which some Galilean pilgrims in Jerusalem
were massacred by Pontius Pilate, the Roman procurator (Luke 13:1–5).
For those who brought up the story with Jesus this was a textbook case
proving the doctrine of retribution. But Jesus, as we discussed earlier, refuted it categorically. He then seemed to go beyond a religious argument
to a political contention. According to Luke's account, Jesus pointedly
referred his listeners to the tragic happening in which eighteen persons
were killed at Siloam when the tower fell on them. The two incidents
were related here — a political massacre and an unforeseen disaster, violence committed by those in power and a tragedy beyond human control.
Was Jesus, after refuting the doctrine of retribution, pointing his finger at
the Roman imperial power as "disaster and tragedy"?[8] After all, Jesus was
also a Galilean and he must have felt acute pangs for his fellow Galileans
who met their tragic death in Jerusalem.

There are also those well-known teachings of Jesus about "turning the
other cheek" (Matt. 5:39; par. Luke 6:29) and "walking the second mile"
(Matt. 5:41) in his Sermon on the Mount. These, with his other teachings,
particularly that of "loving one's enemies," have been held as the model
of nonviolence in situations of hostilities and conflicts. Persons such as
Gandhi and Martin Luther King practiced them in their political struggle
for the national independence of India and for the civil rights of black
people in the United States. This of course is not surrender to violence.
It is to meet violence with moral strength. And what moral strength Jesus
demonstrated in his struggle with the religious and political powers that
opposed him! It is that moral strength that made tremendous impact on
people like Gandhi and Martin Luther King.

There are, however, Christians who consider Jesus' Sermon on the
Mount as meant for the end of time when the reign of God will be completely realized, and not for the present world in which conflicts and
hostilities prevail. But would ethics such as these, lofty and noble as
they are, still be needed when God has brought all things to fulfillment?
Would there still be enemies to whom you should turn the other cheek?
Would there still be those government bullies to force you to walk the
second mile?

Jesus must have meant these teachings of his for the present world
and not for the world to come. He was dealing with the world of realities and not the world of fantasies. What could he have meant, then,

when he said these things? What did he have in mind when he challenged his listeners with those seemingly impracticable ethical conducts? Was he stressing "the *boundlessness* of love, not just for those of a like mind, but even for enemies"?[9] But Jesus here was not talking about how God would deal with us human beings with God's boundless love, but about how we human beings ought to deal with each other in our daily lives. He was dealing with concrete human situations that severely test our love for one another. And he must have been realistic enough to know that our love for one another is not boundless but very much limited.

Perhaps closer attention to the oppressive political situations under Roman rule — the situation in which Jesus lived and worked — could result in a very different interpretation of Jesus' mind and intention. "If one attempts to read tolerance out of these words," it has been pointed out, "then one understands nothing about primitive Christianity. This is not tolerance, but an expression of passive endurance out of spite."[10] This may be an overstatement,[11] but it does point up the need to relate what Jesus said about "loving enemies" to the political realities of his time. Let us first listen to a very unusual interpretation:

> These words of Jesus [about turning the other cheek or giving the shirt as well as the cloak] express the anger of the exploited and oppressed people and their anguish for not being able to give vent to it. Another saying [of Jesus] helps to illuminate this, that is, the saying that "when you are forced by the soldiers of the ruling power to carry their baggage and go one mile, go with them two miles." Put side by side with these words, then "the one who strikes you," "the one who takes your cloak," cease to be abstract nonentities, but those persons who serve as tools of the oppressors of the masses.[12]

We may not agree with an interpretation such as this, but it at least brings out one factor neglected by some commentators in their haste to get to the "ethical" teaching of Jesus, that is, the frustration and resentment of the people subjected to the rule of a foreign power.

Jesus himself, like his disciples and the people around him, must have experienced from time to time the frustration and resentment of being under foreign rule. It is, therefore, conceivable that by "the one who strikes you" and "the one who forces you to go the second mile" he meant "those persons who serve as tools of the oppressors of the masses." This makes us realize how serious Jesus was about what he was saying. He was not just talking about universal ethical principles that good and pious believers must follow. He was addressing a specific social and political situation in which he and his own nation were involved — a situation in which the colonial rulers and their tools, among them people from the

Jewish community, abuse their power and privilege and exploit the colonized Jews. Even in a situation such as this, Jesus must have wanted to drive home to his listeners, we should turn our anger into that power that alone can bring lasting freedom and justice not only for ourselves as individual persons but as a community and a nation. That power is love. Did not Jesus himself demonstrate what he meant when he accepted Zacchaeus, a rich superintendent of taxes and "a tool of the oppressors of the masses," and said: "Salvation has come to this house today!" (Luke 19:1–10)?

Still, the political implications of Jesus' "ethics" in the Sermon on the Mount could not have been lost to the Roman colonialists. In fact, to point to certain people as "tools of the oppressors of the masses" contained a serious political challenge. The point was not lost to Jesus' own people, especially his religious opponents. He was to be accused by them before Pontius Pilate, the Roman governor, of an attempt to subvert Roman rule. This is, as Luke reported in his Gospel, what they said to Pilate: "We found this man subverting our nation, opposing the payment of taxes to Caesar, and claiming to be messiah, a king" (Luke 23:2). In the court of Pilate the expression "our nation" meant of course the Roman Empire, even if it came from the Jewish leaders. That made their accusation even more treacherous, opportunistic, and mean.

If the Jewish religious authorities distorted Jesus' teaching addressed to the specific social and political situation of his day, the Roman officials must have not taken it lightly. To imply that some persons were "tools of the oppressors of the masses," represented, for example, by those who force the helpless Jews carrying a heavy burden for them to walk a second mile, must have sounded "subversive." They must have realized that Jesus was no friend of Caesar, although they might not have reasons to believe that he was a revolutionary capable of leading an armed revolt against Roman rule.

Jesus' political stance, just as his religious conviction, must have been clear to the colonial authorities. His sharp words directed at the abuse of power committed by those who held positions of authority and privilege had strong political overtones. His pronouncements deploring the arrogance and violence of those who served the pleasure of the ruling power must have spoken directly to the people who harbored discontent and resentment deep in their hearts. In the eyes of the Roman rulers Jesus could not have been just a teacher of religion, a reformer of a religious tradition. The discontent and resentment brewing in the hearts of these oppressed masses might, contrary to his desire and intention, explode into a rebellion. For this reason the Roman authorities perhaps did not take Jesus for granted. On the contrary, they might have become worried about troublesome consequences and made an attempt to get rid of him. At one point

Jesus actually received a warning that "Herod is out to kill" him (Luke 13:32).

When the Jewish religious authorities finally took action against Jesus, it could have been regarded at the Roman quarters as a God-sent opportunity. It could be the time for a shrewd political maneuver. They could now proceed to work toward the destruction of Jesus by appearing reluctantly to consent to the demands of the Jewish authorities themselves. They could have been, to use a Chinese proverb, like "the fisherman having his profit while the snips and the clam are locked in a fight" (*yu ong te li*). The death of Jesus on the cross must have also been politically a premeditated and predetermined death.

The Song of the Vineyard

The life of Jesus was maliciously interrupted by the religious authorities with which he openly contended. His life was expediently interrupted by the Roman colonial power with which he was at least at odds. It was cruelly interrupted by the religio-political forces that allowed no dissent, no challenge, no opposition. Did Jesus have a premonition that his life was going to be cut short prematurely? Did he have an inkling that he would meet a violent death? Evidence in the Gospels seems to suggest that Jesus anticipated an untimely end to his life and ministry as his confrontation with the religious and the political authorities grew in intensity. He must have felt more than a premonition about it. He must have taken it not merely as an inkling. He must have come to accept it as inevitable. He did not seem to make it a secret and keep it just to himself. As the writers of the Gospels tell us, he shared it with the people close to him and alluded to it in his teaching on different occasions.

There is, for instance, the parable of the Wicked Husbandmen (Mark 12:1–12; pars. Matt. 21:33–44, Luke 20:9–18). The parable "exhibits an allegorical character unique among the parables of Jesus" as the authors of the Synoptic Gospels tell it and as the primitive church reflects on it and uses it.[13] But there must be an original simple story behind the parable, a story that could have come from Jesus alone.[14] That original simple story can be reconstructed from Luke's and Mark's Gospels put together.[15] What we have here is a story-parable that "tells of a single messenger dismissed by the tenants empty-handed, and on subsequent occasions driven out with contumely and injury."[16] The story, furthermore, is not a pure fiction made up by Jesus. It in fact "bears directly on a definite situation."[17] What is, then, this definite situation? It has to do with "the conditions prevailing in Palestine at the time of Jesus":

Estates in Galilee belonging to foreign owners; the rebelliousness of tenant farmers, working under a share-cropping agreement, against their absentee landlords; the possibility of revolt against and violent treatment of a landlord's produce-collecting agents; even the possibility of the tenant farmers' believing that if they disposed of the landlord's own son, sent as a final recourse, they might take possession of the property.[18]

This being the prevailing situation in those days, the story-parable could not have but made a strong impact on Jesus' hearers.

Who, then, were Jesus' hearers? To whom was Jesus addressing himself with this story-parable? The Temple authorities, especially the priestly members of the Sanhedrin.[19] For "it is very possible that the parable was spoken in connection with the cleansing of the Temple"[20] (Mark 11:15–17; pars. Matt. 21:12–13, Luke 19:45–46). How poignant the story-parable must have been then! We begin to realize its no-nonsense nature when we visualize that explosive scene at the Temple.

"The cleansing of the Temple" might have been greatly exaggerated by the Evangelists in their accounts; it might have been "originally a minor episode in a corner of the Temple court."[21] Perhaps. It may indeed have occurred in a corner, but that does not make the episode minor. The confrontation between Jesus and the religious authorities had always been filled with sharp exchanges. And the confrontation at, of all places, the Temple must have created even sharper exchanges. It must have been filled with foreboding too.

The conflict now takes place where it has to take place — the Temple. The issue is now the Temple itself, that massive concentration of faith, tradition, power, and authority. Is the Temple "a house of prayer for all the nations," Jesus demanded to know from his opponents, or "a robbers' cave" (Mark 11:17; pars. Matt. 21:13, Luke 19:45) for the religious elites who control the life of believers? The question now is the religious traditions that the Temple stands for and guards: Do those traditions empower women and men for the hardships of daily living or make their already hard life even harder? Jesus must have confronted the religious leaders with the question during that episode at the Temple — the question he already raised with them when he most unceremoniously said to them on another occasion: "Alas, alas for you, lawyers and Pharisees, hypocrites, that you are! You shut the door of the kingdom of Heaven in men's faces; you do not enter yourselves, and when others are entering, you stop them" (Matt. 23:15).

The Temple itself is now the issue. It has become the center of the controversy. The Temple, that microcosm of Jewish piety and macrocosm of Jewish history, comes under the scrutiny of that man from Nazareth. The

Temple, that fortress of faith and tower of hope for Jews both in Palestine and in the Diaspora, is now under siege by that man from Galilee with an obscure origin and meager credentials. What unfolds there in the Temple in Jerusalem is the contest of the authenticity of faith between a man who has burst into the religious world of his people out of nowhere and the religious leaders armed with impeccable pedigrees and inviolable traditions. It is a contest between the God of Jesus and the God of high priests and doctors of the law. If Jesus' "cleansing of the Temple" was an "episode," it could not have been a "minor" episode. It had to be a major episode with grave consequences. Jesus must have known what he was doing. Those chief priests certainly knew what they must do. Both Mark and Luke reported that they "began to look for a way to destroy Jesus" (Mark 11:18; par. Luke 19:47).

The story-parable of the Wicked Husbandmen told in the midst of such sharp and tense confrontation must have been like a bomb thrown into the arena of the conflict ready to explode. What Jesus meant in that story-parable should have been obvious to his opponents. For Jesus the round-about manner of speaking is of no use in the thick of the conflict. The occasion demands that Jesus must not "point to east and talk west" (*chi tong hoa si*), as the Chinese expression has it. Otherwise, it would be just like "scratching an itching foot with the boot on" (*ke hsiue sau yang*), again to use a Chinese proverb, having no effect on the opponents. It is a time of direct talk, of not mincing words. That must be the reason why Jesus told the story-parable of the Wicked Husbandmen, a story with a powerful parabolic impact in that particular context.

That story-parable must have, of course, reminded Jesus' opponents of the Song of the Vineyard of Isaiah 5:1–7. And this must have been what Jesus intended. It is not so much the close parallel in the contents of the two story-parables that is important as the way in which they were told to bring the message directly home to the hearers. The Song of the Vineyard, it has been pointed out, "is one of the finest and most powerful examples of a form of teaching of which many occurrences appear in the Old Testament and in the teachings of Jesus. Its function is to engage the attention of the hearers, to invite a judgment on the situation described in the parable; they may then see that the judgment is in fact on themselves and their conduct, and this may lead to repentance."[22]

What is, then, the point that Isaiah the prophet was driving at in that story-parable of the Song of the Vineyard — a story that begins with a love-song (I will sing for my beloved my love-song about his vineyard) and ends with words of judgment on the vineyard for yielding wild grapes? This is what he was saying: "You [people of Israel and Judah] are the worthless vineyard!"[23] And what is the point that Jesus was driving at in that story-parable of the Wicked Husbandmen? This must be what he was saying to the chief priests and the doctors of the law: "You are the wicked husbandmen!" Jesus cornered them. No more prevarication was needed. No recourse to argument on truth and authority was necessary anymore. They "saw that the parable was aimed at them" (Mark 12:12; pars. Matt. 21:45, Luke 20:19). In other words, "they had fully grasped its meaning."[24] But instead of repenting, "they began to look for a way to arrest him" (Mark 12:12; pars. Matt. 21:46, Luke 20:19). Could not Jesus have anticipated such an outcome? Could not he have seen the danger he was inviting?

Jesus did not engage himself in such confrontation unprepared. He did not innocently count on the repentance of his opponents. And he did not walk into his death with his eyes closed. He did not court death. He was not a religious fanatic seeking martyrdom. Nor was he a romantic revolutionary infatuated with death. That is why he, in the garden before his arrest, prayed to his Abba, Father, to take away that cup of death from him. He did not just pray with his lips. He wrestled with his Abba-God and pleaded so hard that "his sweat was like clots of blood falling to the ground" (Luke 22:44). For him death was not an object of aesthetic contemplation either. It was not something about which he could sing with poetic abandon. When the fangs of death were about to close in on him on the cross, he cried out in pain and horror: "My God, my God, why have you abandoned me?" Many a Christian martyr died uttering much nobler words than these.

Even before his decisive confrontation with his opponents at the Temple in Jerusalem, Jesus must have anticipated the worst for what he said and did. This is evident from "the so-called three *passion predictions*" (Mark 8:31, pars. Matt. 16:21, Luke 9:22; Mark 9:31, pars. Matt. 17:22–23, Luke 9:44; and Mark 10:32–33, pars. Matt. 20:18–19, Luke 18:31–32). In all probability these three passion predictions are "variations of the passion prediction" in Mark 9:31. This Markan prediction is "to be recognized as the earliest not only by its brevity and indefiniteness, but above all by its terminology."[25] To the disciples still confused about and ignorant of their master's true mission Jesus announced in words that can be "the shortest and most likely the oldest [pre-Easter] form of the prophecy"[26]: "The Son of Man is now to be given up into the power of men, and they will kill him" (Mark 9:31).[27]

This earliest form of passion prediction is a simple statement of what is likely to happen in the near future. There is no "theological" commentary on why this is going to happen. In most of the variations of this earliest form we find a reference to Jesus' resurrection saying that he would rise again after three days. This must be a post-Easter addition and is not part of Jesus' own original prediction. Perhaps Jesus himself viewed his own death as the result of the message he had proclaimed and the actions he had taken, and not as something divinely ordained.

As he knew well, it was the fate of the prophets in ancient Israel. He could not help bursting into lament: "O Jerusalem, Jerusalem, the city that murders the prophets and stones the messengers sent to her!" (Matt. 23:37). As Jesus saw it, Jerusalem was also a notorious city — a city of God turned into a city of murderers who carried out religious murders. At one point in his controversy with the religious leaders, he even challenged them and said: "So you acknowledge that you are the sons of the men who killed the prophets. Go on then, finish off what your fathers began" (Matt. 23:31–32). He knew whom he was dealing with — the religious authorities who had no scruples about silencing their critics and opponents with death. But nothing held him back from a head-on collision with them during his final days in Jerusalem.

Is it possible that Jesus, besides anticipating his death at the hands of his religious and political opponents, was already also anticipating something beyond his death — something that was going to be far-reaching in its effects on the life and history of humanity? Was he somehow aware that his death was going to have a redemptive power that would endow redemptive meaning to other human sacrifices? Was he conscious that that redemptive power would keep the world from self-destruction and to lead history to the time of fulfillment? In other words, did he believe his death not to be the end but a beginning in a new history that God is forging out of the human history wrecked by the demonic power of human destructiveness?

During his crisis-ridden ministry Jesus must have often pondered questions such as these. These are deep "theo-logical" questions, questions that Jesus had to wrestle with in his communion with his Abba-God. And from time to time he must have been assailed by doubts about the role he was destined to play in this divine-human drama; he must have had to face the temptation to renounce the path covered with insurmountable difficulties and obvious dangers. Can we gain some glimpses into Jesus' mind as he was going through the struggle of the soul in the face of the historical destiny looming larger and larger before him as time went on? This will be the subject of our reflection in the next chapter.

NOTES

1. See *Struggle Against Death*, published by the Editorial Board for the Study Programme, Kottayam, Kerala, India (Kottayam: CMS Press, 1982), p. 140.

2. See Byung Mu Ahn, "The Transmission of the Jesus-Event," in *Gottes Zukunft, Zukunft der Welt*, Jürgen Moltmann zum 60 Geburtstag, ed. Hermann Deusen, Gerhard Marcel Martin, Konrad Stock, and Michael Welker (Munich: Chr. Kaiser Verlag, 1986), p. 95.

3. Ibid., pp. 95–96.

4. See Kim Chi Ha, *Cry of the People and Other Poems* (Hayama/Kanagawaken, Japan: Autumn Press, 1974), pp. 60–71.

5. Nicola Geiger's "Introduction" in Kim Chi Ha's *Cry of the People*, pp. 15–16.

6. A poem by Dong Thien, in *A Thousand Years of Vietnamese Poetry*, Nguyen Ngoc Bich, ed. (New York: Alfred A. Knopf, 1975), p. 199.

7. See *The Interpreter's Dictionary of the Bible* (New York/Nashville: Abingdon, 1956), vol. K–Q, pp. 664–665.

8. This was suggested by Tagawa Kenzo in *A Man Called Jesus (Yi-e-su to yu Otoko): The Life and Death of a Rebel* (Tokyo: San-yichi Shobo, 1980), pp. 118–122. This is a very stimulating study of Jesus by a Japanese New Testament scholar. The author concentrates on the "historical" Jesus. The book should be read with both appreciation and discernment.

9. So Joachim Jeremias, for example, in his *New Testament Theology: The Proclamation of Jesus*, trans. John Bowden (New York: Charles Scribner's Sons, 1971), p. 213.

10. This observation came from Japanese writer Yoshimoto Takaaki and is quoted by Tagawa Kenzo in *A Man Called Jesus*, p. 123. Translation from the Japanese text by C. S. Song.

11. Tagawa Kenzo, though quoting the statement with approval, thinks that it is an overstatement, for according to him the early church did understand this teaching of Jesus in terms of tolerance.

12. Tagawa Kenzo, *A Man Called Jesus*, pp. 125–126. Translation from the Japanese text by C. S. Song.

13. For discussion of the allegorical character of the parable, see Joachim Jeremias, *The Parables of Jesus*, trans. S. H. Hooke (New York: Charles Scribner's Sons, 1955), pp. 55–61. Jeremias explains: "The vineyard is clearly Israel, the tenants are Israel's rulers and leaders, the owner of the vineyard is God, the messengers are the prophets, the son is Christ, the punishment of the husbandmen symbolizes the ruin of Israel, 'the other people' (Matt. 21:43) are the Gentile Church" (ibid., p. 55).

14. Ibid., p. 57.

15. Ibid.

16. Ibid.

17. Ibid., p. 60.

18. Hugh Anderson, *The Gospel of Mark*, New Century Bible (London: Oliphants, 1976), p. 271.

19. Jeremias, *The Parables of Jesus*, p. 124.

20. Ibid.

21. Anderson, *The Gospel of Mark*, p. 264.

22. A. S. Herbert, *Isaiah 1–39*, The Cambridge Bible Commentary (Cambridge: The University Press, 1973), p. 47.

23. Ibid., p. 48.

24. Jan Lambrecht, S.J., *Once More Astonished: The Parables of Jesus* (New York: Crossroad, 1981), p. 130.

25. For a detailed discussion of the view quoted here, see Jeremias, *New Testament Theology*, pp. 281–282.

26. Anderson, *The Gospel of Mark*, p. 232.

27. "The Son of Man" is the title Jesus here used for himself as a circumlocution for "I." See Anderson, ibid., p. 210.

CHAPTER 7

Who Do You Say That I Am?

To have a glimpse into the mind of Jesus is easier said than done. For one thing the writers of the Gospels have not given us accounts of how the mind of Jesus developed, changed, and came to be certain about his mission. They in fact give the impression that they are dealing with a mind deeper than they can fathom, a presence that they cannot fully grasp, and a message they cannot entirely comprehend and explain. What inspires them to pen the Gospels in spite of this is their faith — the faith of Jesus' early followers who came to believe in him as the risen Christ. The Gospels are, in essence, recollections in faith of his teachings accumulated in the memories of that small community that quickly rallied themselves round after the traumatic experience of the crucifixion. And they are witnesses of this community to the extraordinary ways in which Jesus carried out his ministry to bring about radical changes in both the religious and the socio-political culture of a people proud of their history but under foreign domination.

The Gospels are, therefore, not historical records of what Jesus said and did. They are not accounts in chronological order of the life and ministry of Jesus. And they are not attempts to delve into the mind of Jesus and give a "spiritual" development, or even a "psychological" analysis, of the person who has come to command their faith and devotion. The Gospels are literally the gospel, the good news, to a people socially and religiously dislocated, to women, men, and children sick in body, mind, and soul. Jesus himself is the gospel, that good news, to them. For this reason, perhaps, Mark, the author of the earliest of the Gospels, wasting no preliminaries, went straight to the heart of his concern and began his account in this way: "Here begins the gospel of Jesus Christ, the Son of God" (Mark 1:1).

The amazing thing, however, is that although the Gospels are neither historical records nor biographical accounts of Jesus' life and work, we still find in them stories and reflections that are of great historical and biographical importance. It is agreed, for instance, that the Gospels are the only "historical" resource available to tell us directly that Jesus was a historical person born "in those days [when] a decree was issued by the Emperor Augustus for a registration to be made throughout the Roman world" (Luke 2:1), and that Jesus' birth happened to be related to that population census that "took place when Quirinius was governor of Syria" (Luke 2:2). It is a matter of historical fact that Augustus, the Roman Emperor, reigned from 30 B.C.E. to 14 C.E. and that Quirinius governed Syria from 6 to 9 C.E. All such historical information in the Gospels lends strong support to our emphasis on the importance of approaching Jesus as a truly historical person in order to grasp his theological significance for human community at large and for the Christian church in particular.

Another remarkable characteristic of the Gospels is that despite their firm faith in Jesus as the risen Christ, the writers of the Gospels do not hide their ambivalence about the identity of Jesus. And this is of much interest to us here. They could have suppressed their own questions and those of their fledgling community about who Jesus was and what he understood to be his chief mission. This would have been most sensible, and perhaps obligatory, since they were facing a world unsympathetic, if not entirely hostile, to their new-found faith in their master crucified on charges of sedition. It would have been to their interest to leave out those things that might have indicated some uncertainties on their part about Jesus, to whom they were now witnessing as the Christ.

The fact is that in the Gospels we come across Jesus who, from time to time, wrestled with his own uncertainty about his mission. The story of the temptation (Matt. 4:1–11 and Luke 4:1–13) strongly reflects this. We are also led to perceive how his followers and the early Christian community struggled to understand this larger-than-life subject of their faith. At one point his family was reported to have thought of him being "out of his mind" (Mark 3:20–21). The writers of the Gospels were honest enough not to paint a picture of the triumphant Jesus who had overcome the whole world. The fact that candid stories and portrayals such as these were not thought to jeopardize the case for Jesus — the Jesus whom they were witnessing to and proclaiming as the savior and messiah — is important. The memories of Jesus being a very human person close to them did not get completely suppressed in the process of divinizing him. In the minds of his immediate followers Jesus did not cease to be a son, brother, friend, master, or prophet.

For Christians today, especially those of us in Asia and elsewhere in the Third World, the question of who Jesus is again becomes very important. In our world in which religious and cultural pluralism prevails, the question can no longer be dismissed as irrelevant on the ground that it has been settled already. We are forced seriously to look once again at some of the traditional claims the Christian church has made on behalf of Jesus. Even some prominent theologians in the West have come to realize the critical nature of the issues involved. They also acknowledge the far-reaching implications of these issues for the reconstruction of a Christian theology more attuned to the realities of the world in which people of different cultures and religions have to find ways to live in love, justice, and peace. We will address these questions in our third volume.

At this point our interest in Jesus' identity is once again aroused because Jesus is found, as has been highlighted in our previous discussions, to be vitally related to the suffering of men, women, and children in their respective religious and political settings in Asia, for example, to their struggle for human rights, freedom, and democracy, and to their quest for the ultimate meaning of life particularly in adverse social and political situations. Who in the world this Jesus is and why he is deemed to be involved in our problems and struggles are questions of practical importance and not just of academic interest. As a matter of fact, more and more people in the Third World become fascinated with Jesus not out of theological curiosity but out of existential necessity. Jesus who seems to have undergone so much of what we are going through — who is he? Jesus who somehow makes common cause with us in our daily struggle — what can we make of him? Jesus' own disciples and his followers in the early Christian community must have asked similar questions even as they went about proclaiming him as the Christ. And these are the questions with which we want to engage ourselves here by way of letting the stories in the Gospels and our stories today speak for themselves and also speak to each other.

The Identity of Jesus

Let us begin at the mid-point in Jesus' career as a wandering teacher of religion and a social critic. He has been around for some time. From being an obscure laborer in the small town of Nazareth he has risen to national fame. Indeed, he has become an extremely controversial figure. Claiming divine authority for what he says and does, he goes about the business of God's reign with complete abandon. He has won the admiration of many and earned the hatred of some. The lines that divide those who admire him and those who hate him are drawn very sharply — the lines between the poor and the rich, between the powerless and the powerful, between the underprivileged and the privileged, and, last but not least, between the lost and the saved. The polarization seems irreversible. There seems to be no compromise between the groups on either side of the dividing lines.

In the midst of the growing controversy he carries on his ministry of healing, forgiving, and saving as if that alone matters. But he appears to be more than a religious reformer. He does not make a secret of the fact that he is also a social critic, and a very outspoken one at that. What else could he be in a society in which there is no clear division between religious life and political life? In the Jewish community into which Jesus was born, religion and politics blend into each other matter-of-factly. It is, then, not entirely unexpected that for the people who have come to follow him and listen to him in growing numbers, what he says and does has implications beyond religion understood in a restricted sense. He seems to represent their hope as a community and symbolize their aspiration for freedom from foreign rule. He appears to them the fulfillment of God's promise for their national destiny.

His disciples, who live and work with him day and night, share that national hope of a colonized people. It is conceivable that some of them have joined the "Jesus bandwagon" more out of political interest than religious devotion. But Jesus seems in no hurry to take decisive action. He must be aware that people are curious about his identity and even sense that they are expecting from him not merely a "spiritual" leader. The world around him is waiting for something dramatic to happen. He must be aware that he increasingly commands their interest and attention. He must, then, realize that there is a gulf developing between his ministry of God's reign and people's political expectation of him. Did not James and John, two brothers among his disciples, approach him and say: "Grant us the right to sit in state with you, one at your right and the other at your left?" (Mark 10:35–40; pars. Matt. 20:20–28, Luke 22:24–27). This is a situation of "having different dreams in the same bed" (t'ong ch'uan yi mung,") as the Chinese expression has it. How long can he keep them guessing? How should he reveal his true identity to them? How can he bring them to understand the true nature of his mission? He must have wondered.

Jesus seized an opportunity as he and his disciples were on their way to Caesarea Philippi, about twenty miles north of Galilee (Mark 8:27–30; pars. Matt. 16:13–17, Luke 9:18–20). He asked them: "Who do people say that I am?" This is a question about his identity. It could be that this was the first time Jesus posed it to them, but it could have hardly been a new question for them. The question of Jesus' identity must have been in the minds of the people and on their lips for some time. They had been asking who he was. If the question struck the disciples as new, it was because Jesus himself was asking it. The question did not, therefore, take the disciples by surprise. They were prepared for it.

But the question, coming from Jesus, must have been much more complex than the disciples thought, and for that matter, than most Christians have thought. We can only guess what Jesus had in mind when he posed the question to his disciples. It may be that with the question Jesus was, in the first place, gathering a bit of information through his disciples. They must have heard a lot of rumors about him. They must have been aware of endless discussions about what he said and did. It was time for them to tell him what people were saying about him. This could, then, be an *objective* question expecting an *objective* answer. The disciples were, of course, eager to oblige and respond to the question. They told him that people regarded him as one of the prophets.

Christians and churches in all times have also been engaged by Jesus in such an objective inquiry — and this is especially true today. Jesus asks us who people, not Christians alone, say he is. This is a very timely question too, for dialogues between Christians and people of other faiths and religions, if still far from being fashionable for the great majority of Christians, have been going on seriously in some academic circles and are on the agenda of Christian ecumenical endeavors. If we are well-informed Christians, we may be able to tell Jesus that Muslims respect him as a prophet, Hindus have a place for him as an avatar, and many Christians struggling for freedom and justice call upon him as liberator. And for some time now a grandiose name has been added to this growing list of how people call him: cosmic Christ. Even those in the counter-culture once praised him and sang about him as a superstar! In the midst of this proliferation of names that try to identify him, most Christians, East or West, continue to believe him to be the only savior to the exclusion of all other claims to be saviors. "Jesus," perhaps we say to him with some bewilderment but also with a sense of humor, "you are a man for all seasons!"

"Who do people say that I am?" This could also be a question of *historical* nature. Jesus has not appeared out of the blue. Behind him is a long history of Israel. He is, like any other Jew, a product of a religious and political culture with deep and hallowed traditions. To know him people must go back to their history and their traditions. History will give clues to his identity. Traditions will shed light on his teachings. Aware of this, the disciples must have racked their brains to identify who Jesus must have been against the historical backgrounds and religious traditions they shared with him. It must have seemed to them that Jesus was putting to them a historical question that demanded a historical answer. Accordingly, they informed him that some people were of the opinion that he was Elijah, that colorful prophetic figure in the history of ancient Israel.

This is a question most Christians must also feel at home with. History is one of our strong points. We have accumulated much history in the course of two thousand years. No matter where we turn, we run into the history that testifies to the person and work of Jesus — the history of Christianity in the West for many centuries and the history of its expansion in the rest of the world in more recent times. This is why we turn to the so-called normative periods of the primitive church and of the early church fathers (and mothers?) for theological guidance and spiritual inspiration. The Nicene Creed (325 C.E.) is recited in most churches and confessions. In addition, the Lutherans can always appeal to the Augsburg Confessions (1530) and the Presbyterians to the Westminster Confession (1646). Every faithful Catholic is expected to subscribe to the Decrees of the Council of Trent (1563). If this is the case with the traditional churches and confessions in the West, it is no less the case with those in the Third World. This helps to give a semblance of the universality of Christianity. And of course universality expresses itself in uniformity of liturgy, theology, and even church architecture. With perhaps a wry smile we may be prompted to say to Jesus: "We have known you through our historical creeds and confessions."

"Who do people say that I am?" This, of course, is also a *theological* question. Let us not be misled by the simplicity of form in which the question is cast. This seemingly simple question contains a deep theological meaning. Jesus is an expert at formulating profound theological truths in startlingly simple ways. "Render to Caesar the things that are Caesar's, and to God the things that are God's" (Mark 12:17 and pars.) is one example. "The Sabbath was made for the sake of human beings and not human beings for the Sabbath" (Mark 2:27) is another. And what a stir he must have caused among his religious opponents when he declared: "I did not come to invite virtuous people, but sinners" (Mark 2:17 and pars.)! His words and actions are tinged with theological provocation. He must have known that people were raising all sorts of questions about him. Sure enough, the disciples told him that some people take him for John the Baptist, that stern preacher of God's wrath and human repentance.

For theological questions and answers the Christian church is extremely well equipped. Throughout its history the church has produced schools of theology and systems of doctrine. Theological debates are carried on in seminars, conferences, consultations, and in theology classrooms. Out of this emerges Jesus as either humble servant or mighty king, liberator or peacemaker, defender of the powerless or guardian of the status quo. Above all, he is defined as the Second Person of the blessed Trinity. "Jesus," we are able to say to him with some justification, "you are a man for theologians and Christians of all shades and colors."

The objective, historical, and theological Jesus! This is the image of Jesus portrayed in the report of his disciples. Perhaps Jesus expected just such a report from them. The question of who people say that he is tests the objectivity of their observation, the historical accuracy of their knowledge, and their theological sensitivity in relation to the person they are following as their master and teacher. But Jesus in their answers is a second-hand, third-hand, and even a fourth-hand Jesus. They are still to be confronted with a question that opens their eyes of faith to look at Jesus in front of them.

The disciples must have thought that this was the end of the matter, at least for the time being. They might have thought that they had helped make a little clearer the identity of the man on whom people had begun to stake their national aspirations. The veil of mystery surrounding him was being lifted, even if not entirely, at least partially. And perhaps they began to watch with interest and anticipation how Jesus would disclose the true nature of his mission on the basis of the expectations people were entertaining about him.

To their surprise, however, Jesus came at them with a second question: "Who do *you* say that I am?" Now this is not an objective, historical, or even theological question that can be handled as if it were somebody else's business. Jesus has suddenly moved from the objective to the subjective, from the impersonal to the personal, from the third-person to the first-person dimension of faith. A radical shift has taken place. It is no longer a theological debate or a historical investigation that is intended. What counts now is not who people say that Jesus is, but who *you* say that he is. What is decisive now is your direct relationship to the one who stands in front of you and questions you.

This is an entirely new situation — a confessing situation. Most disciples must have been at a loss how to deal with it. They were put off guard by the situation thrust upon them. They did not know how to respond. Only Peter, according to the Synoptic Gospels, retained enough presence of mind to reply: "You are the messiah!" (Mark 8:29 and pars.). He must have said this in great agitation and excitement. That is why his confession was short and crisp — no lengthy discourse, no footnotes, and no commentaries! Jesus, according to the account in Matthew's Gospel, was impressed and addressed Peter with those memorable words: "Blessed are you, Simon Bar-Jona! For flesh and blood has not revealed this to you, but my Father who is in heaven" (Matt. 16:17, RSV). Peter must have felt elated, for this was a well-earned approval from the master.

Jesus Is Not the Davidic Messiah

As it turned out, there was no cause for elation for Peter. Whether it was a sequence in the same episode on the way to Caesarea Philippi or in connection with some other occasions, Jesus gave his disciples a very different picture of his mission. He was reported to have confided to them that he "had to undergo great sufferings, and to be rejected by the elders, chief priests, and doctors of the law; to be put to death" (Mark 8:31; pars. Matt. 16:21, Luke 9:22).

This is part of the passion prediction to which we referred earlier.

Peter, and presumably his fellow disciples also, must have been taken
aback by these words. This is not what they expected to hear. After the
excitement of the confessing encounter subsided, Peter regained his com-
posure and his "good" common sense returned. Compulsively, he "took
Jesus by the arm and began to rebuke him: 'Heaven forbid!' he said. 'No,
Lord, this shall never happen to you' " (Matt. 16:22; par. Mark 8:32). But
Peter's effort to restrain Jesus from facing suffering and death only drew
the sternest rebuke Jesus had ever given to his disciples. "Away with you,
Satan," he said. "You think as human beings think, and not as God thinks"
(Mark 8:33; par. Matt. 16:23). In Matthew's account Jesus was even more
blunt with Peter and said: "You are a stumbling block [skandalon] to me."
    What had gone wrong with Peter, the other disciples, and the people
who followed Jesus with expectation? What blunder did Peter commit
in front of Jesus in those otherwise memorable moments on their journey to Caesarea Philippi? It must have had to do with the time-honored
word "messiah," the anointed one (christos). Jesus must have known what
Peter, and by inference people at large, meant by the word and found it
impossible to share the religious and political aspirations that prompted
Peter's confession about his own person. For "on the lips of Peter the title 'Christ' would have referred to the messianic Son of David.... The
coming of a Davidic Messiah, who would restore the political fortunes
of Israel and establish her national supremacy over the world, was a
widespread hope."[1]
    It must have been most difficult for Jesus to contradict people's ex-
pectations. He did not hesitate to set himself in opposition to the religious
leaders who monopolized and dictated both the spiritual and the material
welfare of the people. He could also express himself strongly in relation
to the Roman authorities. But he had always been on the side of the men,
women, and children who lived in fear of the religious leaders and in submission to the colonial authorities. Their longing for freedom from fear
and servitude was a legitimate longing. He must have fully shared it with
them. If Jesus was in solidarity with them in matters related to their place
and welfare in their religious community, would it not be fair to expect
him to be also in solidarity with them in their political aspirations? Could
he afford not to heed a call to be a national messiah coming from the
people he had befriended and for whose rights he had spoken out without
hesitation?
    But Jesus wanted no part in this messianic euphoria of the people.
Why? Is he saying that his involvement in the political struggle of his
people has to give way to his efforts for a religious reform? Is he intimating that his solidarity with people is more of a religious nature than of a
political nature? It is hard to find evidence in the Gospels to support such
a conjecture. Jesus must have been aware of the political implications of

his religious activities. And he must have also been conscious of the fact
that the political stance he took came from his religious convictions.

Or perhaps his faith dictated that he dissociate himself completely
from involvement in the political affairs of his nation and devote himself
entirely to the religious affairs of his community, as some Christians think
and claim. Such a view reflects certain ideological presuppositions of
these Christians much more than the faith of Jesus found in the Gospels.
Unfortunately, this view continues to prevail in the churches in the West
and in the Third World, making the witness of the Christian church a divided witness. Such a view is, in fact, an illusion that has no basis in the
realities of life in the world, not even in the realities of the life Christians themselves live as members of society. How could Jesus, having
said what he had to say and done what he had to do, share such a view,
much less such an illusion?

It is in the question of the church's involvement in the affairs of the
world that the divided mind of the church becomes evident. At the same
time the question reveals a lack of integrity on the part of Christians in the
practice of their faith and in their witness to Jesus in the eyes of the world.
The most obvious example is the discrimination practiced by Christians
against one another and against other people on account of race, sex,
caste, or creed. Christians may think that the church is above the world,
but they will be hard pressed not to acknowledge how much of the world
they themselves bring into the church, making church a caricature of the
body of Christ.

If Jesus wanted no part in the messianic euphoria of the people who
had begun to focus their national hope on him, it was not because he re-
nounced his involvement in the destiny of his nation as no part of his
faith. Nor is it because he decided that his mission was to take care of the
spiritual welfare of the people over against their material welfare in the
world. He must have found it impossible to share their messianic aspirations first on the ground of his reading of the history of his own nation
particularly with regard to the Davidic kingdom, and then on account of
the theological convictions he had gained from his pursuit of God's reign
in his ministry.

Jesus must have read the history of his nation much more deeply than
most of his compatriots. Like his fellow Jews, he must have known that
King David "created a major state such as had no precedent in history
on the soil of Syria-Palestine."[2] It was an empire of power, glory, and
pride that

> included all of Palestine, east and west, from the desert to the
> sea, with its southern frontier deep in the Sinai desert along a
> line from the Gulf of Aqabah to the Mediterranean at the River

of Egypt (Wadi el-'Arish). The Canaanites of Palestine had been incorporated into the state, the Philistines restricted to a narrow strip along the southern coastal plain, while Moab, Edom, and Ammon, under one arrangement or another, yielded tribute. All of southern and central Syria was embraced in the empire, apparently under provincial administration. David's frontier ran northward with that of Tyre along the back of the Lebanon range to a point near Kadesh on the Orontes, where it bent eastward with the frontier of Hamath . . . into the desert. David probably exercised a loose control . . . over Aramean tribes to the northeast as far as the Euphrates valley; certainly, with Zoboah disposed of, no power was there to stop him.[3]

A very impressive achievement! It is perhaps surpassed only by the achievement of Alexander the Great of ancient Greece a few centuries later or by the unification of China under the Emperor Kao, who created the Han Empire (206 B.C.E.–220 C.E.). Just as the name "David" came to have a messianic overtone for the Jews of Jesus' time, the name "Han" is a household word in China even today, although the Han Empire ceased to exist nearly eighteen hundred years ago. The largest segment in the composite make-up of Chinese people is called Han people, the people of Han.

But the glory of the Davidic kingdom was short-lived. It lasted for a very brief period of time "like the night blooming cereus" (*t'an hwa yi hsien*, as the Chinese would say). In less than a hundred years that kingdom became divided never to regain its greatness again, with Israel in the north and Judah in the south. The divided kingdoms were progressively to be weakened by internal corruption and mutual conflicts, dangerously exposed to the interference and invasion of outside forces. The northern kingdom of Israel disappeared from history in 721 B.C.E. and its people were deported to Assyria. In 586 B.C.E. it was the turn of the southern kingdom of Judah to come to an end as a political entity at the hands of the Babylonian Empire. And when Jesus appeared on the scene Palestine was under Roman domination.

Despite this turbulent history as a nation, or perhaps because of it, King David came to live in the mind of the people as a legendary hero who would come again to restore their nation to its past glory. He became "the model of the Messiah who was expected to unite in himself the fullness of secular and religious powers."[4] It is possible that Jesus too in some way shared this vision of Israel restored and reunited as a sovereign nation. How could a nation survive the oppression of foreign rule without such a vision? How could a people deprived of a political power-base maintain their national identity without a political culture focused on an idealized personality revered as the founder of the nation? How could there be a nation and a people, humiliated, colonized, and oppressed, that would not dream of a national savior (messiah) personifying the glory and pride of the ancient days, embodying the cause of the present political struggle, and promising the advent of freedom and independence?

But a sober historical consciousness must have told Jesus that the Davidic kingdom could not be resurrected from the past to replace the Roman Empire. This was not merely a matter of political realism. It must have had to do with a deep reflection on the history of his nation from the time of King David to his own time. Jesus must have perceived the history of the Davidic kingdom in a light very different from most of his fellow Jews chafing under Roman rule. In his historical hindsight he must have shared the view of the psalmist who, in Psalm 89, extolled King David as the one anointed of the Lord with holy oil (v. 20) but ended on "the downbeat of lament in which the Anointed One (Messiah) suffers humiliation. The promises of grace to David are in question, for apparently the history of the throne succession is a history of failure."[5]

That history of the Davidic kingdom, the history that failed, has now become a legend to live in the memories of the people and to shape the consciousness of the nation. A Davidic messiah, a messiah-king who combines the religious devotion and the political hope of the Jewish people, becomes an intense focus of people's expectation. It must be this expectation that is implied in Peter's confession of Jesus as the Christ, as one anointed to be a Davidic messiah. But how could Jesus consider himself to be such a Christ and proclaim himself to be a messiah in the line of King David? This would contradict what he believed to be his mission in the service of God's reign and not in the service of the Davidic kingdom. A deep contradiction must have developed between him and his followers — a contradiction between Jesus' own understanding of his identity and his followers' perception of it.

Differences Between the Exodus and the Davidic Kingdom

Jesus as a Davidic messiah would, furthermore, frustrate God's mission among the nations and peoples through Jesus. The idea could not have occurred to his disciples, much less to the wider group of his followers. For Jesus, however, acceptance of that messiahship would have been a serious hindrance, a stumbling-block (*skandalon*) to his mission beyond his own national boundaries. In fact he chided Peter precisely for being such a stumbling-block. He would have been no more than a national savior, a revolutionary hero, with no further significance for the larger human community.

This contradiction, developed between Jesus and his followers concerning messiahship, teaches us the importance of distinguishing those historical events that can be significant beyond their immediate contexts from those that cannot. No history of a nation as such, even that of Israel, can be taken as a whole to be of universal significance. How could particular happenings in that history, then, be applied to other settings without further ado? This becomes obvious if we study the difference, for example, between the Exodus and the Davidic kingdom.

In the Exodus we have a history as an event of faith, that is, a historical happening appropriated through faith. This is why generations of Jews relive the Exodus in faith as a "historical" experience. Here faith and history become closely interrelated. Faith interprets history and understands it to be related to divine intervention. In this way faith saves history from itself, that is, prevents it from becoming a thing of the past. Faith resurrects history from the past, makes it live in the present, and extends it to the future. Faith, in this sense, is the power that enables history to become contemporary. The history that comes under the impact of the power of faith ceases to be a mere history. It becomes a history filled with meanings. This is the case with a historical happening such as the Exodus. Its central meaning consists in liberation from oppressive powers.

History as an actual happening is localized in a certain intersection of time and space, but its meaning can be lifted from its immediate historical context and applied to other situations. The history imbued with meanings seen through the eyes of faith can, however, be transmitted from one generation to the next and resonate in the community of nations. For this reason the historical experience of the Exodus in the Hebrew Scriptures becomes a central motif for people of varied cultural, ethnic, and historical backgrounds struggling for liberation from oppression of different sorts. Black theologians in the United States do not make a secret of their profound indebtedness to the Exodus as the heart of the history that led black people from slavery to freedom. Feminist theologians too find in the Exodus the inspiration for their struggle to be free from centuries of oppression within patriarchal society.

Black South African Christians who fought the evil system of apartheid that humiliated their humanity and enslaved them to unjust social and political structures is another case in point. In the Kairos Document, a theological comment on the political crisis in South Africa, the Exodus was a living experience that fortifies the determination of black South African Christians to struggle for deliverance from enslavement in that inhuman religious, social, and political structure of apartheid. It says in part:

> The Bible describes oppression as the experience of being crushed, degraded, humiliated, exploited, defrauded, deceived, impoverished,

and enslaved. And the oppressors are described as cruel, ruthless, arrogant, greedy, violent and tyrannical and as the enemy. Such description could only have been written originally by people who had a long and painful experience of what it means to be oppressed. And indeed nearly 90 percent of the history of the Jewish and later the Christian people whose story is told in the Bible is a history of domestic and international oppression. Israel as a nation was built upon the painful experience of oppression and repression as slaves in Egypt. But what made all the difference for this particular group of oppressed people was the revelation of Yahweh. God was revealed as Yahweh, the one who has compassion on those who suffer and who liberates them from their oppressors.[6]

For black South Africans South Africa was the contemporary Egypt. The white South African rulers were the modern pharaohs. The black South Africans are the enslaved Hebrews of today. Struggle against apartheid was struggle for an exodus. It was struggle for freedom from oppression. Here a meaning generated by a particular historical happening joined in the universe of meanings transcending temporal and spatial particularities.

Every nation in Asia too has its own exodus experience. In modern history the year 1945, for instance, can be regarded as the exodus year for most Asian nations and peoples. In that year Asia was delivered from the tyranny of Japanese imperial ambition and from the devastation of the Pacific War. That deliverance was followed by the beginning of the end of the Western colonial era. The Philippines won independence from the United States in 1946, India from British rule in 1947, Indonesia from the Dutch in 1949, to mention just a few examples. The road to exodus for Indochina was tortuous and bloody. French colonialism ceased after the Geneva agreement in 1954. But soon after Indochina was to be engulfed by the Vietnam War, which cost more than one million Vietnamese lives. Almost sixty thousand American troops also lost their lives.

For many nations and peoples in Asia, and for that matter in Africa and Latin America, struggle for exodus goes on — liberation from political oppression, from economic exploitation, from poverty and hunger. It is in such exodus struggle that the redemptive meaning of history is manifested. And that redemptive meaning with liberation at its heart enables the histories of nations and peoples to be linked with the historical experience of the Exodus told in the the Hebrew Scriptures, remembered by the succeeding generations of Jews, and given a prominent place in the Christian faith.

Thus occurs a creation of a common zone of meanings with the Exodus as the chief emphasis. If the Hebrews enslaved in Egypt experienced it, other nations and people also go through an exodus experience of one kind or another in the course of their history. They may not call their experience "exodus"; still it is the experience of deliverance from bondage both in the physical and in the spiritual sense. African Americans in the United States, women in the long tradition of male-dominated culture, most nations and peoples in the Third World today, find themselves in that common zone of the meaning derived from the Exodus. Christian theologians in the West as well as in the Third World are now facing the challenge to reexamine their traditional theological concepts and presuppositions and to engage themselves in theological activities that make sense in light of that common zone of exodus experience.

The Davidic kingdom, however, is not the Exodus. It is an integral part of the history of Israel like the Exodus, but its meaning contradicts that of the Exodus and other exodus experiences. The Davidic kingdom is primarily a political system built on a religious ideology of theocracy. And how different is a theocratic political system from a totalitarian state? Very little. This is the experience of almost all theocratic states in history, the most recent example being Japan. How Japan turned into a fierce political and military machine — with the emperor as god at the pinnacle of the pyramid of power serving as the mobilizing spirit — and let loose its demonic power against peoples of Southeast Asia is a history to be long remembered. The history of the Davidic kingdom is also the history of a theocratic state with power concentrated in its ruler. That power could become an idol that corrupts those in power and abuses the rights of people to be free and human. The history of the Davidic kingdom was a history of failing God and people. Amos the prophet saw that as early as the eighth century B.C.E. when he said:

> Shame on you who live at ease in Zion
> and you, untroubled on the hill of Samaria,
>   men of mark in the first of nations,
> you to whom the people of Israel resort!
> Go, look at Calneh,
> travel on to Hamath the great,
>   then go down to Gath of the Philistines —
> are you better than these kingdoms?
> Or is your territory greater than theirs?
> You who thrust the evil day aside
> and make haste to establish violence.
> You who loll on beds inlaid with ivory
>   and sprawl over your couches,
> feasting on lambs from the flock
>   and fatted calves,
> you who pluck the strings of the lute

and invented musical instruments like David,
    you who drink wine by the bowlful
and lard yourselves with the richest of oils,
but are not grieved at the ruin of Joseph —
    now, therefore,
you shall head the column of exiles;
    that will be the end of sprawling and revelry.
                                                    (Amos 6:1–7)

This is what those who operated the theocratic political machines inherited from the Davidic kingdom had done to the nation called into being through God's saving love. They compromised the future of a nation with material gains of the present. They corrupted the religious basis of their community and destroyed the vision of a people inspired by love, truth, and justice.

The history of the Davidic kingdom was, like the history of any other theocratic state, a history marred by corruption and oppression. But the Jews under Roman colonial rule did not want to remember this. They remembered the glory and pride of their ancient kingdom and idealized David as the savior-king who accomplished the political and military feat of building a powerful nation. Conquered and ruled as a colonized people, they were awaiting the return of the Davidic kingdom with religious fervor. In their struggle for political independence they were looking for a "Davidic messiah" to lead them to victory against the Romans. Even the disciples of Jesus and the early Christian community injected this national aspiration into their perception of who Jesus must be. They said to Jesus: "You are the Christ, the messiah, the Davidic messiah!"

The fact, however, is that the messiahship inspired by the ancient kingdom built by King David cannot be a part of the universe of meanings in which the Exodus plays a crucial role. Messianism is a pseudo-religious faith that excludes people of other religious traditions and backgrounds. It is a political ideology that creates antagonistic relationships among the nations. It is the heart of a religious and political culture that has no room for people of other religious and political cultures. And it is a nationalistic religion that identifies religious allegiance with political allegiance. How could Jesus respond to the demand to be a Davidic messiah and restore ancient glory to his nation? The window to the universe of meanings opened by the Exodus, for example, would be closed again. Conformity to a particular religious and political culture would be a necessary part of believing in God. God would become a God of that culture only. God would have an exclusive ethnic identity. The universe of meanings would be broken, fragmented, and destroyed. In its place would come into being domination of one particular meaning over other meanings. Is not all this already implied in the expression "Davidic messiahship"? A Davidic messiah would be a crowned political ruler and king, a legitimated despot. Surely this would have contradicted everything Jesus believed to be his mission of God's reign entrusted to him by God.

Promise and Fulfillment Reconsidered

We are speaking of a "messianic syndrome." Not only the religious ethos of Jesus' time was visibly shaped by it; the early Christian community was also deeply affected by it. Some stories in the Gospels, as has been shown above, give us an idea of how that syndrome created a tension between Jesus and his followers. It has been pointed out that for the early Christian community "the stream of tradition associated with David and Zion survived intact and provided a major resource, if not hermeneutical guide, for understanding the messianic identity of Jesus."[7]

It is this "messianic syndrome" of the early Christian community, among other things, that the Christian church has inherited. With the theocratic tradition represented by King David and symbolized by Zion as "a major resource for understanding the messianic identity of Jesus," the Christian church has built its strength on exclusivistic faith. It has established systems of belief on the basis of its claim to absolute truth. It has appropriated to itself the sole right to interpret the saving will of God for humanity.

In due time exclusivism has become deeply engraved on the Christian mind. It has shaped the mindset of Christians. It has even become an organic part of the ways in which we view the world. The Christian church has thrived on it. It has been proud of it. It is the criterion of truth by which one's orthodoxy is tested and judged. Many Christians have become mentally and spiritually incapable of appreciating people of other cultures and religions as "children of God." God the creator of *all* human beings in a real sense has disappeared from their teachings about God. God is worshipped as the redeemer of only those who believe in Jesus as their personal savior. God the redeemer negates God the creator. God the creator is abrogated by God the redeemer. God becomes a truncated God. But God is not redeemer without at the same time being creator. And God is not creator if God is not at the same time redeemer. God is the creator-redeemer and the redeemer-creator. It is this God the creator-redeemer and God the redeemer-creator who is the center of the universe of meanings that can be shared, explored, and enjoyed, by women, men, and children who live, breathe, and have their being in God's world. Christian exclusivism is an abolition of this universe of meanings. It is a reduction of God the creator-redeemer. It not only serves Christian spiritual arrogance but distorts the gospel of Jesus.

The most common framework used by Christians and theologians alike to define the messianic nature of Jesus' life and ministry is expressed in the two related concepts of promise and fulfillment. It has worked splendidly until recently when some thinking Christians outside the West began to question the theological validity of those concepts in light of their experiences of cultures and histories not related to Christianity. They have discovered that a theological framework such as this does not quite explain how God is related to them in their own cultures and histories. It is one of the sacred cows of traditional theology. But does it really have a sound biblical ground? And is it universally applicable?

In the Hebrew Scriptures, we are told, God's promise is given to Abraham and his descendants — the promise of a land "flowing with milk and honey." And what a history was unfolded in pursuit of that promise! It was a long, tortuous history filled with human hopes and tragedies. The story of the burial of Sarah, Abraham's wife, was a most touching episode in this history. After having taken the risk to leave his home in Mesopotamia and undergone many hardships in the new land, Abraham did not even own a piece of land to bury his wife. "I am an alien and a settler among you," he said to the Hittites, aborigines of the land. "Give me land enough for a burial-place," he asked them, "so that I can give my dead proper burial" (Gen. 23). The story goes on to tell us that Abraham refused a free offer of a burial ground from the Hittites and bought it for what seemed an exorbitant price. At last Abraham was able to claim as his own a piece of land in the "promised" land.

It is this history of the settlement of Abraham and his descendants that the Christian church has come to view with theological romanticism. The process of spiritualizing that history began already in the early Christian community. In the words of the writer of the letter to the Hebrews, "By faith Abraham obeyed the call to go out to a land destined for himself and his heirs, and left home without knowing where he was to go. By faith he settled as an alien in the land promised to him" (Heb. 11:8–9). The parallel of this "patriarchal" history to the beginnings of the Christian community in the inhospitable world of the Roman Empire is evident. The history of "the people of God" in the Hebrew Scriptures became a hagiography. Many elements that made up that history — social, political, cultural, or even ideological elements — though retained abundantly in the Hebrew Scriptures, were seen as serving the cause of the promise on its way to fulfillment. In the centuries that followed, Christian theology, based on the hagiographic understanding of the history of Abraham and his descendants, constructed the theological concepts of promise and fulfillment to explain God's saving activity culminating in Jesus Christ.

For the Christian church the long history of ancient Israel as promise has finally found fulfillment in Jesus Christ. This of course is not a simple and direct process. The focus has to be shifted from a land to a person. The promise of a land has no actual meaning for Christians. The idea of the promised land does not work for them in a literal sense. It has to be replaced by the promise of God's salvation realized in Jesus. What happens, then, is that the twin concepts of promise and fulfillment are detached from land and attached to Jesus. This is a major shift, but Christian theology has not grappled with it and continues to be preoccupied with the concept of continuity between Israel as promise and Jesus as fulfillment. This, incidentally, is one of the critical issues that divide Jews and Christians. Christians must learn to understand how God's promise is fulfilled, partially to be sure, even within Israel. They must also learn that that same promise of God is also *only* partially fulfilled in the history of Christianity. The concentration of promise in others and that of fulfillment in oneself is both historically and theologically wrong. This has important implications for our appreciation of the history of the nations and peoples in relation to God's saving activity. This will be one of our concerns in our third volume.

Did Jesus consider himself to be the fulfillment of God's promise to Israel, first in terms of the possession of a land in the Hebrew Scriptures and then in relation to God's salvation granted to Israel and the Christian church? Evidently, he did not. As will be discussed in detail later, Jesus introduced a startling new element into the religious tradition of his time — the Gentiles! In his life and ministry he made it abundantly clear that the Gentiles and those Jews who made themselves Gentiles — such as tax-collectors, prostitutes, sinners, swineherds, for example — persons excluded from the scheme of the promise of salvation, figured prominently in God's reign. God's salvation is now offered to all, especially to the Gentiles. The original promise, claimed to be closely bound to a particular land and to a certain nation or people, is suspended. Something new began with Jesus.

If Jesus superseded the idea of promise and fulfillment as pivotal to the understanding of God's saving activity in the world, traditional Christian theology reconstructed it and made it central in the life and mission of the church. The church is the new Israel. God's promise to the old Israel is now fulfilled in the church as the new Israel. Israel and church are believed to be interrelated closely and form a very special history within history. The Christian Church now plays the key role in this new history. It is this church as the new Israel that moves to the center stage of world history and overshadows other histories. The Christian church considers itself the principal actor in the drama of God's saving activity in the world.

In this way, the relationship between promise and fulfillment offers the clue to the complexity of history. It is the key to unlocking the mystery of God's dealing with the world of nations and peoples. The Christian church itself comes to appropriate the messianic nature it has attributed to Jesus. It even acts "messianically" toward Israel and specifically toward Jews. This explains why for some Christians "Christian mission to the Jews" is part and parcel of their calling to be followers of Jesus. An autobiographical account of a Jewish rabbi points out sharply how misdirected this kind of "Christian messianic calling" can be:

> I suspect that few Christians recognize the pervasiveness of Christian missionary efforts to the Jews. Here I do not speak about generalized programs of witness or mission to all the "unconverted," but of specific programs of conversion targeted to the Jews *as Jews* ...
>
> Here I must speak autobiographically. From my earliest childhood, I remember being importuned, evangelized, or witnessed to in one fashion or another by all kinds of people who professed to have my best interests at heart. I often felt as if the very fact of my Jewishness constituted me as a special challenge to these people ...
>
> I have myself been a rabbi for a little over a decade, my name being added to the various lists of rabbis. Scarcely a month has gone by since my ordination when I have not received one form or another of those conversionary solicitations. They have become, in my mind, one of the intrinsic features of the American rabbinate, though certainly not one of its more edifying aspects....[8]

The rabbi who shares this experience remembers that his father, also a rabbi, was frustrated and embarrassed by the Christian mission to the Jews. Jesus would surely have no part in it. The conversion he urged was not conversion from being Jews to something else. It was the conversion of the heart to the saving love of God. If he were here today, he would most certainly urge the same conversion of heart on the part of Christians. He perhaps would do the same with Buddhists and Hindus as well.

If some Christians and their churches have persisted with their "mission to the Jews," they have likewise behaved messianically toward people in the Third World. The missionary expansion of the churches in the West to Asia and Africa in the nineteenth century and the early twentieth century reflected strongly this messianic complex on the part of Christians. And of course the messianic complex that expresses itself in missionary calling is not without the political and military backing of the nations from which they come. Perhaps this is justified on the grounds that the Jesus they believe to be king and messiah comes as a victor decked with power, might, and authority. But this is a far cry from how that Jesus of Nazareth rejected pressures to be a Davidic messiah and went about the business of God's reign in the midst of mounting forces hostile to him.

If, then, Jesus did not consider himself to be the messiah in the religious-political meaning understood by his own people, how did he take himself to be? And equally important, if Jesus is not the king-messiah that most Christians believe him to be, how do we take him to be? Jesus' question "Who do you say that I am?" remains a challenge to us Christians today.

NOTES

1. Hugh Anderson, *The Gospel of Mark*, New Century Bible (London: Oliphants, 1976), p. 214.

2. Ernst Ludwig Erlich, *A Concise History of Israel*, trans. James Barr (New York: Harper & Row, 1965), p. 36.

3. John Bright, *A History of Israel*, 3d ed. (Philadelphia: Westminster Press, 1981), pp. 204–205.

4. Erlich, *A Concise History of Israel*, p. 38.

5. Bernhard W. Anderson, "The Messiah as Son of God: Peter's Confession in Traditio-historical Perspective," in *Christological Perspectives*, Robert K. Berkey and Sarah A. Edwards, eds., Essays in Honour of Harvey K. McArthur (New York: Pilgrim Press, 1982), pp. 167–168.

6. See *Challenge to the Church: The Kairos Document and Commentaries* (Geneva: Programme to Combat Racism/WCC, 1985), p. 24; see also *The Kairos Covenant: Standing with South African Christians*, Willis H. Logan, ed. (Oak Park, Ill.: Meyer-Stone Books, and New York: Friendship Press, 1988).

7. Bernhard Anderson, "The Messiah as Son of God," p. 169.

8. Daniel F. Pulish, "Contemporary Jewish Attitudes to Mission and Conversion," in Martin A. Cohen and Helga Croner, eds., *Christian Mission — Jewish Mission* (New York: Paulist Press, 1982), p. 161.

CHAPTER 8

Great Temptations

Messianism abounds in history. It persists in religion and in politics. And when religion and politics fuse in messianism, the result is political messianism. The temptation of political messianism is almost irresistible. Especially in a politically oppressive situation, it may be heard by certain charismatic leaders as a call from God. They convince themselves that a divine mandate has been thrust upon them to bring freedom, justice, and peace to their people. Divine mandate or not, this is how the history of a nation is made and unmade, created and undermined.

Political messianism must have been the prevailing political theology among Jews in Jesus' day. Can Jesus embrace it without betraying his cause? Can he accept it and not do disservice to God and people? Is it what his call really is? Is a messiah-king what he is called to be? But has he not aroused such expectation in people by healing the sick? Has he not raised much hope in religiously and politically oppressed women and men in his confrontation with the authorities, whether religious or political? How can he leave them in the lurch to fight for their survival and independence?

What Jesus has to deal with is the history of a people. What is at stake is the destiny of a nation. Questions such as these must have engaged Jesus' mind from time to time. He must have wrestled with them while carrying on his ministry of the reign of God. He must have been very much preoccupied with them as his conflict with his religious opponents intensified. It becomes more and more evident that this mandate of the people is the mandate of political messianism. But is this also a mandate from God? Is the voice calling him to lead his people in the struggle for liberation from Roman rule also the voice of God? Jesus must have had to face such questions during his ministry. The story of the temptation in the Gospels of Matthew and Luke gives us some idea of how Jesus wrestled with them. Obviously, that story does not only mark the beginning of his ministry. It is in fact the story of his life — a story that gives us some idea of how seriously Jesus had to deal with the political implications of his ministry. The temptation to which Jesus was exposed, it has been pointed out, "was repeated, in part, at Gethsemane [according to Luke], and, according to Mark, at Caesarea Philippi."[1]

One of the critical issues that must be raised here seems to be this: How is Christian political theology related to Christian political ethics? This is the question of the relation of theology and ethics with a particular focus on political commitments and conducts. In recent years Third World theologies have made it clear as never before that theology cannot be ethically neutral, that Christian doctrines cannot but be accountable to the ethical decisions and conduct of the Christian church and its believers. The reverse is also true. Ethics is not just a practical application of what the church has decided to be the truth. It compels the church and its theology to direct questions to that truth.

In recent years the Christian church has had to learn a sober lesson when its theology has been put to the acid test of ethics, not only in matters related to racism or sexism, but also concerning its alliance with oppressive political powers. The alliance takes different forms. In a nation in which Christianity is a dominant religion, such as in the Philippines in Asia and in most countries in Latin America, the Christian church used to ally itself with the ruling power and render theological justification for political authoritarianism. When Christianity is a minority religion, as in most countries in Asia, the church tended to acquiesce in the political status quo and kept the practice of faith entirely within the four walls of the church building. In either case the Christian faith was discredited as a religion of the powerful and the opiate of the powerless.

A dramatic change has now taken place for an increasing number of Christians, thanks to the social and political awakening of the oppressed and marginalized people in their own society — the change that has thrust the Christian church into the struggle for justice, freedom, and democracy in solidarity with people. Christian theology has no alternative but to reexamine critically its inherited presuppositions and drastically restate the contents of the Christian faith on the basis of the church's involvement in the painful process of transition from authoritarianism to democracy.

"Political theology" has thus come to preoccupy Christians and churches in the Third World. It is a theology of action and not of speculation, of involvement and not of detached reflection, of critical analysis of social and political realities and not projection of a utopian world based on a Christian apocalyptic vision. It even has to concern itself with programs, strategies, and goals. For this reason Christians, pastors and theologians among them, are found sitting at the table with opposition political leaders, in political rallies, in street demonstrations. The experiences gained through such involvement give them new vantage points to draw fresh insights from the Bible and to strive for fresh theological articulations.

As this doing of political theology continues, Christians and churches are bound to be faced with some of the fundamental issues with which they, in solidarity with the people, have confronted authoritarian social and political forces: issues such as the relation between means and ends in achieving political goals, the nature and function of the power expected to replace the old power, the place of moral ideals and values in the struggle for change. Christian political theology has raised such ethical issues against the ruling powers. Will not these same issues have to be also directed to the forces of change in which Christians are involved? Just as theology cannot set aside ethics, can Christian political theology ignore what may be called Christian political ethics without detriment to its integrity and credibility?

Jesus had to face what we call political ethics in his involvement in political theology. In actual fact, the more he became politically involved, the more he had to wrestle with the ethical issues his involvement generated. We already discussed why he rejected the pressures to be a Davidic Messiah, even though he must have fully shared the political aspirations of his people. It is even possible that he was also involved in certain political actions that might have attracted the attention of the Roman authorities. And he must have agonized over the political leadership role people expected him to play. How did he deal with all this? How did he wrestle with ethical issues related to his political involvement?

In the Gospels we do not find a wealth of material explicitly disclosing how Jesus reflected on such questions. There is, however, an invaluable source that gives us a clue, perhaps more than a clue, as to how Jesus had to come to terms with the ethical issues that posed a challenge to political messianism. I am referring to the story of the temptation in the Gospels of Matthew (4:1–11) and Luke (4:1–13). What can we still learn from it today? What is Jesus in the story telling us? And perhaps it can shed some further light on Jesus' identity.

Turn These Stones into Bread!

What a noble cause! Temptation is not temptation if it does not appear noble and worthy. A temptation must sound estimable enough to be able to move the heart of the tempted. And it must be relevant to the prevailing situation. All this is subtly implied in this command to turn stones into bread. And its imperial tone is only barely disguised in the note of urgency demanding that the situation requires immediate attention.

Looming large in Jesus' mind must be, for example, those emaciated children in the arms of their tired and helpless parents. The image must have tormented him. He could have jumped at the command. He could have even been impatient to have a try. Why not? An extraordinary situation requires extraordinary measures. Besides, this might have been a voice from God. But Jesus gave a disappointing answer: "Human beings cannot live by bread alone; they live on every word that God utters." This sounds like a typical answer given in the traditional church.

Has Jesus retreated into a theology of "abstract word" — word not accompanied by deed? Has Jesus given up praxis and gone back to the theory of God's word? Has he decided to develop a theology of the word of God instead of a theology of bread and rice? Has he now opted for spirituality and not for materiality? Has a fundamental theological change taken place in his theology — a change resulting from the power of God's word over bread for humanity? Has Jesus' mind changed from involvement to detachment, from engagement to disengagement, from earth to heaven, from human beings to God? Is it now God-talk without human-talk all over again?

Jesus' theological mind has not changed: his Abba-God is still Immanuel, God-with-people, and not God-without-people. His orientation has not shifted: his theology is still an earth-bound theology and not a heaven-bound theology. His theological course has not altered: for him the word is not the word of God until it makes the sick person well, comforts those in sorrow, empowers the weak, and defends the victims of injustice. His theology of the word of God is still theology of bread and theology of rice. In short, his theology is a theology of God's word precisely because it becomes audible in human words of pain and suffering.

Jesus must have known from his own experience that those in dire need of bread must be fed with bread first and not with the word of God; for those people bread is the word of God. He also knows that those women, men, and children suffering from malnutrition must be given rice first and not the word of God; for them the word of God has to take the form of rice and comes in a bowl filled with rice. James, the brother of Jesus and possibly the author of the letter that bears his name, had certainly understood Jesus when he exhorted his readers: "Suppose a brother or a sister is in rags with not enough food for the day, and one of you says, 'Good luck to you, keep yourselves warm, and have plenty to eat,' but does nothing to supply their bodily needs, what is the good of that? So with faith; if it does not lead to action, it is in itself a lifeless thing" (James 2:16–17).

The power of bread! Is there spirituality apart from it? The power of rice! Does the word of God mean anything without it? Word and bread. Word and rice. What God has put together let no one put asunder! Not even Jesus! That is why he taught his disciples to pray God to "give us today our daily bread" (Matt. 6:11; par. Luke 11:3). The word has become flesh. Even God cannot reverse this and make the word flesh-less; much less can Jesus do so. The word has become rice. Even God cannot undo this and turn the word rice-less; how could then Jesus? The word has become bread. What is done is done. It is futile even for God to regret this and to remove rice from the word. If it is futile for God to attempt this, how much more futile would it be for Jesus? It is not only futile, it would be for Jesus a denial of God-Immanuel. It would be a rejection of his calling. It would amount to giving up the theology of incarnation and slipping back into the theology of disincarnation. Jesus could then sit down and write an essay, even a book, on how his theological mind has changed. But then it would not be *theo*-logy any more, for it would have nothing to do with what God has done and continues to do in history, in human community, in the world of conflicts and tribulations. It would be an *apologia* of why the subject of his theology is not Abba-God from whom we human beings can ask for such mundane things as daily rice and bread. It would be an apology of why the center of his theology is not the God who feeds the birds of the air and who considers human beings worth more than the birds (Matt. 6:26; par. Luke 12:24).

Jesus has not left us such an *apologia*. His God was Abba-God, not only at the beginning of his career when he was an unknown village preacher, not only at the height of his career when he was popular among the masses and rose to national prominence in the eyes of Jewish leaders and Roman authorities. His God remained Abba-God right to the end when his career was cruelly brought to a close on the cross. It is there on the cross, as we have seen, that God disclosed God's own self to the dying Jesus to be totally, one hundred percent, with the suffering Jesus and with suffering humanity. God went even further. There when the demonic power lurking in the depths of humanity turned the world into a God-less world, when that power enabled godlessness to gain an upper hand, God was perceived not only being with Jesus, but God was that Jesus. There God was recognized not only as with the suffering human beings, but God was the suffering human beings. God as Immanuel is not just God-*with*-Jesus, but God *is Jesus*. God as Immanuel is not only God-*with*-suffering-human-persons, but God *is* suffering human persons. This is the decisive meaning of the incarnation. It is there that *theo*-logy begins and ends, since it is there that God begins and ends. Theology has to reckon with God fully present with humanity and to reflect deeply on the theological consequences that presence entails.

Then why did Jesus refuse to turn stones into bread? And why did he say we human beings live not by bread alone but by the word of God? Was he trying to weigh which is heavier — the word of God or bread? Was he now making a value judgment as to which is more important —

the word of God or rice? Faced with the enormous challenge of world
hunger, yes, world hunger even in the days of Jesus, hunger caused not
by ill harvests but by mismanagement and exploitation of those in power,
was Jesus now trying to readjust his theological stance and focus on the
word of God that contains no bread or rice? Was he now refocusing his
emphasis from social transformation to spiritual transformation, recasting
his ministry solely in terms of reforming individual persons? Was he intimating that his feeding of as many as four or five thousand famished
men, women, and children (Mark 6:32–34 and 8:1–10) is a thing of the
past and that he is now launching an evangelistic campaign to feed people
with spiritual food?

There is nothing in what Jesus said and did during his life and ministry
that would indicate such a turn-about in his faith and theology. The problem for Jesus, I suspect, is not with bread but with stones. The question
for him does not lie with rice but with turning stones into rice. This must
be the heart of his rejection of the temptation. To grasp this is essential to
understanding the real meaning behind that rejection.

There is something so obvious in this that it should not have been
missed by us. Stones are stones and not bread. For that matter, bread
and rice are bread and rice and not stones. To turn stones into bread? To
change them into rice? Is this not magic?[2] This is the real secret behind
the challenge posed by the temptation. The challenge is *not* to turn stones
into bread or rice, but to turn Jesus into a magician! And there is a world
of difference between turning stones into rice or bread and turning Jesus
into a magician. This is a serious challenge to who Jesus must be. It is to
make a mockery of what he considers to be the essential part of his mission: to restore integrity to religion and to reassert the credibility of faith
in his Abba-God.

Are we Christians not also subject to such a challenge from time to
time? We also speak of the poor, the hungry, the malnourished. But how
we wish, in moments of desperation, we could turn stones into bread and
rice to save them from starvation and death! There must be a short cut to
solving the problem of world hunger. There must be a less painful way
of solving the problem. Our "Christian" heart may be in the right place,
but we want to believe that there should be a magical way for hunger and
starvation to disappear overnight. We cannot wait endlessly for time to
mature, for programs to take shape, for logistics to be in place.

This is not a groundless criticism of what Christians sometimes do
to alleviate what they consider to be the malaise of the world. Think of
some well-meaning Christian groups who tried to smuggle Bibles into the
Communist countries they deem to be atheistic. This often turns out to
be a risky operation. It was not as easy as waving a magic wand. But
the basic attitude was the same: there must be a quicker way for Chris-

tians to deal with the forces that militate against Christian conscience and
Christian principles. But does our Christian conscience represent God's
conscience? Are our Christian principles God's principles? Besides, what
we Christians do in obedience to our conscience and principles may prove
to be counter-productive and even offensive to the Christians and other
people we try to help. Much worse, we impose our conscience and principles on them in such a way that we become a burden to them and an
obstacle (*skandalon*) to what they seek to do in their own way to serve
God in very different cultural and political situations. It is not, then, entirely unexpected to hear, for example, Christian leaders in China saying
to those Christian groups engaged in smuggling Bibles into their country:
Please do not smuggle Bibles to us. We need Bibles, but not smuggled
Bibles. Besides, we are doing our best to print Bibles ourselves and make
them available to our people.

The challenge posed by the temptation, however, is not always well-
meaning, its intention laudable, nor its aim commendable. It proves, in
fact, to be very sinister in both intent and aim. It is very demonic, too.
The real and dreadful intention hidden in this challenge is not to change
one physical substance into another physical substance. What is called
for is not even an "alchemical" operation. We know something of what
alchemy is about and its history. Alchemy, "a blend of science, magic,
and religion . . . practiced in China and India before the birth of Christ,
developed into a major system in Egypt during the next three hundred
years, and popular from the time of early Christianity until about 1700
[in Europe], tried to change less costly metals into silver and gold and to
find the *elixir of life*, a substance that would cure disease and lengthen
life." It might be considered a kind of science fiction in practice in
those old days. As we all know, science fiction of yesterday may become scientific and technological reality of today and tomorrow. And
this is what alchemy proved to be despite many abuses and misuses
associated with it. Its "work in preparing and studying chemical sub-
stances helped the development of the science of chemistry."[3] Alchemy
might have been a pseudo-science; still it was a precursor of modern science. It involved painstaking experiments day and night. It went through
trial and error for months and years. It was not an instant happening
like magic.

Turning stones into bread would be something totally different. It
would be pure magic. What is expected is an instant "transubstantiation,"
a change of the substance or essence of things, a transformation of a set
of elements that constitute stone into another set of elements that make
up bread or rice, in a twinkle of an eye, in a flash of a second, before the
audience in public and not in a private laboratory hidden from the public
eye. What is presented would be an illusion, for if magic is not an illusion,

what is it? It is an optical illusion. Once the trick is exposed, it becomes evident that no "transubstantiation" has taken place and no stones have turned into bread. Magic is also a mental illusion. It creates a mental state that takes unreality for reality. But when that mental illusion is broken, the cruel fact appears: rice is not rice but stone. Performed as a stage show in which both the performer and the audience know it is not real, magic is a harmless pastime. But displayed as a serious demonstration of religious power and political leadership, magic is an inexcusable hoax involving deception and cunning. It is a betrayal of the trust of people and enforced prostitution of their conscience. Sadly, history is not short of such magicians who practice their art of deception and betrayal, bringing infinite sufferings and miseries to people.

If the temptation meant some of the things mentioned, how could Jesus have responded to it in ways other than what he did? Should he agree to perform the magic of turning stones into bread or rice, he would become a magician. He would be a magician-messiah, deceiving the masses with illusion and false promises. He would be a magician-savior deluding people with a fantastic vision of a future free from hunger. He would be a magician-teacher misleading women, men, and children about the suffering of this world as unreal. His would be a theology of no pain and no tears, a theology of all comforts and ecstasy. It would be no different from the theology of a Sunday preacher with a fresh rose on his chest in a shining multi-million dollar cathedral greeting his congregation and beaming: "Good morning. How good and marvelous God is to us!" What a sad spectacle! The Christianity of affluent churches has made a magician of Jesus. For the Christians who have grown used to riches, Jesus is a magician who could turn stones into bread or rice. For them the world of people with stones but no bread or rice is not real.

This kind of magic Christianity and magic theology may still work in the First World, but it does not work in the Third World. For the majority of people there the hardship of life is so real, shortage of food so severe, that magic has no power even to create an illusion of peace and prosperity. Here is a little poem from India that illustrates what I mean.

> Sitting near the dust bin from morning
> not a scrap have I found
> not even a slice of bread —
> from that big white window.
> My little sister is hungry.
> How can I stop her cries?
> Will mother get her pay today
> I wonder —
>   I'm so hungry.[4]

Magic theology has no place in such a situation. A magic preacher is of
no use to a girl like this waiting for her mother to come home with her
pay while trying in vain to stop her hungry little sister from crying. Magic
faith will not work for her.

Who would not wonder whether stones could be turned into rice for
this family in dire need for some nourishment? But the long history of
poverty and hunger in that country tells us that no magical formula would
cure that disease. Religion in a society such as this had no better thing to
do than to offer spiritual compensation for the people stricken with material deprivation. This is religion serving as opium of the people. Hinduism
is such a religion to the masses of people in India. In the case of Christianity, Marx had to tell this to the Christian church. It was a bitter pill
for the church to swallow. In actual fact, the church did not have to wait
until the nineteenth century to be told this by Karl Marx. Well before him,
nineteen hundred years before him, to be exact, Jesus knew there was no
such thing as magic faith or magic theology. The reason is simple: his
God was not a magic God. His God did not give him the power to turn
stones into bread or rice.

But there is one thing God has given him: the word of God that is to be
heard in the suffering of people, the word of God that strives with hungry
men, women, and children in search of daily rice and bread, the word of
God that is the flesh of human beings tortured and mutilated and done to
death. This must have been what Jesus meant when he said: "Human beings cannot live by bread alone; they live on every word that God utters."
Jesus must have said the word "live" with force. The word of God on
which people can *live* must not be a hollow word. It must be the word that
does not spiritualize their daily bread. It must be the word that does not
despise their daily rice as materialistic. And it must be the word that does
not theologize the flesh of Jesus out of its historical reality and divinize
his humanity.

That word of God is human history. It is humanity. It is the life of
human beings. Jesus must have believed that he himself is that word of
God. He is human history. He is humanity. He is the life of human beings.
He is, in short, people and people are him. This must be his theology of
the incarnation, a theology that does not seek an instant success. He has to
refuse to turn stones into bread. No, he *cannot* turn stones into bread. But
he may be able to turn the heart of stone into the heart of love. He may be
able to awaken in those who hold religious and political power the desire
to change their ways and work to redress oppression and injustice. This
must be what he decided to do. This, as it turned out, is not an easy way.
No political glamor and no religious pomp, but opposition, slander, and
danger will follow him every step of the way. Jesus had to face all this.
He did face all this. He did not allow himself to be seduced by economic

messianism and to exchange the miracle of the incarnation for an economic miracle — the miracle that enlarged the distance between the rich and the poor, whetted greed and opportunism, and created a culture that debases human values in the Third World today.

Throw Yourself Down from the Parapet of the Temple!

The scene has changed. It is no longer the desert covered with sand and stones. It is the Holy City decked with glories of the past. The scenery has shifted. It is not the wilderness where solitude invades one's soul with fears and temptations. It is Jerusalem filled with the sound of life and noise from the marketplace. The stage has moved. It has moved from the wasteland that menaces one's life with death and threatens one's mind with nothingness. It is now the city of David, the center of the national and spiritual life of a people under Roman occupation.

This is the city where Jesus is to be led eventually. Jesus must have shared the aspiration of his fellow Jews who considered the journey to Jerusalem the height of their religious life. For the Jews in the Diaspora and the Jews in Palestine the city is no mere tourist attraction. It is the *holy* city, a city set apart from all other cities. That city is their history — their personal history and the history of their nation.

This applies to non-believing Jews as well as to believing Jews. In his book *One Generation After* Elie Wiesel, the well-known writer and survivor of Auschwitz, recounts how Colonel Mordecai Gur (Motta Gur) led his troops to liberate Jerusalem in the Six-Day War in 1967:

> Shells ripping through the waning night. Men blown to bits. The wounded among them moaning and crawling ahead on their knees. The paratroopers were running from street to street, from turret to turret, propelled by an irresistible, unrelenting force, every one of them obscurely aware of having lived for this moment, for this race. And suddenly, over the deafening clangor, Motta Gur was shouting his report to Headquarters. "The Har Habayit is ours! Do you hear me? The Temple Mount is in our hands...." And everywhere, on every front, in every home, officers and soldiers, children and old people wept and embraced. And in those tears, those explosions of feeling, there was an element of the unreal which made the event unique, and changed all those who lived through it.

This was not just a military operation. It was also a spiritual experience. Jerusalem had the magic to turn a military struggle into an experience with spiritual dimensions.

Then a conversation took place between Motta Gur and the narrator. Motta Gur turned out to be *not* religious.

"You make it sound too poetic," says Motta Gur. "I don't buy that."

"In other words, for you, this was just another episode, another battle among many?"

"I wouldn't go that far.... After all, it was Jerusalem, wasn't it? But ... why are you laughing?"

"And in what way was Jerusalem different from any other military objective?"

"Jerusalem was not just a military objective. It was something else. Jerusalem is ... Jerusalem."

"And what makes Jerusalem ... Jerusalem?"

"Its history, of course. It's Jewish, isn't it? It touches me. It concerns me."

"Jericho too has a history linked to ours. And so does Hebron. And Gaza. And Bethlehem."

"Your comparisons are boring. Jerusalem defies comparison."[5]

Jerusalem is more than a city. It defies comparison, even comparison with other cities such as Jericho and Hebron, cities deeply engraved in the memories of the nation and on the hearts of the people.

What is Jerusalem? Jerusalem is power — power that sustains the nation of Israel through thick and thin. Jerusalem is life — life that vibrates in their veins and in the veins of their tradition. And Jerusalem is hope — hope that enables them and their nation to rise again and again from the ashes of destruction. All this power, all this life, and all this hope come to a most impassioned expression in the words of a poet exiled in Babylon:

> If I forget you, O Jerusalem,
>   let my right hand wither away;
> let my tongue cling to the roof of my mouth
>   if I do not remember you,
> if I do not set Jerusalem
>   above my highest joy. (Ps. 137:5–6)

This is an oath — the kind of oath exchanged between husband and wife. The relation between Jews and Jerusalem is almost a kind of marital relationship. Jews are married to Jerusalem and vow not to forget it.

These are noble words Jesus must have been able to share. The passion that takes form in these verses must be his, too. The spirit that inspired the exiled poet with love and longing for Jerusalem must be the same spirit that compels him to weep over the same city in deep anguish, saying: "O Jerusalem, Jerusalem, the city that murders the prophets and stones the messengers sent to her! How often have I longed to gather your children, as a hen gathers her brood under her wings; but you would not let me" (Matt. 23:37; par. Luke 13:34). Yes, Jerusalem is not without its faults.

Its sins are many. Jesus himself is to die in that city. In spite of this, and perhaps because of this, Jesus wants to hold it in his arms, cuddle it on his breast, embrace it with all his love.

This is Jerusalem. No matter what it does to you, you cannot hate it; you can only love it. Despite its rejection of you, you cannot reject it. You still would want to hold it close to your heart even if it were to deal you a death blow. This is Jerusalem. What mysterious power! Even though you were to die at its hand, you would still long for salvation to come out of its very midst and give you a new life. What a faith Jerusalem has been able to foster in you! Because of faith such as this, for Jews Jerusalem has never ceased to be the center of God's saving activity among the nations. An unknown prophet-poet during the Babylonian captivity put it most marvelously in these words:

> Arise, Jerusalem,
> rise clothed in light; your light has come
> and the glory of the Lord
> shines over you.
> For, though darkness covers the earth
> and the dark night the nations,
> the Lord shall shine upon you
> and over you shall the Lord's glory appear;
> and the nations shall march towards your light
> and their kings to your sunrise. (Isa. 60:1–3)

What a vision of God's salvation with Jerusalem at its very center! If God will not fail Jerusalem, Jerusalem will not fail God either.

With this faith, this hope, and this power, miracles can happen in Jerusalem. Jesus, believing Jews, even unbelieving Jews such as Colonel Mordecai Gur, cannot but believe in the miracle-power of Jerusalem. This is what Elie Wiesel testifies:

> I saw Israel at War [the Six-Day War]. I can therefore testify in its behalf. In the Old City of Jerusalem, barely reconquered, I saw hardened paratroopers pray and weep for the first time in their lives; I saw them, in the thick of battle, gripped by an ancient collective fervor, kiss the stones of the Wall and commune in silence as elusive as it was pure; I saw them, as in a dream, jump two thousand years into the past, renewing their bond with legend, memory and the mysterious tradition of Israel. . . . Their experience was of a mystical nature. Even the non-believers felt transcended by their own acts and the tales they told about them afterwards. The words on their lips sounded fiery and distant. It is as if they had all started to believe in miracles, or just — believe.[6]

This mystical power of Jerusalem! Even nonbelievers start believing in miracles. This is Jerusalem. Colonel Gur, that non-religious Jew, was right. Jerusalem defies comparison. There is no other city like Jerusalem on earth.

Why, then, did Jesus refuse to throw himself down from the parapet of the Temple of Jerusalem? Is not that miracle-power of Jerusalem concentrated in the Temple? Does it not stand for the mystical power of faith on behalf of the people? Is it not the bastion of hope for the liberation of the nation? Surely God "will put God's angels in charge of you, and they will support you in their arms, for fear you should strike your foot against a stone" (Matt. 4:6; par. Luke 4:11). A divine miracle! And Jesus would be an instant Messiah. Even Roman rulers and their soldiers would be terrified. Jerusalem would be liberated from their hands with no cost of Jewish lives.

But this is not the kind of miracle that deeply gripped Colonel Gur and his fellow soldiers. They were not spectators of a miracle that liberated Jerusalem. They were part of that miracle. That miracle was not performed by a miracle-worker who had descended on beleaguered Jerusalem from nowhere. Colonel Gur and his soldiers were co-makers of that miracle. Blood was shed to make that miracle happen — their own blood. Bodies were blown to bits for that miracle to become a reality — their own bodies. Even tears of children and old people had to be poured out in abundance to make that miracle happen. This was true in that Six-Day War in 1967. It had been true for centuries before that war in the history of that nation. It must be also true in the time of Jesus. To jump down from the parapet of the Temple is to betray that history of miracles. To throw himself down from the pinnacle is to defile the tears of millions and millions of people who enabled that history to happen, to desecrate the memories of those women, men, and children whose blood was shed and whose bodies were broken to make that miracle possible. And above all, it is to put the Lord to the test — the Lord who has not instituted an instant miracle in the entire creation and therefore is *incapable* of it.

Jesus cannot be a miracle-messiah without betraying people. A miracle-messiah suffers no pain, but people have to deal with pain that accompanies them throughout their lives. A miracle-messiah does not have to toil and labor, but for the people toil and labor is their lot. A miracle-messiah pays no such costly price as blood and life, but people have to shed their blood and lose their lives to gain their freedom and to achieve their independence. A miracle-messiah would, then, be a messiah without people to save just as a general with no troops to lead. But is a messiah still messiah without people to help and save? He would be a self-appointed messiah who does not command their faith and trust. In refusing to throw himself down from the parapet of the Temple, Jesus is also declaring: I am no miracle-messiah!

If "economic miracles" have happened in some Asian nations, political miracles have not taken place. One military regime replaces another military regime, repeating the oppression of the people. At last some form of democracy has come, for example, to Korea, Taiwan, and the Philippines. Even China has to reckon with people's yearning and passion for an open society in which freedom of speech is guaranteed and political rights of people are respected. But it has been a long process, and a very costly one too. And the Christian churches have learned that "thy kingdom come and thy will be done" in the Lord's prayer does not mean a miraculous intervention of God but the assurance of God's presence in the painful and costly struggle for social and political changes. They have also learned that genuine long-lasting changes are not brought about by one or two so-called charismatic leaders, but by those anonymous men, women, and children who earn their daily living by the sweat of their brow and at the call of time dare to stand up and defy the oppressive powers. This must be a humbling thought especially for Christians who desire to play a "messianic" role to bring the justice and peace of God to their society.

And Jesus cannot be a miracle-messiah without betraying God. He would be a messiah without God on his side. What kind of messiah would he be, then? He would not be a Christ, an anointed of God. He would be a messiah anointed by the devil. He would be subservient to the satanic power that has usurped God's anointing power. He would be a usurper-messiah. A usurper-messiah must be a devil in disguise. He would be a scourge of people and blasphemer of God. History is not short of such usurper-messiahs.

Jesus must have shuddered at the thought of it. He must have realized that the most sacred spot on which he stands can turn into the most profane spot in God's creation. Before too late he must have come to know that the most holy place can become a most dangerous place. It could hypnotize some people to believe that they are endowed with special power to change the world as easily as turning over the palm of one's hand. It could delude them into thinking that they have the mandate of heaven to rule, the mandate used, almost without exception in human history, to justify the abuse of power. It does not seem to make the slightest difference whether that mandate comes from Buddhism, Hinduism, Confucianism, or Christianity.

In response to that temptation to be a miracle-messiah, Jesus must have shouted at the top of his voice: "You are not to put the Lord your God to the test!" (Matt. 4:7; par. Luke 4:12). His voice must have echoed loudly in that holy city of Jerusalem, so loudly that it must have awakened his supporters and opponents alike from their messianic dream of a Davidic kingdom. Jesus is no miracle-messiah who would bring about socio-political change entirely through his own feats, without people and without God. The reign of God (*basileia tou theou*), the heart of his message and ministry, is literally the reign *of God*. And because it is the reign of God, it is the reign of people. To bring about this reign of God and people is a miracle. It is a miracle of miracles. But it is a miracle of a totally different sort from that of throwing oneself down from the parapet of the Temple in Jerusalem. It is a miracle that can be achieved only through the toil and labor of people and through God toiling and laboring with people. A miracle-messiah would be anti-God's reign. He would be a rejection of Immanuel — God-with-people. It would be anti-people's mandate too. Jesus had to reject the temptation to be a miracle-messiah.

All These Kingdoms Will Be Yours, If...

Besides the seduction to become a miracle-messiah, there is a temptation to become an all-powerful king. "All the kingdoms of the world in their glory I will give you, if..." Jesus would have been able to claim kings and emperors as his illustrious predecessors.

There was Alexander the Great of Greece in the fourth century B.C.E. He "was a creative mind, but self-absorbed, obsessed with his pursuit of glory."[7] For ten years he pursued that glory relentlessly, first in Greece and then in Western Asia.

> Legend says that after crossing to Asia Minor he cut the Gordian knot. He then defeated the Persians at the battle of Issus. This was followed by a campaign which swept south through Syria, destroying Tyre on the way, and eventually to Egypt, where Alexander founded the city still bearing his name.... He pushed into the desert, interrogated the oracle at Siwah and then went back into Persia to inflict a second and decisive defeat on Darius III in 331 B.C. Persepolis was sacked and burnt and Alexander proclaimed successor to the Persian throne.... On went Alexander, pursuing the Iranians of the north-east into Afghanistan (where Kandahar, like many cities elsewhere, commemorate his name) and penetrating as far as the Punjab and a hundred miles or so beyond the Indus.... Alexander returned to Babylon. There he died in 323 B.C., thirty-two years old, just ten years after he had left Macedon.[8]

What a glorious career! And in such a short time and at such a young age! Coincidentally, that was about the same age that Jesus was most active and came to his untimely death.

Alexander's kingdom in its glory. It is still remembered today, but only in history books and in scattered ruins. The glory of the kingdoms offered to Jesus could be as great, if not greater. The pursuit of personal glory and national grandeur could have obsessed Jesus, too, as it did Alexander the Great before him. In more recent times it did obsess Mao Zedong, who led the Chinese Communist revolution against the Nationalist regime and established the People's Republic of China in 1949. His poem "Snow," written probably in the winter of 1944–45, extols the beauty and glory of nature that is China:

> The northern scene:
> A thousand leagues locked in ice,
> A myriad leagues of fluttering snow.
> On either side of the Great Wall
> Only one vastness to be seen.
> Up and down this broad river
> Torrents flatten and stiffen.
> The mountains are dancing silver serpents
> And hills, like waxen elephants, plod on the plain,
> Challenging heaven with their heights.
> A sunny day is needed
> For seeing them, with added elegance
> In red and white.

China is great. China is glorious. But is not China's greatness Mao's greatness? Is not China's glory Mao's glory? Or perhaps, is Mao's greatness and glory going to be China's greatness and glory as he envisions the victory of his revolution? A visionary and a shrewd and relentless politician combined in one, Mao could have been seeing with his mind's eye his own glory and China's glory merge into each other while the struggle for supremacy over China raged on.

Mao's vision, then, turns from the beauty of nature to the mystery of history that has given birth to kings and emperors to rule China. His poem continues:

> Such is the beauty of these mountains and rivers
> That has been admired by unnumbered heroes —
> The great emperors of Ch'in and Han
> Lacking literary brilliance,
> Those of T'ang and Sung
> Having but few romantic inclinations,
> And the prodigious Genghis Khan
> Knowing only how to bend his bow
>   and shoot at vultures.

All are past and gone!
For men of vision
We must seek among the present generation.[9]

These were all heroes. China can be proud of them. They were great and glorious. But they all are past and gone! The present generation needs a new hero, a greater hero, a more glorious hero, a hero with literary brilliance, plenty of romantic inclinations, and prodigious power and energy.

Who would that hero be? Mao himself? This is not entirely a capricious thought. For the poem "drips with Mao's sense of personal destiny. The heroes of the past are all gone. They do not count as the sun rises on a new arena of battle. Is Mao alone the trustee of China's beauty [and glory]?"[10] The answer may be yes. During the last years of his life, Mao, through the Great Proletarian Cultural Revolution, mustered his waning life force and his diminishing political power to wage a perpetual revolution, to make himself immortal in the life and history of the Chinese nation.

His poem "Snow" is, then, not just a nature poem. It "is a very nationalistic poem. It was China's beauty [and glory] that inspired in Mao the extraordinary belief in the present moment as more glorious than any in four thousand years of history."[11] The glory of the kingdom called China fascinated Mao. That glory, instead of liberating him for the freedom and democracy of the long-suffering people of China, imprisoned him in a personality cult that was to bring about deep wounds and tragic deaths to tens and hundreds of thousands of men and women and to set China back from the movement of history for decades. Mao's is a tragic case of power and glory turned inward to serve a personal ambition and to devour the children given birth by a revolution that cost millions and millions of lives.

Still, the lure of the glory of the earthly kingdom is irresistible. As long as human history lasts, there will be "heroes" who fall on their knees to be slaves of that lure in exchange for earthly power and glory. It is this power and glory that is offered to Jesus now. "All these I will give you." Jesus was told. What an offer! His nation in travail under colonial rule. His people languishing under a foreign power. His was a glorious nation in the past. His was a great people in the days gone by. There was King David who founded the unified kingdom of Israel to dominate the Near Eastern world of his day. And there was King Solomon, his son and successor, who brought about the economic miracle of unprecedented prosperity to the nation, although with great human cost. They are all past and gone. For persons of vision we now must seek among the present generation! Jesus might be that "hero" in the present generation to bring back greatness and glory to the nation. "All these kingdoms will be yours," he was told.

But the offer does not end there. It goes on to lay down conditions. "All these kingdoms in their glory I will give you." This is only the first part of the offer. Then comes the other half: "If you will only fall down and do me homage." What a condition! What an if! It is an IF with capital letters. It is an if with enormous weight. And that if is fraught with risks. That if links the first part of the offer with the second. It makes the first half of the offer predicated on the second. Together, only together, they make up the offer. But why is the "if" clause said in the second part and not in the first part of the offer? It could have been said to Jesus: "If you only fall down and do me homage, all these kingdoms in their glory I will give you." There must be a reason for the order in which the offer is made.

When the sovereign power is the object, when the glory of the kingdom is the goal, one does not care how one achieves that object and reaches that goal. One even can be in league with Satan to attain that power and glory. There should be no thought wasted on ethical concerns. So-called political ethics is not the ethics of a victor but of a loser. Politics should be a-moral, if not im-moral. It should be conducted from the position of strength and not of weakness. If this is what politics is, why should one bother with that if-clause that says, "if you only fall down and do me homage"? But to do homage to the devil is not the same as doing homage to God. It cannot be regarded merely as a political expediency, only as a means to attain an end. Before you know it, you find yourself enslaved by the power given to you and blinded by the glory bestowed on you. You lose the ability to act according to your conscience. You forfeit the freedom for the truth. And you begin to worship the devil instead of God.

That is when the glory of the king becomes a curse for the people. It is a glory that judges and condemns. It is a glory that divides and rules. As to the power of the king, it is used to intimidate people, incarcerate the opponents, and carry out political murders. Is this not the history of the kingdoms and empires of almost all countries in Asia and in other parts of the world? We do not know how the devil got into empire-building and nation-building. All we know is that political power and glory contain in themselves the demonic elements that all too easily get out of control. This is not only true of an autocratic nation. It can also be true even of a nation with the democratic system of checks and balances.

Jesus must have heard the offer of all the kingdoms of the world in their glory to the end with patience. He must have waited until the "if" part was finished. He must have then realized that the if-clause was a powerful challenge to his political ethics as well as to his political theology. Accepting that challenge, he would have to pay homage to the devil instead of God. He would be compromising truth and justice. He could be another example of a revolutionary turned despot, a visionary turned dictator. Jesus could not have failed to perceive the sinister nature of the temptation.

Begone, Satan!

How could Jesus, then, fall down and worship the devil in order to gain all the kingdoms of the world in their glory? His response has to be a resolute No. Politics is an art of compromise. If this is true today in the geopolitical world of ours, it must have also been true in the no less complex world of Jesus' time. Jesus could have struck a compromise with various religious and political factions within his own community. He could have played a shrewd politician, outwardly paying homage to the Roman power but in reality working toward the political goal of his nation. Why not? The end justifies the means. One who aspires to national leadership must be a master power-player. One who pursues a political career should learn to be a tactician among varied interest groups. Of course one has to be ruthless too. Politics is a matter of give and take. More accurately, it is more a matter of taking than giving. To give is just the means. To take is the end. To be engaged in politics one has to be prepared to be exposed to the demonic in human nature and to face the dark abyss in human community. That demonic, that dark abyss — did it not begin to play havoc, for instance, with French politics when King Louis XIV started to say, "L'Etat c'est moi" (I am the State)?

The marriage between state and religion invariably gives birth to a state religion that enhances the power of the state and diminishes the integrity of religion. Here again history is an eloquent witness. Take, for instance, the Ch'ing dynasty of China (1644–1912). Its laws stipulated:

> Those who make private appeal to Heaven and worship the Seven Mansions (of Ursa Major), burning incense at night, lighting the Heavenly Lamp and the Seven-Star Lamp, shall be punished with eighty strokes of the stick. The head of the family shall be held responsible for violation of this law by female members of the family. Buddhist monks and Taoist priests setting up religious services with written appeals to Heaven shall be administered the same punishment, to be followed by reversion to secular status.[12]

This is political dictatorship combined with dictatorship over religious beliefs and practices. It controls the whole human person — body, soul, spirit, mind, all.

This is a clear example of how easily, comfortably, and logically, politics and religion can pass into each other, working hand in glove (*lan pei wei chien*, in Chinese idiom) to invade people's innermost lives and to keep a powerful control of society. As late as "in 1853 imperial armed guards were posted around the altar grounds [the Altar of Heaven] at the time of the grand sacrifice to keep the curious mob from obtaining a glimpse of the unfathomable mystery of the worship of the mightiest of gods, Heaven, by the mightiest of human beings, the monarch."[13] Politics takes on a religious aura. Victims of this marriage between politics and religion are people, common men and women, who are deprived even of their rights to worship God not only in public but also in private. Political religion such as this, or religious politics such as this, is both against God and against people.

But a strange thing happens. The more politics-religion tries to drive people away from God, the more people experience the closeness of God. The more religion-politics sets about distancing God from people, the closer God is drawn to people. There is no power on earth, not even political power and religious power combined, not even that of "the mightiest of human beings, the monarch," can separate God from people and drive people away from God. Why is this so? The reason basically must be this: God is not God without people, and people are not people without God. God is God-with-people and people are people-with-God. The word "God" contains the word "people," and the word "people" implies the word "God." God is in the "definition" of people and people are in the "definition" of God. Human beings cannot be "defined" and described apart from God on the one hand, and on the other God cannot be "defined" and described with no relation to human beings. In the language of ancient Hebrew writers, human beings are created "in the image of God" (Gen. 1:28). This must be also what John the Evangelist meant when he said, "the Word became flesh" (John 1:14). Could this be what Jesus implied too when he said to the Pharisees who asked him when God's reign would come: "The reign of God is within you" (Luke 17:21)?

This is what God is and this is what human beings are. Is there any other way to explain the origin of human religious consciousness? Is this why human beings are, and must be, *homo religiosus*? Is this not the reason why in Christian theology if we want to take God seriously, we must also take human beings seriously, and if we want to take human beings seriously, we must also take God seriously? Is it then not true to say that from the perspective of Christian theology the theology of the incarnation is where theology of religions should be developed, where the roots of *homo religiosus* can be explored?

God is "fated" to be with humanity and humanity is also "fated" to be with God. To deny God to people is to denude people. Whether this is done by political powers in a ruthless manner — confiscating Bibles, infringing upon freedom of worship, infiltrating churches with secret agents — or it is carried out by religious authorities in subtle ways — erecting the holy of holies to keep people away from God, stifling the religious conscience of believers in the name of orthodoxy, taking advantage of people's fear of divine judgment — it amounts to the same thing. Human beings deprived of God become dehumanized. You can then treat them as subhumans or even nonhumans. You can arrest them, imprison them, and execute them. You can also persecute them, burn them at the stake, and condemn them to eternal punishment in hell.

Further, to deny people to God is to denude God. God is naked without people. An imposing cathedral may be built to house God, but it will not cover God's nakedness. A gorgeous temple may be erected and dedicated to God, but God still feels lonely without the company of human beings. To deny people to God is also to "denature" God. Since people are in the "definition" of God, to deprive God of people is to make God other than God. No liturgy, however, elaborate, can make that God-other-than-God God. A religion that makes people inaccessible to God becomes a crisis of God. And political power that severs people from God is a catastrophe to God.

Although this is a long detour from our discussion of Jesus' political ethics, it is closely related to it. At least some of what has been discussed above must have deeply concerned Jesus as he faced the challenge to become "professionally" involved in political activities and to take up the role of a Davidic messiah. Finally, he had to reject the inducement to be a king-messiah. His rejection was total and final. It was even defiant. "Begone, Satan!" (Matt. 4:10), he shouted. The shout was so loud and determined that Satan must have been shocked into speechlessness. It must have been such a powerful shout that Satan must have trembled. Peter too, Jesus' own disciple, heard that shout. He too must have been shocked and trembled. As we saw earlier, Jesus had just told Peter and the other disciples, following Peter's confession, that what was waiting for him was not the glory of the Davidic throne but suffering and death. Peter disagreed wildly and proceeded vigorously to dissuade Jesus from it. But Jesus directed at him that same shout with which he rejected Satan's temptation: "Away with you, Satan!" (Mark 8:33; par. Luke 16:23). Peter might have been taken aback, but he was not mortified, at least not until Jesus' death. He might have trembled, but he did not grasp its meaning, at least not until his experience of the risen Christ. He and his fellow disciples deserted their master to face death on the cross, alone.

What have we learned from all this? We can put it this way: Jesus' political theology does not have room for Satan, and his political ethic does not contain homage to political powers. For power is not God, although

God is power — power of love, not power of violence, power of justice, not power of injustice. His political ethic does not teach political cunning. It teaches truth. Truth is not God, although God is truth — the truth that God loves the world, that God's utmost concern is the well-being of people, that God loves them so much that God suffers with them. Politics with God and people, Jesus must have decided, cannot be done from the throne of kings and emperors and under the shadow of the power and glory of the kingdoms of this world. There must be a different way of doing politics with God and people. And Jesus chose that different way.

Jesus' involvement in political affairs of his people is to make politics as the art of the impossible into politics as the art of the possible. "Love your enemies" is a supreme impossibility in politics, not only in authoritarian politics but also in democratic politics. Jesus believes that it could be a supreme possibility. But how? Through the redemptive power of suffering and death! That power alone could mobilize the oppressed people to move the hearts of their enemies. And if the hearts of their enemies are not moved, which is often the case, then the systems and structures built to carry out oppression and exploitation must collapse in the end. Politics for Jesus and for those who follow him must be a matter of faith — faith in the redemptive power of the cross, the cross Jesus had to bear and the cross oppressed people have to carry.

NOTES

1. G. W. H. Lampe, "Luke" in *Peake's Commentary on the Bible*, Matthew Black and H. H. Rowley, eds. (London: Thomas Nelson, 1962), p. 827b.

2. See Krister Stendahl, "Matthew" in *Peake's Commentary on the Bible*, p. 774a.

3. For the quotations on alchemy in this paragraph see *World Book Encyclopedia* (Chicago: World Book, Inc., 1983).

4. The poem is by S. Pragsam of Bangalore, India. It is to be found in *Stree*, an occasional Newsletter of the All India Council of Christian Women (Madras, National Council of Churches in India), no. 9, September 1985, p. 10.

5. Elie Wiesel, *One Generation After* (New York: Schoken Books, 1982), pp. 139–140.

6. Ibid., p. 136.

7. J. M. Roberts, *The Pelican History of the World*, rev. ed. (Middlesex, England: Penguin Books, 1983), p. 218.

8. Ibid., pp. 217–218.

9. The poem is translated by Michael Bullock and Jerome Ch'en and included in Jerome Ch'en, *Mao and the Chinese Revolution* (London: Oxford University Press, 1970), p. 340. The chronology of the dynasties referred to in the poem is as follows: Ch'in: 221–206 B.C.E.; Han: 206 B.C.E.–220 C.E.; T'ang: 618–907; Sung: 860–1279. Genghis Khan (1167–1227) was the chief of a small Mongol tribe who "became the

greatest conqueror the world has ever known" (Roberts, *The Pelican History of the World*, p. 364).

10. Ross Terrill, *Mao: A Biography* (New York: Harper & Row, 1980), p. 143.

11. Ibid., p. 144.

12. Shen Hsun (Imperial Instructions), chuan 46–50. Quoted by J.J.M. de Groot, *Sectarianism and Religious Persecution in China* (Amsterdam, 1903), pp. 487–550. See C.K. Yang, *Religion in Chinese Society* (Berkeley: University of California Press, 1961), p. 183.

13. Yang, *Religion in Chinese Society*, p. 185.

CHAPTER 9

The Last Supper at Round Table

For Jesus involvement in social and political activities is redemptive involvement. This is the conclusion we reached at the end of our study of Jesus' temptation in the last chapter. Jesus must have decided that he had to be with the people oppressed politically and religiously to carry out his redemptive activities.

Jesus is right. A king cannot be with such people. He is above them and lords over them. Even a king-messiah — is there a king who does not fancy himself to be a messiah of one kind or another? — cannot be with the people. His "messianic" ambitions set him apart from them. His "messianic know-how" must command their respect and obedience. His "messianic vision" must dictate how they live and what they strive for. People are only the means to achieve his ambition for power and his vision for glory. Jesus could not have been more right. He refused to be a messiah in the line of King David. He decided that his vocation was to be with people because his God was God-with-people. With him a new chapter on political ethics is written and a new history of political theology begins. The focus of that chapter is the last supper he had with his disciples and followers shortly before his crucifixion. The heart of that history is the reign of God he proclaimed and practiced during his ministry.

Last Supper with People

For Jesus it had been a long and hard struggle. He had finally reached the last station of his ministry — Jerusalem. His active ministry lasted only three years. But what a three years! As a chronological time, it is a mere three years. In relation to eternity it is just a fraction of a second, a twinkle of an eye. But when it comes to the impact he has made, the values he has advocated, the presence of God he has evoked in the life of people, his ministry cannot be measured in terms of its length of time.

189

What he said and did is deeply rooted in his time, but also transcends it. It has to be understood in relation to the background of his society and the tradition of his religion, but it goes beyond them. It is, in short, thoroughly contextual, but it can be transposed to other space and time exerting as much, if not more, force as it did in its own space and time. Jesus was someone his fellow Jews, followers and opponents alike, and even Roman colonial rulers, had to reckon with. At the same time he has proved to be someone the powers and principalities of other nations also have to take with utmost seriousness.

As human history after Jesus testifies, not only the history of the North and the West that has come under his direct impact, but also the history of the South and the East that has developed differently are affected by the redemptive power the death of Jesus generated. The meaning of Jesus as a supreme redemptive power, as the Christ, stretches backward into the beginning of creation and forward into the fulfillment of creation. This must be the reason why Jesus as that redemptive power is perceived to be in interaction with forces that are at work in human community and in the universe. History within histories is thus made through such interactions — the history redeemed from ruin and led forward to its destination in God.

In this movement of history within histories there is one thing that becomes more and more clear to us today: that history is incomprehensible apart from the men, women, and children of each and every generation whose lot is to suffer and whose passion for freedom and justice is the power that changes the status quo. We now have begun to realize that the history of a nation is not just a history of its kings and princes but a history of its people — the men and women whose names are not recorded in history books and will never be known. In the same way, it also begins to dawn on us that the history of a religion is not just a history of its priests, ministers, leaders, and thinkers, but a history of its believers who struggle to live and believe within the realities of this world and against the hardships of everyday life. As Jesus meant so much to such people in his day, so he means just as much to such men and women today.

With Jesus in Jerusalem for his final encounter with the religious and political powers of his time, this history of people has reached a climactic hour. The history of people that preceded him and the history of people that is to come have converged, as it were, in that extraordinary place for a few days, creating a tremendous tension, anxiety, and also expectation in the whole of God's creation. And as Jesus and his followers sit down at table for their Passover meal,[1] that history is acted out in the words of Jesus and in the sharing of bread and wine in anticipation of his death. It is as if time has come to a standstill in Jerusalem and become an eternal time — time conscious of eternity, time filled with people and God. A massive space of redemption is created in that small space in which the last act of sacrament takes place.

The holy city, that navel of the earth, has also become transformed dramatically because of the influx of pilgrims from near and far, from Palestine and from beyond it. "In the days before the passover," it is pointed out, "and still more during the festival itself, Jerusalem was filled to overflowing with pilgrims, . . . an estimate would be of between 85,000 and 125,000 pilgrims, to which must be added the population of Jerusalem, which would number about 25,000–30,000."[2] Jerusalem, the city of God, has become visible as the city of people. Without knowing it, these people are soon to be witnesses of a great drama of redemption unfolding itself before their eyes. They are in fact going to be more than witnesses. They are to be part of that drama, either as onlookers, as sympathizers, as participants, or as adversaries.

If Jerusalem at the Passover time is a city that belongs to people, and not just to the ruling religious and political elites, then what about the feast of Passover? It should be the feast of people also. How can it be something else? The event it commemorates is the Exodus. It celebrates the deliverance of their ancestors from the oppression of the pharaoh in the land of Egypt. The Exodus was a people-event. And the celebrations of this people-event in Jerusalem year after year, generation after generation, must also have been people celebrations, people celebrating with God and God celebrating with people. It is an annual reliving of people together in the communion of one another and in communion with God.

Jerusalem during the feast of Passover becomes, in this way, a very crowded festive city. A city of thirty thousand has swollen overnight into a city of more than one hundred thousand! How can it not become a city bubbling with excitement? People touch each other, smell each other, hear each other. There must have been a lot of talking, yelling, and laughing, too. It is into this city crowded with people — people he loved, enjoyed, and had compassion for, that Jesus came with his disciples to have their Passover supper. What could that supper have been like? How did they celebrate it? What kind of supper could it have been? And who were present at that supper? Questions such as these are of great importance in helping us to know who Jesus was, how he died, and what his death meant and still means today.

Who Were at the Last Supper?

The story of the Last Supper begins this way: "In the evening he [Jesus] came to the house with the Twelve. As they sat at supper Jesus said . . ." (Mark 14:17; pars. Matt. 26:20, Luke 22:14). This reading at once reminds us of that famous painting *The Last Supper* by one of the greatest painters of the Italian Renaissance, Leonardo da Vinci (1452–1519). Jesus is seated at the center, with his twelve disciples on either side. Jesus looks pensive with his eyes downcast. Perhaps he is saying, with deep anguish and tremendous pain in his heart: "I tell you this: one of you will betray me — one who is eating with me" (Mark 14:18; pars. Matt. 26:21, Luke 22:21). These words, said most probably without anger and perhaps with a sigh and even with compassion, must have caused quite a commotion among the disciples. The painting, though still, seems to stir with their consternation and become filled with their anxious question to themselves, to each other, and to Jesus: "Not I, surely?" (Mark 14:19; par. Matt. 26:22). The great painter has captured this tense atmosphere of the Last Supper on a monastery wall where he, with his brush and colors, poured out his artistic genius and deep faith in his interpretation of Jesus' Passion.

The tense atmosphere depicted in this world-famous painting enhances the privacy of the Last Supper. It was a supper Jesus had with his disciples alone. The supper was the occasion on which he shared his last thoughts and concerns with his disciples and with them only. There is a sense of inviolability in this privacy. It does not seem to allow intrusion from outside. For once Jesus seems to shut himself off from the crowds, from the masses, from women, men, and children. Now are these last hours Jesus has reserved for himself to be with his disciples and no one else. And this, it seems to me, makes the Last Supper of the painting a little too sober, a little too remote, and somewhat inaccessible to the beholders. It is something you can watch from a distance, but you are not part of it. You are a spectator but not a participant.

I do not know how much this great masterpiece from the great Italian painter in the fifteenth century has affected the thoughts and practice of the Lord's Supper in the Christian church during the following centuries. It must have, one way or another. For the Lord's Supper, or the Eucharist, observed in the church today is sober, orderly, and tense. Believers are spectators. There seems to be a gulf separating them from the Table or the Altar on which the Last Supper is symbolically enacted. Only the celebrants — ministers and priests — seem to feel at home. Even the elders sitting near the table to assist in the celebration of the Lord's Supper look a little uncomfortable, not to say members of the congregation waiting in their pews to be served with the elements or going forward to the front to receive them from the hands of the celebrants.

This has created a situation in which believers are not active members of the drama, not actors in the play. They are outsiders who have gained entry into the solemn and exclusive observance with special permission, yes, with a special permission, because they have to be communicant members! And in some confessions children, even though baptized, are not permitted to receive the elements. It is as if people are not inside the conspiracy going on before their eyes, as if they are not good enough, not important enough, to be part of that great thing supposedly done for them. Is this what Jesus intended? Is this what he wanted the Last Supper, or now the Lord's Supper, to be? I wonder. Maybe not.

The problem is that in that painting of the Last Supper, and in most paintings of it, there is no one else to be seen beside Jesus and the twelve disciples. Of course the great master Leonardo is not to blame for this absence of other persons. Nor are the other artists. They were merely following what the writers of the Gospels — Mark, Matthew, Luke, and John — recorded for later generations of believers. Still, the question can be asked whether there were no other persons present at the Last Supper, if not sitting with Jesus and the disciples at the table, at least on the floor near the table or somewhere in the room in which the Supper was being held. And knowing how much Jesus enjoyed the company of people, would it be entirely fanciful to suppose that the small room might have been filled to capacity with people, not only with men, but also with women, not only with adult women and men, but also with children?

Perhaps this is not totally fanciful, for the question has been actually raised by some erudite New Testament specialists. It has, for instance, been pointed out, with much imagination:

> According to Mark 14:17 (par. Matt. 26:20) Jesus celebrated the Last Supper with the Twelve. It is not possible, however, to assume from this that the women mentioned in Mark 15:40, Luke 23:49, 55† were excluded; in Eastern texts the argument from silence is inadmissible in such cases.[3]

Argument from silence! Is it totally inadmissible? Perhaps not. As a matter of fact, in some cases this seems the only way to recover facts and truths left out in biblical texts and to gain deeper insights into God's purpose for that small community of Jesus' followers in the early days and for human community at large. After all, what we can read in the New Testament must only be a fraction of what actually happened around Jesus and what he actually said and did. Even this fraction tells us much, and it has in fact told us much, thanks to the early Christian community and thanks to centuries of tireless efforts of students and scholars of the Bible. Of course, we could have been told much, much more, if more stories

---

*"A number of women were also present, watching [the crucified Jesus] from a distance. Among them were Mary of Magdala, Mary the mother of James the younger and of Joseph and Salome..."

†"His [Jesus'] friends had all been standing at a distance; the women who had accompanied him from Galilee stood with them and watched it all. The women who had accompanied him from Galilee followed; they took note of the tomb and observed how his body was laid."

about Jesus had been preserved and made available to us on the pages of
the New Testament. But omission of what must have been a large amount
of original source material is not our only problem. What makes it more
difficult for us to gain entry into "the mind of Jesus" is that even what
has been written down and passed on to us through the centuries is the
outcome of a selection from theological "biases" that had shaped the faith
and ethos of the early church *and* the social-religious world deeply en-
trenched in patriarchism and androcentrism. Feminist theologians have
made us keenly aware of this. The result is both encouraging and exciting.

It really is a marvel, in spite of this, that there are hints and allusions
in the Gospels showing how Jesus challenged, for instance, the ethno-
centrism of his own religion. It is not difficult to assume that Jesus must
have said much more, done much more, in relation to this. This is very
important particularly for Christians in parts of the world not assimilated
into the "Christian" culture of the Western nations. And our understanding of Jesus becomes even more problematic and complicated for us since
the traditions about Jesus, after having been screened and interpreted by
the early Christian church, finally reached us rescreened and reinterpreted
by the Christian church in the West. The traditions arrived in a package
bearing every mark of "the spirit and the letter" of Western culture.

Since this is the case, argument from silence cannot be set aside as un-
scientific, unhistorical, or purely subjective. It is an indispensable way,
along with other critical methods, to reach the "authentic" Jesus who
rekindled the vision of God's reign in the company of the marginalized people and the oppressed women and men in the society of his
day. This way of surmising the mind of Jesus and discerning the purpose of God's saving activity in the world from what is *not* directly and
explicitly read in the texts of the Bible has begun to tell us fascinating
stories we have not heard before. It will play an increasingly important
role in our efforts to reconstruct Christian theology in the social-historical
and religious-cultural world outside the world of traditional Christian
theology.

Some feminist biblical theologians have called this argument from
silence the "hermeneutic of silence." It has contributed enormously to
their fresh understanding of the Bible, to their liberation from male-
dominated Christian theology, and to their reconstruction of the Christian
faith. Consider, for instance, this forceful insight:

> If the locus of revelation is not the androcentric text but the life
> and ministry of Jesus and the movement of women and men called
> forth by him, then we must develop critical-historical methods for
> feminist readings of the biblical texts. If the silence about women's
> historical and theological experience and contribution in the early

Christian movement is generated by historical texts and theological redactions, then we must find ways *to break the silence of the text* and derive meaning from androcentric historiography and theology. Rather than understand the text as an adequate reflection of the reality about which it speaks, we must search for clues and allusions that indicate the reality about which the text is silent. Rather than take androcentric texts as informative "data" and accurate "reports," we must read their "silences" as evidence and indication of that reality about which they do not speak. Rather than reject the argument from silence as valid historical argument, we must learn to read the silences of androcentric texts in such a way that they can provide "clues" to the egalitarian reality of the early Christian movement.[4]

To break the silence of the text. How well put! Silence cannot be used as an alibi to prove that androcentric biblical scholarship and traditional theology is not guilty of misrepresenting what Jesus understood the will of God to be.

In this silence is the history of women suppressed by the history of men. In this silence are the stories of female members of the community ignored by the stories of the male members of the community. In this silence is the contribution of women to the faith, life, and work of the early church — the contribution buried out of sight by the faith, life, and work of men. And of course this history, these stories, and these contributions are important and indispensable parts of God's story with humanity. How much we have missed in these two thousand years because silence remains silent! How much we have misunderstood God and what God wants from us human beings because that silence has been forced to keep silent by the male-dominated church and its theology! How much we have been misled about the church, a hierarchical structure dominated by male priests who have monopolized "the sacrament of ordination" because that silence is condemned to silence!

That silence must be broken, and it is being broken. To be an apostle, for example, was not the divine prerogative solely reserved for men in the early church. For a "woman in Rom. 16:7 . . . does receive this title [of apostle]. Like Prisca and Aquila, Andronicus and Junia were missionary partners — Jewish Christians, perhaps from Tarsus. Since they had become Christians before Paul in Antioch and even shared imprisonment with him, it can be conjectured that they belonged to the circle of apostles in Jerusalem who, together with James, received a vision of the resurrected Lord (see 1 Cor. 15:7). Paul even stressed that they were outstanding members of the circle of the apostles."[5]

The early Christian community could not have been a community organized, run and dominated solely by men. It must have been a community of "men *and* women" bound together in the same faith for the service of God in the name of Jesus Christ. The *"Christian* spirituality" fostered in that community must have meant

> eating together, sharing together, drinking together, talking with each other, receiving each other, experiencing God's presence through each other, and, in doing so, proclaiming the gospel as God's alternative vision for everyone, especially for those who are poor, outcast, and battered. As long as women Christians are excluded from breaking the bread and deciding their own spiritual welfare and commitment, *ekklesia* as the discipleship of equals is not realized and the power of the gospel is greatly diminished.[6]

How much the Christian church of today, whether in the East or in the West, falls short of this *ekklesia* (community or church) of women, men, and children, not to say the *ekklesia* of *all* people of God!

People Supper

But the silence of the biblical text has been broken. The voice from the depths of that silence is growing louder and louder. That voice is being heard from Latin America, from black churches in the United States, from Africa, from Asia, as well as from feminist theological communities. There are many voices, not only one. The traditional church and its theologians may choose not to hear these voices; they cannot force them back into the depths of silence from which they came. And these voices are forcing them, whether they like it or not, to re-examine the teachings and doctrines they have developed under the conditions determined by their social-historical realities and religious-cultural idiosyncrasies. How can they assume their understanding and expression of faith to be true and valid for all human beings — women as well as men, blacks as well as whites, the powerless as well as the powerful, the poor as well as the rich, Orientals as well as Occidentals? These voices from the depths of silence are not concerned about peripheral issues, but essential ones. They are "radical" voices — voices that disclose and point to fundamental realities about God and what God has been doing in creation.

In the case in which we are especially interested here, those voices are telling us that the Last Supper Jesus had with his followers before he left for the last mile of his life's journey must have been a "people supper." And since that Last Supper has developed into the Eucharist, or the Lord's Supper — the all-important sacrament of the Christian church, the sacrament that defines what the church has been in its life and ministry, in its faith and order, in its relation to the world and people outside it, disclosure of that Last Supper as "people supper" will surely compel us to take a hard look at the "rubrics of faith" prescribed by the traditional church and its theology.

"People supper" it must have been. Others besides the twelve disciples have followed Jesus to Jerusalem. Mary, his own mother, was one of them. At that critical hour of his life, could Jesus have excluded her from what was going to be his last Passover meal? This would be unthinkable, knowing the importance of strong family ties in those days. Surely this would have been impossible in the context of Asian familial relations. With all her hope mixed with deep anxiety since the birth of her son, Mary must have been there, her heart filled with silent prayers to God, asking God to remove from her son the cup he was about to drink. And like Jesus later in Gethsemane, might not she have also prayed that not her will but God's will be done?

And what about Martha and Mary? They too must have been there — those two sisters who had often entertained Jesus at their home. As a matter of fact, Jesus was reported to have stayed not in Jerusalem itself, the city trying to cope with "population explosion" during the Passover festival, but at Bethany, about one and a half miles southeast of Jerusalem (Mark 11:11, par. Matt. 21:10–11; Mark 14:3, par. Matt. 26:6), most probably in the home of Martha and Mary.[7] Could they have been excluded from the Passover meal?[8] Further, if to find a lodging in Jerusalem was difficult during the feast of the Passover, it must also have been difficult to find a place to eat the Passover meal. But Jesus "had friends in the city and had arranged to eat the Passover in the house of one of them" (Mark 14:13–16; par. Matt. 26:18–19). Would it, then, be entirely unreasonable to think that the friend in whose house the Passover supper was held and members of his family could have been invited to join Jesus and the others? In that case, there could have been children also, if not sitting at the table, at least in the room of the Passover meal. All this seems to indicate that Jesus must have eaten his last Passover meal not just with his twelve disciples.

Oriental custom tells us that a festival such as Passover is not an exclusive occasion, but a communal one. It is a time of hospitality to strangers as well as to friends and relatives. How pointedly Jesus made this clear is to be found in a story in Luke's Gospel. According to the story, he said to the Pharisees and lawyers who had invited him to a dinner in the house of one of them on a Sabbath day:

> When you are having a party for lunch or supper, do not invite your friends, your brothers or other relations, or your rich neighbors; they will only ask you back again and so you will be repaid. But when you give a party, ask the poor, the crippled, the lame and the blind; and so find happiness. For they have no means of repaying you; but

you will be repaid on the day when good people rise from the dead. (Luke 14:12–14)

What an exhortation! And to the hosts who have invited him! The atmosphere must have grown uncomfortable. An expression of displeasure must have flitted across the face of the host and the faces of those prominent guests. A lively conversation must have come to an abrupt stop before it was picked up again. The only person in the room who did not lose composure must have been Jesus. These words must have come from him quite naturally, not accompanied with an affected moral tone. His host and other important guests might have scowled, but Jesus must have looked as serene as ever. I do not think Jesus intended to embarrass them, or to teach them a lesson. He was with "the poor, the crippled, the lame, and the blind" so much and ate with them so often that it just came to his mind that they should have been there at dinner with him. A dinner without them is incomplete. A supper that does not include them is sinful. A meal that keeps them out is a meal prepared and eaten without love.

This must have been what Jesus meant when he addressed the religious leaders sitting at table with him. What Jesus said should not have been entirely strange and new to them. In later rabbinical literature we find an exhortation: "Let your house be opened wide and let the needy be members of your household."[9] In fact, it was already enjoined explicitly in the Torah (the Five Books of Moses in the Hebrew Scriptures), which they knew inside out:

> When you reap the harvest in your field and forget a swathe, do not go back to pick it up; it shall be left for the alien, the orphan, and the widow.... When you beat your olive-trees, do not strip them afterwards; what is left shall be for the alien, the orphan, and the widow. When you gather grapes from your vineyard, do not glean afterwards; what is left shall be for the alien, the orphan, and the widow. (Deut. 24:19–21)

Is this designed to teach the people of Israel to be charitable? Maybe. But it must have been more than charity that was intended. Is this an appeal to our goodness of heart? Perhaps. But it goes beyond the goodness of our heart. Or is this to inspire humanitarianism? Again, maybe. But it is rooted in something much deeper than humanitarianism. Concern for the needy is related to the most important event that goes all the way back to their beginning as a nation. "Remember," they are reminded, "that you were slaves in Egypt; that is why I command you to do this" (Deut. 24:22). The Exodus! This is the foundation of their ethical codes and conducts. That manifestation of God's saving love that gives birth to the faith of Israel must in turn give birth to the concern for the needy. And that people-event of the Exodus must inspire us to be identified with those who need exodus from hunger, injustice, humiliation, pain, and suffering.

The faith developed from the Exodus is communal in nature. It has to do with the history of a community of people from diverse backgrounds bound together in faith in God as the Lord and Savior. And it is this faith of the community that brought pilgrims, Jesus among them, to Jerusalem for the feast of the Passover. Most of them have come not just to remember the old Exodus that happened once upon a time, but to renew their hope for a new exodus from Roman rule. At any rate, the longing of the people for a community with a clearer sense of faith and purpose must have affected Jesus. It was perhaps not his intention to celebrate the Passover as an exclusive feast just for himself and his twelve disciples. As he was conscious of the great ordeal waiting for him, he must have needed a community of his loved ones and his faithful followers as well as his disciples to celebrate with him the feast for the last time.

There must have prevailed, then, a strong sense of "eschatological-ness," of finality, at the Passover meal Jesus had with his followers in Jerusalem. That sense of finality was very much heightened and intensified, although it was not totally new. As a matter of fact, every meal Jesus had with people during his ministry had an eschatological flavor to it, for it could have been their last meal. Jesus and the people eating and drinking with him did not know whether there would be food for them tomorrow. Each meal for them could have been an "eschatological" meal, a last meal. It had an ultimacy to it. It might not be repeated. It might not be possible again.

This ultimacy, this "eschatological-ness," this "last-ness," could have given them a special kind of freedom — freedom from worry about themselves and freedom to entrust themselves to God. Is this what Jesus had in mind when he said to the people: "I bid you put away anxious thoughts about food and drink to keep you alive, and clothes to cover your body. Surely life is more than food, the body more than clothes" (Matt. 6:25; par. Luke 12:22). How do we understand a saying such as this? This could not have been just a moral exhortation not to worry about material things, not a high-sounding teaching not to mind daily needs as something beneath spiritual concern.

With words such as these Jesus must have been affirming their freedom — the freedom the rich do not have. They were celebrating their freedom — the freedom the privileged are not capable of. Without that freedom we are slaves of what we possess and of what we do not possess, prisoners of what we are and of what we are not. And without that freedom we are not able to face the uncertain future and dare not embark on adventures of faith. But that freedom frees us for what we can be and what we must be. That freedom is the power of our being and the ground of our hope. God is that freedom. And with that freedom that is ours, we can do what we must do. We can venture into the unknown with faith in the God of freedom. That is why Jesus referred his friends to the birds of the air and to the lilies of the field (Matt. 6:26–30; par. Luke 12:24–28). Birds and flowers live and die on that freedom of God. They bloom and wither, abandoning themselves to it. If this is how birds and flowers live and die, how much more we human beings must let the freedom of God be our freedom! In that freedom is the secret of what it means to live and live fully. That freedom is the fulfillment of life. Faith is to accept that freedom and learn to live in it as God's grace. As Jesus faced that great unknown, how much he needed the assurance of that freedom that is God's, which he himself taught and practiced! He needed that community of freedom of God and people to embark on that journey of no return.

Those religious authorities who had no inkling of what that freedom meant called Jesus "a glutton and a drinker" and accused him of being "a friend of tax-gatherers and sinners" (Matt. 11:19; par. Luke 7:34). They were totally wrong, of course. They missed the point completely. Their religion, their faith, not able to free them from their attachment to life, was not capable of what Jesus said to the people eating and drinking with him: "So do not be anxious about tomorrow; tomorrow will look after itself. Each day has troubles enough of its own" (Matt. 6:34).

If this was Jesus' faith and the faith he imparted to the men and women who followed him, would he not have wanted his last meal to be a meal affirming and celebrating that freedom with people? And since it was a Passover meal, a meal remembering liberation from bondage, there would have been all the more reason for it to be a meal with more people than just the twelve disciples. The last Passover meal should have been a "people supper," a supper prepared by the community for the community, a supper in which Jesus was surrounded by that community with which he identified himself.

Supper at Round Table

If the Last Supper was a Passover meal that Jesus had with a community made up of women and children as well as men, of other followers of Jesus as well as the disciples, it could not have been as pensive as we have been led to think. Jesus was aware of the danger waiting for him, but the fellowship and sharing with people at table and in the room could have heartened him. During the supper a lot more conversation must have taken place between Jesus and the people. Jesus must have said more than those words about the betrayal by Judas and those words alluding to his death. None of the other things Jesus might have said can be found in the

Gospels. In most cases all we see in the paintings of the Last Supper is a "literal" representation of the Passion stories told by the Gospel writers. I already referred to this in regard to Leonardo's classic painting of the Last Supper.

But would not the Last Supper as a "people supper" enable a different picture to appear before our mind's eye? Would it not give us quite a different visual perception? A Chinese writer from Taiwan shares his reflection on the scene of the Last Supper he saw in a Chinese calendar he had received among the Christmas and New Year greetings:

In this small calendar some Bible stories are reproduced in Chinese paintings. Their style is special and their taste is of quite a different nature, giving those Bible scenes a completely new impression. These scenes are familiar, but at the hands of Chinese painters they seem to reveal meanings that we have not realized before. Take the Last Supper, for example. Leonardo da Vinci's painting has made us think that the table of the holy supper must be rectangular, just as the table for Western meals must be rectangular. But in this Chinese painting of the Last Supper, the table is round and the twelve disciples sit around it like the eight Taoist immortals sitting around a Chinese style table. At the head of the table is Jesus. The painting is not filled with a tragic sense of life. It looks more like the reunion of a large Chinese family on New Year's Eve.

From this little Chinese painting of the Last Supper I suddenly realized why Chinese people are able to contain tragedies of life. Just as a rectangular table differs from a round table, Westerners stress absoluteness while Chinese prefer roundness. Pursuit of absoluteness will turn into tragedy at a certain point. In the love for roundness, however, tragedy is encircled and contained.... China has not produced works on tragedy. I think this is a remarkable thing. In this one finds wisdom, vision and maturity. The long suffering Chinese people understand tragedies not less than Sophocles or Euripides. There is in fact more tragedy than comedy in *The Twenty-Four Books of History*.[10] We are a very old people, but we have learned to look at the world with serenity and to accept it without fear. In comparison, the West does look a little younger and tends to make much ado about nothing. The great master Leonardo was able to depict brilliantly the consternation on the faces of the disciples, but he was not able to express Jesus' peaceful and serene face and had to stop painting for a long time. Leonardo should have come to China. He could have found such a face in the face of an old farmer in the farm-land of the north, a model that could have been close to his ideal.[11]

Not everyone would agree with what is said here. Leonardo da Vinci would not have had to come all the way to China to find an ideal model for Jesus. He could have found that serene and peaceful face containing deep pathos in an old farmer in Italy, his own country. There is something universal about this kind of face — the face that tells the stories of how women and men have finally made peace with hardships of life, pain and suffering.

But it is quite true that the Chinese people and, for that matter, people of Asia in general, have learned to contain tragedies of life much better than people in other regions of the world. By containing them, tragedies have not disappeared. They are still there, in the inmost parts of the heart. They are still there, gnawing at the very being of the sufferer. One of the colloquial sayings in Taiwan, "swallowing tears into one's stomach," describes how people internalize and contain pain and suffering. This does not solve the problem they face, right the wrong done to them, or injustice inflicted on them. Often time is a healing factor. When time does not heal and pain cannot be contained, tragedies cannot be prevented.

Even in traditional Asian society such individual persons are not left completely to fend for themselves. Within the very community that causes them much pain and suffering there is a community that brings healing to them. There is a community within the community in which the wronged individuals may take refuge. That community may be a close circle of friends, an informal association of like-minded people, or a religious community detached from society. Still, it has to be acknowledged that in an Asian society in which pain and suffering are expected to be contained, taking one's own life is often the only solution to be free from the oppressive family system and social structure. But then this is regarded as a form of freeing oneself from worldly worries and getting rid of the shackles of life. At any rate, since there will always be suffering, it has to be contained and transcended. And if possible, reconciliation with one's suffering and peace with oneself and the world are to be attained. This is the central concern of the Buddhist faith. The ideal of that faith is the Buddhist projection of the face of the Buddha whether in painting or in sculpture. That face is serenity itself. It is peace itself. But that face contains the sufferings of the living multitudes. It encircles the tragedies that fall upon people in the sea of bitterness.

This is a spiritual experience one may come away with after visiting, for example, the Borobudur Temple in Central Java, Indonesia. The Temple is truly a marvelous sight. The massive construction, rising as it were out of the depths of the earth, is an enduring monument to the powerful Buddhist kingdoms in Indonesia during the eighth and ninth centuries. It is breathtaking to behold from the distance. To climb to the top takes one's breath too.

Eight interconnected stone terraces rise in pyramidal form to cap a natural hill. The five lower terraces are covered with the texts of Mahayana Buddhism. From base to summit the structure rises to a height of more than 100 feet. A pilgrim visiting the Borobudur had to walk for nearly three miles along its terraces and pass more than four hundred images of the Buddha before he [or she] reached the summit....[12]

After walking three miles, meditating on four hundred images of the Buddha and reaching the summit of one hundred feet, one's pain and suffering, if not resolved, at least is forgotten in that strenuous physical exercise and is transcended in spiritual contacts with the images of the all-merciful Buddha.

The main Buddha statue at the Borobudur invites special attraction. It is the only Buddha statue left open to full view. The Buddha, seated cross-legged in lotus fashion, his eyes lightly closed and his lips gently pressed, faces the pilgrims and tourists from far and near, from Indonesia and from overseas, who have climbed the hill toward him for more than one thousand years. How much woe and joy, how much despair and aspiration, of his fellow human beings he has absorbed into his body, soul, and mind! Behind his closed eyes he has seen the vicissitudes of human history. His closed lips have uttered words of comfort and hope to many a perplexed soul. His whole frame, though maintaining supreme serenity, has contained the suffering and pain of those men and women who have come to him for rescue from the miseries of life and for deliverance from the tyranny of death. In that Buddha statue we find the secret of how Buddhist believers are able to accept the tragedies of life and continue their journey on earth.

The Buddhist ideal is to learn to encircle, to contain, and to overcome the tragedies of life and the world and eventually to achieve Nirvana here and now, to attain the Pure Land in the present time and in the present world. It is to realize that:

> There is no difference at all
> Between Nirvana and Samsara.
> There is no difference at all
> between Samsara and Nirvana.[13]

Nirvana contains Samsara (the continuing cycle of life). It has not done away with the sufferings of this world. But it is the power of serenity in the midst of tragedies. It is the bliss of peace in the midst of suffering in this world.

The Chinese representation of the Last Supper at a *round* table gives us deep insights into the Last Supper. Suffering is a fact of life. Tragedy is very much a part of history. We cannot wish them away. We cannot think and act as if they did not exist. Even Chinese people, with their almost infinite capacity to contain them, cannot deny that for most of their long history they have lived from one tragedy to another, whether personal or national. Suffering has been their lot as individuals and as a nation. But they have survived all this and will continue to survive all this. They have contained all this and will not stop containing them. If suffering and tragedy have not in the past destroyed their power to grow into a face that is as serene and peaceful as that of an old farmer in northern China, they will not be able to destroy that face either in the days to come.

But what is the secret of this? How does this happen? It is in fact very simple and closely related to daily life. The secret has to do, among other things, with the round table and what it symbolizes in Chinese culture. A round table is a family table at which members of the family, young and old, women and men, can seat themselves. That circle around the table begins with any person — the eldest person or the youngest person. And that circle can end with any person — mother, sister, father, or brother. There is, in fact, no beginning and no ending for a round table. You as a member of the round table give to all other members sitting at the same table what you are, while at the same time you receive from them what they are. This giving and receiving move and circulate around the table. You do not have to strain your neck, as in the case of a rectangular table, to see those others sitting at the far end of the table. At a round table you see everyone and everyone sees you. You talk to everyone and everyone talks to you. You enjoy everyone and everyone enjoys you.

This round table is a table of hospitality. It symbolizes an extended family — extended not just to first cousins and second cousins, but also to nth cousins, not only to close relatives and friends, but also to remote relatives and friends. It is even more: the extended family formed at a round table extends also to strangers. Once joining the meal at a round table by invitation or by chance, even a stranger quickly becomes a member of the extended family after a few moments of shyness or embarrassment. This is the mystery of a circle. This is the miracle of roundness. You are encircled and contained by others and you in turn encircle and contain others. The circle becomes even more circular and the roundness becomes even more round. In this encircling and in this containing, what is encircled and what is contained is not only your physical selves and the physical selves of others. It is your total self and the total selves of other persons. It is the self that has sustained and survived sufferings and tragedies as well as happiness and blessings. It is the self that has gone through many a night of sleeplessness and torment as well as many a day of joy and happiness. It is the self that harbors in its inmost part both fear and hope, despair and vision.

If this is what a *round* table is capable of, the communion it creates has to be a delicious communion. The food placed in the middle of the round table can be reached by all from all directions. To reach the food you must "extend" yourself, not only your chopsticks and your arms. The chopsticks you hold in your hand are the extension of your own self. As you reach the bowls for the food, you participate in a communion of human relationships. That communion at the round table is not merely a communion of chopsticks, of physical appetite, but a communion of human persons, of their souls, spirits, and minds. This communion of human persons around a round table makes the delicious food even more delicious. By tasting the food from the common bowls, they taste each other, each other's pain and happiness. That communion is also a nourishing communion. It nourishes their bodies, but it also nourishes their spirits. It makes their stomachs full, but it also makes their souls full. It cures their hunger, and it can alleviate their pain and suffering.

That communion is, then, a sharing communion. The medium is not a kiss, not elaborate words, but the food on the round table. This is a very "primitive" sharing. And because it is "primitive," it is real, not empty; concrete, not abstract; genuine, not phony. It is a very "physical" sharing, not a verbal sharing. When it comes to the sharing of each other's person, Oriental people are not good at words; they are lost for words; they are not capable of words. Instead, they become shy, reticent, tight-lipped. They stammer. They become incoherent. But salvation comes from the food on the round table. That food is their words; it speaks volumes for them. That food is their speech; it is their eloquence. That food is their trust; they entrust themselves to each other through it. That food is the medium of their hearts, souls, minds, and bodies. This is the miracle of a round-table communion.

A round table communion is an empowering communion. The family feast on New Year's Eve is a feast of renewal of communion. The power that binds them together as a family is weakened as they go separate ways for business, school, and work. That power needs to be strengthened for another year to come. A wedding feast at a round table is a feast celebrating a new communion. And what a celebration it can be! There will of course be the round table seating the bride and the bridegroom and their immediate kin. And there will be round tables, from several to twenty, thirty, and even more, forming communions of friends and relatives. The power and love of these communions will be transmitted to the communion of the family newly created, empowering it for the days to come, for better or for worse.

And of course there is funeral feast at round table that creates a communion to support and empower the bereaved family in time of sorrow and loss. The power of communion in the bereaved family is dissipated and dangerously weakened. They cannot live on the memories of the dead alone and allow the power of communion to be drained away. The communion at a funeral feast around round tables refills the communion of the bereaved family with new strength, enabling them to cherish the memories of the dead and to start a new journey of life for the living. The communion strengthened at a funeral feast at round table makes a cycle of life seriously endangered by death not to stand still, not to fall backward, but to forge ahead for the present and for the future.

This is what a round-table communion can make real. It is sacramental, because it renews life. It lifts up the despondent and gives them the energy to go on living. It removes from the frightened souls loneliness and isolation, and restores to them faith in the meaning of life. It also enables them to envision a communion of communions — a communion of the living and the dead, a communion of the living with the world beyond this world. This sacrament of life is very much at the root of ancestor rites in China and in other Asian countries strongly influenced by Chinese culture. Understood in this way, ancestor rites can help Christians to have a deeper understanding of life as a communal event extending from the past to the future through the present. Does not the communion of saints also include communion with ancestors to whom we are related both biologically and spiritually?

What would, then, be more fitting for Christians in Asia than to set their Lord's Supper at a round table? But this is not what we see in churches in Asia. The altar in the chancel is without exception rectangular. The communion table, too, is invariably rectangular. It is a pattern imported from the churches in the West, where a dinner table is rectangular and not round, square and not circular. As to the "communicants," they sit in rows of rectangular benches, separated from the celebrants and from the rest of the communicants except their immediate neighbors. It is a communion service, but there is little communion between celebrants and believers, or among communicants themselves. Is there, then, communion between them and Jesus? But how can there be communion between them and Jesus unless there is communion among themselves? They are communicants, but they are hardly communicating with each other. And if they are not communicating with each other, how can they communicate with Jesus?

Does this alone not tell us that the theology and practice of the Lord's Supper in most churches in Asia needs a radical change? The Lord's Supper is supposed to be a most "hospitable" supper that can take place in the very hospitable society of Asia. But it is not noted for hospitality. It in fact becomes a very inhospitable Supper. It is a mark of how different Christians are from their neighbors. It takes place within the church not visible from the world outside the church. Neighbors who are not Christian are not invited. It is the least accessible part of the life of the Christian church to people outside the Christian community. Is this what the Lord's Supper should be? Should it be a sacrament made available only to Christians? If it represents the reality and symbol of God's saving love through Jesus Christ, is not there something to be said for making it available in some manner to the people outside the Christian church? This is one of the questions Christian churches in Asia and elsewhere in the Third World can no longer avoid. It is essentially a question of how Christians and churches should practice, and not just believe, the "Word become flesh" in a world not directly related to Christianity.

The Lord's Supper should also be an empowering supper. But how much of what is actually done at the Lord's Supper empowers the weak, comforts the sorrowful, uplifts the downtrodden? And when we sin, especially if we sin gravely, then we are barred from the Lord's Supper, cut off from the holy communion. The emphasis is on "holy" rather than on "communion" — holy in its original sense of setting apart. The communion is set apart from the sinful ones. It is forbidden to them. The Lord's Supper becomes a supper of judgment — stern and cold judgment like its stern and cold looking rectangular altar or communion table. Is this not far from the intention of Jesus, who reached out to sinners and outcasts, who always went out of his way to eat and drink with them? Is the Lord's Supper meant only to strengthen those who are already strong, to empower those who are already powerful, to give assurance of God's salvation to those who are already saved? But did not Jesus say that it is not the healthy but the sick who need a doctor, and that he came not to invite the righteous but sinners (Matt. 9:12)? How does a Christian church put this into practice, not only in its programs of social service but in its celebration of the Lord's Supper? A question such as this compels Christians and churches to look more deeply into some of their basic beliefs and practices.

There is no reason for the churches in Asia, or at least for the churches in a society shaped and influenced by Chinese culture, not to use an altar or a communion table that is round and not rectangular. I am not saying that change in the physical shape of the altar or communion table will at once bring "communion" to the people at the Lord's Supper and reinforce sacramental power within the Christian community. But at least it will be a beginning of it. For that sacrament of the Lord's Supper to be sacramental, it has to be life-generating and life-giving; it has to be empowering; it has to be hospitable. The symbol of a round table and the meanings it symbolizes in Asia have an important role to play for churches and Christians in rediscovering what must have been in Jesus' mind when he sat at table for his last Passover meal with his own mother, relatives, friends, as well as the twelve disciples — women as well as men, children as well as grown-ups. His Last Supper had to be a "people supper."

The Last Supper is, of course. the "Lord's" supper, the supper at which Jesus is the host. It has to be observed and celebrated by Christians and churches in such a way that his will be respected, his intention fulfilled, and his concerns given a priority. But in most instances in our churches we have replaced Jesus' will with our will, his intention with our intention, and his concerns with our concerns. We have developed a theology of the Lord's Supper that reflects only vaguely what Jesus intended and did at the Last Supper. Is this not the reason why Christian churches of different confessions still cannot be fully united even at the Lord's table? Do they not behave as if the Supper is the Lord's in name only but in reality theirs? The authenticity of the "Lord's" Supper they celebrate must be questioned. It has to be tested in the light of all that Jesus, the master of the Supper, said and did during his ministry. The test will, in all probability, show us how much the Lord's Supper has become our supper, the supper of the church, the supper of a particular denomination or confession.

And of course the Lord's Supper was not the disciples' supper — a supper claimed by the disciples as a special privilege. The Supper stipulates no privileges for anyone, not even for the disciples. It does not give special privileges to priests and pastors, to popes and bishops. It does not endow them with "sacramental" power, enabling them to mediate God's saving love to the people. People need no such mediation, for the Lord's Supper is a "people" supper — a supper shared by Jesus and people. As such, the Last Supper becomes a powerful symbol of the incarnation: "the Word became flesh and dwelt among us" people.

NOTES

1. Jesus' last meal with his disciples, according to New Testament scholars such as Jeremias, Benoit, and R. E. Brown, was the Passover meal, although in the account of the Synoptic Gospels the meal took place on the night before Jesus' death, i.e., the 15th of Nissan, while for John it took place before the Passover. See Raymond E. Brown, *The Gospel according to John XIII–XXI*, Anchor Bible (New York: Doubleday, 1970), pp. 555–558.

2. See Joachim Jeremias, *The Eucharistic Words of Jesus*, trans. Norman Perrin (London: SCM Press, 1966), p. 42.

3. Ibid., p. 46.

4. Elisabeth Schüssler Fiorenza, *In Memory of Her: A Feminist Theological Reconstruction of Christian Origins* (New York: Crossroad, 1983), p. 41.

5. Ibid., p. 172.

6. Ibid., pp. 345–346.

7. Sherman E. Johnson, "The Gospel according to St. Mark, Introduction and Exegesis," in *The Interpreter's Bible* (New York/Nashville: Abingdon-Cokesbury Press, 1951), p. 573.

8. "According to the *Apostolic Church Order* 26g (A. Hilgenfeld, *Novum Testamentum extra canonem receptum* IV2, Leipzig, 1884, 118f.), Mary and Martha were present at the Last Supper, but were not allowed to partake of the sacrament because Mary laughed"! (see Jeremias, *The Eucharistic Words of Jesus*, p. 46, footnote 9).

9. This saying is attributed to R. Jose b. Yohanan (m. abot 1:5). See Joseph A. Fitzmeyer, S.J., *The Gospel according to Luke X–XXIV*, Anchor Bible (New York: Doubleday, 1985), p. 1048.

10. *Er su shu*, an official history of China up to the end of the Ming dynasty (1368–1644), consisting of twenty-four books, authorized by Emperor Kao Chung of the Ch'ing dynasty (1644–1912).

11. Kao Ta P'en, "La Pietà" (*she mu pei tzu t'u*), in the *United Daily News* (*Lien ho pao*, Taipei/Taiwan), overseas edition, December 24, 1986. Translation from the Chinese text by C. S. Song.

12. John A. Garraty and Peter Gray, eds., *The Columbia History of the World* (Harper & Row, 1981), p. 360.

13. From *The Wisdom of Buddhism*, Christmas Humphreys, ed. (London: Curzon Press, 1979), p. 261.

CHAPTER 10

Jesus Is the Crucified People

Who are the main characters in the divine-human drama of salvation? Traditional Christian faith and theology give us a ready answer: God is the chief actor in this drama. It was initiated by God, is carried out by God, and is to be brought to fulfillment by God. From beginning to end God alone plays the active role. The salvation drama is God's solo act.

Then enters Jesus on the stage of the drama. The focus of our faith and theology is directed to him. He is the visible alter ego of God in this divine-human drama. He is also the representative of human beings before God. He is the mediator between God and humanity. It now appears that a second actor is added to the drama. Salvation is a drama played by God and Jesus. Does this change the drama from a sole act to a dual act, from a solo to a duet? Perhaps not. As we discussed earlier, the cross, which is the heart of this salvation drama, is seen in traditional theology as devised by God to get human beings off the hook of the devil. In a more sophisticated form, it is something that happens between God as the First Person and God as the Second Person within the Trinity.

We have stressed, by contrast, the role and place of people in the drama of salvation. After all, it is people who are the objects of God's saving activity. It does not make sense to leave them out of the drama. But they are not just objects passively waiting for something to be done to them and for them. Again one of the characteristics of traditional Christian faith and theology is to relegate human beings to a passive state, not capable of playing a positive role in God's design of salvation. Faith and theology such as this have reduced believers to inactivity not only in matters of faith but also in relation to their social and political responsibilities. How easy it is, then, for them to become, on the one hand, objects of exploitation and, on the other, unconscious or unwilling collaborators of evil social and political forces!

But people must not be just passive objects of forces external to them. They ought not to be mere playthings of the vicissitudes of historical movements within their own countries and in the world. On the contrary, they must be awakened to the positive role they are entitled to play in their society. They have to become aware of the fact that history is not just made for them but that they are, in a real sense, makers of history. They are not merely objects of history, but, to use the expression of theologians in the Third World, are subjects of history. With the end of the Second World War the world entered the era of the people awakened to their rights as human beings and prepared to strive for these rights. And Christian theologies in the Third World have learned to take seriously the implications of people's awakening for the Christian faith and theology. People, then, loom large even in the drama of God's saving activity. They have come to be recognized as actors on the stage of the salvation drama together with God and Jesus. Their suffering has a positive meaning and plays an active role in God's saving work. That is why Jesus tried, in what he said and did, to empower people for the part they must play in God's reign.

Who, then, are the people? How are they to be identified? Where can they be found? People rediscovered in Third World theologies are not people in general. They are not abstract humanity. They are human beings who are oppressed, exploited, disadvantaged, and marginalized, socially, politically, economically, culturally, and also religiously. If this is still not specific enough to tell us who we mean by "people," we only need to refer ourselves to the people with whom Jesus was associated during his ministry. They were those women, men, and children who suffered not only social and political discrimination but also religious discrimination. By identifying with them Jesus broke the social and religious taboos and revolutionized what God's salvation must mean for human beings.

It is this Jesus that we found celebrating the Passover meal and his last meal not just with his twelve disciples but with an enlarged community of his followers. How did he celebrate that Last Supper with them? How is the suffering he went through repeated over and over in a variety of ways in the life of people in ancient times and today, in the East and in the West? It is to questions such as these that we will now turn.

Jesus Means Crucified People

The Passover meal must have begun in the customary way. Although those present with Jesus might have sensed something unusual in the air, they must have expected nothing different in the Passover ritual they had come to know so well.[1] They waited for Jesus, acting as a *paterfamilias*, to share with them his Passover meditation on that familiar yet always exciting story of the Exodus from Egypt. That extraordinary event had taken place a long, long time ago. It had happened to their ancestors many,

many generations back. But each time they heard that story, it became their own story, their own experience, their own vision. And each time they shared the story with each other, they renewed and strengthened their faith in God to set them free from the bondage of foreign domination, just as God delivered their ancestors from slavery in Egypt. The Passover meal was their spiritual meal. It nourished their soul and spirit for the hard realities of their life. It was also their "political" meal. It enabled them to experience liberation and renew their commitment to it. They were ready to hear from Jesus once again what the special elements of the Passover meal meant: "the unleavened bread was...a symbol of the misery that was endured, the bitter herbs as representing the slavery, the fruit-puree which resembled clay as recalling the forced labor, the passover lamb as a resemblance of God's merciful 'passing over' Israel."[2]

Jesus could have said all this, although the writers of the Passion story in the Gospels give us no record of it. These familiar words were to be "followed immediately by the grace over the unleavened bread, the eating of the passover lamb and the grace over the cup."[3] It is at this point that Jesus did something totally unexpected and "contrary to all custom."[4] After saying the grace over the unleavened bread, Jesus broke it and distributed it. It was while the bread was being passed out to those present that Jesus said: "Take this; this is my body" (Mark 14:22; pars. Matt. 26:27, Luke 22:19). Similarly, after the cup of wine had been passed around and drunk, Jesus referred to the wine as "my blood shed for many" (Mark 14:22; par. Matt. 26:28). My body and my blood! This is Jesus' own person! This is Jesus himself! Jesus is the Passover lamb. This is no part of the Passover ritual. Those present must have been struck by the intrusion of something new into what they knew so well.

Does Jesus mean that he himself is the Passover lamb to be slaughtered? But how is he linked with that ancient Exodus? How is he to be related to the lamb killed to pave the way for their ancestors to escape from Egypt? Those in the room must have wondered. As it turns out, Jesus is going to be a very different Passover lamb. In the historical Exodus the lamb was killed and its blood smeared on the lintels and on the door posts of the house so that, seeing it, God passed over (*pasah*) that house to spare the Hebrew family from destruction (Exod. 12:21–27). But here is Jesus — himself a Jew, a member of the Jewish people who were supposed to be spared from destruction and led to freedom from foreign domination — talking of being broken and destroyed. Not only this, it is the leaders of his own people that are conspiring against him and plotting his death. Jesus as the Passover lamb is not the same as the Passover lamb slaughtered as part of the divine instruction to save the oppressed Hebrews in the land of pharaohs in the ancient time. He is not ordained by God to suffer and die. He is not just a means used by God to achieve the purpose of human salvation, just as the Passover lamb was a means to attain freedom for the Hebrew slaves in Egypt. By referring to the bread as his body and the wine as his blood — words not found in the Passover ritual — Jesus must be intimating that there is something fundamentally different between him and the Passover lamb killed for the Exodus and for the Passover festival.

How different are they one from the other? The blood of the lamb in the historic Exodus is just a sign, an important sign to be sure, but nothing more than a sign for the Lord to pass over the house concerned. But Jesus, whose body is to be broken and whose blood is to be shed, is not just a sign. He is more than a sign. The metaphor of God's passing over at the sign of the lamb's blood does not apply to Jesus. God did not pass over Jesus on the cross; God was with him. God did not leave Jesus behind; God, as we have seen, remained with him even on the cross. God did not move on from Jesus hanging on the cross as if he were of no ultimate concern for God. Jesus concerned God in an ultimate way — Jesus who had shown the world what God was like, that God was love, that God wanted justice for the poor and oppressed. Because of his deep faith in this God and because of his firm commitment to the people God loves, Jesus was marked out by the religious and political powers to be broken, to be destroyed.

At this point I must draw attention to the fact that in the accounts of the Passover meal in the Gospels Jesus did not refer to the historical Exodus in his own words. This seems an important difference between him and the prophets in the Hebrew Scriptures. For all the prophets the theme of the Exodus was paramount in their thought and message. Jeremiah, for instance, complained bitterly that his people no more asked the question, "Where is the Lord, who brought us up from Egypt, and led us through the wilderness..." (Jer. 2:6). In his indignant refrain of "for crime after crime" directed at Israel, Amos declared God as saying, using the powerful first person singular of the divine I: "It was I who brought you up from the land of Egypt, I who led you in the wilderness for forty years" (Amos 2:10). And Hosea, that prophet who likened God's love for the faithless Israel to the yearning love of a husband for his unfaithful wife, left us these heart-rending words he had spoken on God's behalf:

> When Israel was a child, I loved him;
> I called my son out of Egypt;
> But the more I called, the further they went away from me.
> (Hos. 11:1–2)

The Exodus was the central focus for the prophets. It was on the foundation of the Exodus that they constructed their theology and ethics. They understood the relationship between God and people and human relation-

214

ships in light of the Exodus. It was through the Exodus that they identified theo-logical forces of redemption working in the life and history of their nation.

Isaiah the prophet conjured up a vivid picture of the Exodus in his discourse relating to foreign nations: "See how the Lord comes riding swiftly upon a cloud," he said in his warning against Egypt. "The Lord shall descend upon Egypt; the idols of Egypt quail before the Lord, Egypt's courage melts within her.... The waters of the Nile shall drain away, the river shall be parched and run dry; its channels shall stink; ... reeds and rushes shall wither away..." (Isa. 19:1–10). Some three centuries later, Ezekiel, the prophet in the land of exile, had all the more reason to remind his fellow exiles in Babylon of the Exodus. "I revealed myself to them," he said, again using the divine I, "by bringing Israel out of Egypt. I brought them out of Egypt and led them into the wilderness" (Ezek. 20:10). Ezekiel was, of course, alluding to their own exodus, this time not from Egypt, but from Babylon.

No such reminders of the Exodus, however, occurred in the stories of the Last Supper in the Gospels. How are we to understand Jesus' silence about that most important historical and spiritual experience of Israel? Why was Jesus reticent about it? Perhaps in Jesus' own mind the traditional meaning of the historical Exodus is now to be transcended. He in fact gives a new meaning to the Passover meal by relating it to his own body about to be broken and to his blood about to be shed on the cross. The historicity of the Exodus is going to be superseded by the new meaning to be created by the cross. Both the Exodus and the cross are powerful historical happenings. But the Exodus has to yield its place to the cross at the critical juncture of history inaugurated at the Last Supper Jesus had with his followers.

The relationship between the Exodus and the cross that I have tried to recapture seems to disclose to us a pattern in which the world of meanings organizes and reorganizes itself. That pattern appears to follow at least a few stages not necessarily in chronological order but interweaving one with the other. In the first place, there is a historical happening experienced by a particular group of people at the intersection of a particular time and space. Second, in due time — it may be decades or centuries — the importance attached to the historical framework of a particular happening is gradually replaced by the importance of the meaning derived from that happening. Third, when the meaning originally generated by that happening is applied to a new group of people in their different circumstances, it undergoes change and acquires new meanings. And last, it is on this level of meanings pressed into symbols and expressed in images that the historical experiences of a particular group of people can interact with the other groups of people from different backgrounds and traditions.

With this process of transition from the Exodus to the cross in view, let us ask once again what the cross means. How did Jesus himself understand his own death on the cross? The answer to such questions has to be found in the eucharistic words of Jesus. "Take this," he said, breaking the bread in his hand, "this is my body" (Mark 14:22; pars. Matt. 26:26, Luke 22:19). Then he took the cup saying: "This is my blood, the blood of the covenant, shed for many [*huper pollon*]" (Mark 14:24; par. Matt. 26:28). The phrase "for many" in Jesus' pronouncement in relation to the wine is a key phrase here.

First of all, the word "many" (*polloi*), it has been pointed out, is "used in an inclusive sense . . . that is, in the sense of 'inconceivably many, the whole host, all.' "[5] Was Jesus referring to people outside his own community as well as inside it? Did he have in mind Gentiles as well as Jews? There is no definite answer. But did Jews alone make up "inconceivably many" people? Were not there in his company both Gentiles and Jews considered by the religious authorities to be Gentiles? The number in "inconceivably many" is, of course, not of primary importance. "Many" in Jesus' eucharistic pronouncement must have meant the breaking down of barriers between Jews and Gentiles, the regrouping of people not according to their ethnic origin and their religious affiliation, but according to the boundless love of God.

There is the preposition "for" (*huper*). Jesus' body is to be broken and his blood shed *for* many. Jesus is to die for us. In Paul's words, "Christ died for (*huper*) us while we were yet sinners, and that is God's own proof of God's love towards us" (Rom. 5:8). This is the basis of the traditional theology emphasizing the sinless Jesus dying for sinful humanity. We already discussed this at some length before. But this little Greek preposition *huper* has another meaning. It means "in behalf of."[6] Now this prepositional phrase carries the simple preposition "for" a step further. "For" presupposes someone in a superior position doing something for others who are in an inferior position, in the case we are discussing here, the sinless Jesus doing something for the sinful human beings. Jesus, in this sense, stands over against human beings. He is above us and different from us. From that superior position he condescends to do something for us. Essentially, he is *not* one of us. But the prepositional phrase "in behalf of " is not the same. The person who can say and do things "in behalf of " us must be one of us to begin with. Because he or she is one of us, he or she can speak and do in our behalf. The representative character of that person is not imposed from outside but grows from within the community of people. Could it be this "in behalf of," this representative meaning of the preposition *huper*, that Jesus wanted to express in his eucharistic words?

Furthermore, the Greek preposition *huper* also means "to be on someone's side."[7] So the preposition *huper* carries an even stronger meaning. It does not just mean "for." It even goes beyond "in behalf of." It implies being in the company of, making common cause with, or in solidarity with someone. We have here a progression of meaning from "for" to "in behalf of" to "being on someone's side." This progression may be indicative of Jesus' life and ministry. He must have had a strong urge to do something for the people and been exposed to the temptation of becoming a king-messiah. He certainly was a strong spokesperson in behalf of the marginalized people. But finally he was found in their company, on their side and in solidarity with them. In actual fact, when he was crucified, "two bandits were crucified with him," we are told, "one on his right and the other on his left" (Mark 15:27; pars. Matt. 27:38, Luke 23:32). Both symbolically and in reality Jesus lived and died *with* suffering people.

The analogy of Jesus as the Passover lamb breaks down. Jesus is *not* the Passover lamb. He is "people" in the sense we described above. In the loving Jesus we see people capable of loving each other. In Jesus who is in pain we perceive people in pain. In the angry Jesus we encounter the angry people. In the suffering Jesus we witness the suffering people. In Jesus crucified on the cross we behold the crucified people. And the reverse is also true. In the people in pain and suffering, in the people tortured and put to death, we witness Jesus tortured and nailed to the cross. And in this Jesus and in such people we encounter the loving and suffering God.

Jesus, in short, is the crucified people! Jesus means crucified people. To say Jesus is to say suffering people. To know Jesus is to know crucified people. A critical christological conversion takes place here. Traditional Christian theology tells us that to know Jesus we must know God first. But we stress that to know God we must know Jesus, because Jesus makes God real to us. Now we must go even farther: to know Jesus we must know people. We cannot know Jesus without knowing people at the same time. We cannot talk about Jesus if we do not talk about people simultaneously. By "people" I do not mean people in general. I already pointed this out. In fact I do not know what people in general means. It is an abstraction; but people are not abstraction. It is not a common noun; people with flesh and blood are a proper noun, a noun with a particular name and a special identity. By people I mean those women, men, and children whose company Jesus enjoyed, with whom Jesus liked to eat and drink, to whom, Jesus declared, God's reign belongs. By people I mean those men, women, and children, in Jesus' day, today, and in the days to come, economically exploited, politically oppressed, culturally and religiously alienated, sexually, racially, or class-wise discriminated against.

History is made up of the stories of such people. There are countless such stories. Here is one of those stories told in a poem dedicated to the memory of a young Sindhi student leader by the name of Nazir Abbasi from Pakistan. He was tortured to death while under detention at the Mauripur Investigation Center in Karachi.

Forlorn in a corner
Of the jail house
It stands
With dreadful calm

For its solitary inmate
Dark dingy
Suffocating suffering reality
His cherished goals
Freedom liberty
A faraway dream

Surrounded by concrete
Parched and chipped
Like his body —
He lies
Beaten battered shattered

Tattered clothes
blood congealed
Smudged all over
Like art abstract

For the tiny window
In that mass of concrete
Allowing:
A ray of light — a hope
The scenario clears

A thin frail starving
Breaking youthful body
Lies apparently
Tragic and pathetic
Possessed of:
A fierce fighting dauntless spirit
Glaring challenging threatening

From within those watery eyes
— the spirit bursting
Shimmering shining shooting
To greet the ray
Emerging through the window.[8]

Is this not a story of a cross? Is not here a life given "for" many, "in behalf of" many, and "in solidarity with" many? That life, battered and shattered, lying motionless in the torture chamber, joins with other lives also given "for" many, "in behalf of" many, and "in solidarity with" many in Pakistan and elsewhere. That life and these other lives — are they not part of that supreme life of Jesus given for, in behalf of, and in solidarity with, "inconceivably many, the whole host, all"?

Where these "inconceivably many, the whole host, all" are, where these people are, there Jesus is, whether two thousand years ago or two thousand years from now. In the midst of these people Jesus is to be found, yesterday, today, and tomorrow. This is the "historical" Jesus. Jesus is historical because people are historical. The life of Jesus is, in this way, linked with the life of people, with all that life means and brings — despair and hope, suffering and joy, fear and reality of death overcome with faith in resurrection. The history of Jesus becomes *historical* in the histories of people. In the meeting of these histories — Jesus' history and histories of people — the perimeter of God's saving power working in the whole of the world is broadened and deepened. Jesus is released from the captivity of the Christian church. He is liberated from the historicism of traditional Christian theology — historicism that defines and restricts God's salvation first in relation to Jesus as a Jew who lived, worked, and died in Palestine two thousand years ago, then in relation to Jesus made in the image of the white Western male who has enjoyed centuries of advantage over women, and later in relation to Jesus domesticated by the Western "Christendom" that dominated many nations in the Third World as colonies since the beginning of the modern era. The fetters of that historicism have been shattered and Jesus is now recognized as "the historical Christ" among women, men, and children across the boundaries of nations and transcending barriers of time. From the historical Jesus to the historical Christ! This is a "christological conversion" of great significance. The conversion restores theological wholeness to God's saving love. It enables us to feel the reverberations of God's saving power in all parts of God's creation.

The Historical Christ

The historical Jesus is risen as the historical Christ — Christ who is born, lives, heals, comforts, saves, dies, and rises again, not only once, not only ten times, not only a thousand times, but as many times as there are people who have to be healed of their ailments, who long to be saved from their misery, who need to be given power to live in the midst of suffering, and who seek the assurance of life in face of death. But traditional Christian theologians are not good at such "christological conversion." It is those women, men, and children — though "unprofessional" in academic theology yet very "professional" in their home-made theology inspired by their pain and hardships of life — who are capable of it. And it is novelists and writers, moved by the history uncovered from its buried past and feeling in their bones and in their sensitive hearts the suffering of their fellow human beings, who tell us how they encounter the historical Jesus as the historical Christ in human community wherever it may be.

"This Ugly, Emaciated Man"

One such writer is Shusaku Endo, a Japanese Roman Catholic Christian. He wrote a startling historical novel called *Silence*.[9] The fierce persecution of Christian converts under the Tokugawa shogunate in seventeenth-century Japan sets the stage for the author to explore two themes that even today have no ready answer: conflict between the Christian faith and Japanese culture, and the meaning, or rather puzzlement, of God's silence for Christian believers in the inferno of horrendous persecution. Shusaku Endo has written another historical novel, *The Samurai*.[10] The setting is familiar. It is feudal Japan of the seventeenth century. But unlike in *Silence*, here the in *The Samurai* reader is not confronted with the horrifying picture of the naked power of the sword over helpless Christians and the latter's desperate waiting for God to break silence and save them from cruel torture and painful death. The author unfolds before our eyes a subtle politics that involves the Japanese government's desire to gain trading privileges with "Christian" Europe despite its conflict with the Christian religion and a Catholic missionary willing to serve the political authorities of the "pagan" nation in exchange for the right to make converts.

Conscripted into this struggle was a samurai, an impoverished warrior in the service of Lord Ishida, a wealthy vassal with the rank of a general, and three other Japanese emissaries. Father Velasco, an ambitious Franciscan missionary, and the samurai with his companions set out on a long, tortuous, and fruitless voyage to Rome. The turbulent voyage turned out to be the samurai's own turbulent spiritual voyage. Baptized by the missionary on their way to the West, not out of his own personal conviction but for the sake of the mission entrusted to him by his feudal lord, the samurai was to be haunted by the crucifixes he inevitably saw on the walls of the monasteries where they stayed during their journey — haunted by that "emaciated man with both hands nailed to the cross hung with drooping head."[11] That man never left him in peace. He had to tell himself: "This ugly, emaciated man. This man devoid of majesty, bereft of outward beauty, so wretchedly miserable. A man who exists only to be discarded after he has been used. A man born in a land I have never seen, and who died in the distant past. He has nothing to do with me."[12] But he was not able to put that man out of his mind.

During that long painful voyage little did he know that he himself in the end was to become like that ugly, emaciated man. After his return to Japan, he found himself in a country grown hostile to Christianity again. And being a "Christian," he was humiliated and ordered to die. Yes, like that ugly, emaciated man, he was to be discarded after he had been used. He should have known that that man was not born in a land he had never seen; that man was born in his own land. He should have been aware that that man did not die in the distant past; that man was to die in his own time. Yes, that man had everything to do with him; that man was he, the samurai.

The samurai never understood this, but there were times during his voyage when he came close to understanding it. When he saw a crucifix on the bare wall of his room at the Franciscan monastery in Madrid, where he and his companions were staying, his mind wandered into the past and he

> remembered that he had once seen a prisoner in a similar condition. Riding bareback, he had been paraded about with both his hands lashed to a pole. Like this man on the crucifix, the prisoner was ugly and filthy. His ribs protruded, and his stomach had caved in as though he had not eaten for a long while; he wore only a cloth about his loins, and he supported himself on the horse with spindly legs.

This was not just a memory from his own land that had nothing to do with the crucifix he was gazing at in the monastery room in a strange land. For "the more he looked at it, the more the image on the wall reminded the samurai of that prisoner."[13]

Extraordinary, is it not? That Jewish man and that Japanese prisoner. They should not have the slightest connection in time and in space — the one lived in the first century and the other in the seventeenth century; the one from Palestine, the other from Japan, one entirely foreign to the other. They were arrested for totally different reasons. That man on the crucifix was innocent. He did not commit any crime. But that prisoner the samurai saw back in Japan could not have been innocent. He must have committed some kind of crime, or at least an offense, that deserved death in those feudal days. If they are so different, poles apart as a matter of fact, why do they get connected in the samurai's memories? They must have something in common. Yes, they are both ugly, filthy, miserable, emaciated. They carry the same marks of suffering on their person. That is why the man on the crucifix reminded the samurai of the prisoner and the prisoner reminded him of the man on the crucifix. They have everything to do with each other. The samurai fell short of putting himself in the place of the prisoner he had seen back in his own country. Otherwise, he would have been able to relate himself to that ugly, emaciated man on the cross and also to relate that man to himself.

"I Discovered Jesus among These Indians"

The samurai's spiritual voyage continues. After what seemed an endless voyage over the stormy Pacific Ocean, they reached the shore of Nueva España, what is now called Mexico, sick and exhausted. There in that first foreign land they had ever seen, they met, by sheer chance, a strange Japanese man in the village of Tecali near Puebla. Born in Japan, orphaned in a war at an early age, adopted by a Christian priest to become his servant, then sent to Manila to be trained as a monk at the seminary, the Japanese man became "disaffected with the clergy ... boarded a ship bound for Nueva España.... After a long, difficult voyage he arrived in Mexico City, where for a time he did odd jobs at the monastery. Here, too, however, he found it impossible to feel close to the fathers, and grew disenchanted with everything." He fled and joined a group of Indians and now lived with them in the settlement at Tecali.[14]

The renegade Japanese monk was scarcely able to conceal his powerful emotions. To meet compatriots from the land he had left many years before! To be able to speak his mother tongue after he had almost given up hope of being able to speak it again! Amid surprise, joy, and nostalgia, the conversation between him and the samurai turned to the question of the Christian faith.

"Won't you ever return to your home in Japan?" the samurai asked. The renegade monk smiled sadly. "I have no relatives. Even if I returned, there would be no one to welcome me. And Christians are ... "

"But you've abandoned Christianity, haven't you?" "No, no, I am still a Christian. It's just that ... " He stopped. Then a look of resignation came into his eyes, suggesting that he could not convey his feelings in words. "It's just that ... I don't believe in the Christianity the padres preach."

"Why not?"

"Atrocious things happened here in Nueva España before the padres came. The foreigners snatched away the lands of these Indians and drove them from their homes. Many were brutally murdered; the survivors were sold into slavery. Everywhere you look there are villages these people had to abandon. Nobody lives in them now — only the stone houses and stone walls still stand.... "

"But war is like that," the samurai muttered. "It's the same in any defeated country."

"I'm not talking about a war." The man made a grimace. "It's just that the padres who came to this country later on have forgotten many sufferings of the Indian people.... No, they haven't forgotten. They pretend that nothing ever happened. They feign ignorance, and in seemingly sincere tones preach God's mercy and God's love. That's what disgusted me. Only words of beauty come from the lips of the padres in this country. They never soil their hands in the mire."

"Is that why you abandoned Christianity?"

"No, no!" The renegade monk glanced behind him. Several Indians were standing in front of the hut to the rear, staring at the Japanese.

"No matter what the padres might say, I believe in my own Jesus. My Jesus is not to be found in the palatial cathedrals. He lives among these miserable Indians.... That is what I believe.... "

The man stopped talking and fingered Nishi's [one of the four Japanese envoys] clothes. He stroked them again and again and cried, "Ah, these smell of Japan!"

"Why don't you go back?"

The samurai felt pity for the man, no longer distinguishable as either a Japanese or an Indian.

"The merchants who came with us are taking a ship back to Japan at the end of the year. Wouldn't you like to go with them?"

"I'm too old to return." The renegade monk lowered his eyes to the ground. "I...wherever the Indians go, I shall go; where they stay, I shall stay. They need someone like me to wipe off their sweat when they are ill, to hold their hands at the moment of death. The Indians and I — we are both without a home.... "

The renegade monk accompanied them to the edge of the fields. The dusty corn stalks swayed languidly in the breeze that blew from the marsh. A carved wooden image of a man on a cross stood at the edge of the fields like the guardian deity of this settlement. The emaciated man on the crucifix had pigtails and a pug nose, and eyes filled with dark endurance just like those of the Indians who had been sold into bondage by the Spanish. At his feet lay a pool of melted wax, like tears shed by the man himself.[15]

No, the renegade monk did not abandon faith in Jesus — Jesus who "has pigtails and a pug nose, and eyes filled with dark endurance just like those of the Indians...." Would Christians in Japan today, renegade or not, find Jesus who bears marks of pain and longing behind the stoic faces of the Japanese and underneath the surface of affluence and prosperity? Maybe this is a question Shusaku Endo, the author, wanted to project on that emaciated man on the crucifix who had pigtails and a pug nose and whose eyes were filled with dark endurance just like those of the Indians.

That Jesus with pigtails, however, is not merely a cultural adaptation of an otherwise "Jewish" Jesus or "European" Jesus. That Jesus is not just a piece of native Indian art work. That Jesus is an Indian! This is what that renegade monk discovered in his life with the Indians — the Indians wronged, deprived, impoverished. And it is this Jesus that enabled him to keep his Christian faith. He said to the Japanese envoys: "Jesus lives among these miserable Indians." In the face of the sick Indians he saw the face of Jesus. In the agony of the destitute Indians he perceived the agony of Jesus. And in the compassion that kept the flame of life and hope burning in the Indian community he encountered the compassion of Jesus. The renegade monk grasped the central truth of the Christian faith he had failed to grasp within the religious establishment — the truth that the Word became *flesh*, the truth that that same Word became *Indian* flesh. What a theology of the incarnation! It is closer to Jesus' own theology of the incarnation than most christologies concocted by academic theologians.

The renegade monk said the same thing again to his Japanese compatriots the second time they met in Tecali on their return voyage after their unsuccessful mission to Rome. The very sick former monk said as if making a confession: "Because of my condition, the Indians have been good enough to stay behind here in the swamp." "Otherwise," he smiled embarrassedly, "I would have moved far from Tecali. Sometimes I discover Jesus among those Indians."[16] Jesus does not have to be imported from outside. He is not a product made in Palestine, remanufactured in the West, and then exported to the rest of the world. Jesus was a Jew and remained a Jew. But this Jesus, when he means Christ, anointed of God, filled with the Spirit of God, this Jesus-Christ the lover of God and lover of the sick, the sorrowful, the downtrodden, the poor, the helpless, does not have to be a Jew, not to say an Anglo-Saxon. He can be an Indian, as that renegade Japanese monk found out. He can be an Indonesian, a Chinese, a Filipino, a Thai....

And this Jesus-Christ, Jesus hyphenated with Christ, Jesus who stands for God's love for the world that manifests love and compassion between human beings, can be that renegade monk, too, although he might not know it himself, or rather he would not dare to know that he knew it. As he told the Japanese envoys, the Indians "need someone like me to wipe off their sweat when they are ill, to hold their hands at the moment of death." This at least he knew. But is there anything more important than this to know? Is this not the heart of what is called "theology of the incarnation" in Christian theology? And should not the question of "who Jesus is" stop here? Should not, then, the "theological ethic" of God's reign be more important than the metaphysical theology of the nature of Jesus or hermeneutical squabble over the Jesus of history and the Christ of faith?

The old sick former monk chose to stay with his Indians. "Don't you have anything you would like us to say to your family back home?" the samurai asked him for the last time. "Nothing," was his reply. Then he added: "I have finally been able to grasp an image of Him that conforms to my own heart." These were his words of farewell to the samurai. The Japanese envoys had to leave without the monk. "The swamp glimmered in the sunlight. The horses plodded slowly along its banks."[17] The swamp of Tecali! Does this not remind us of another swamp — the swamp of Japan — in *Silence*? In *Silence* Shusaku Endo made Lord Inoue, governor of Chikugo, say to the apostatized missionary priest: "You were not defeated by me. You were defeated by the swamp of Japan."[18] The swamp of Tecali and the swamp of Japan. There is a vast difference between them: in the swamp of Tecali the Japanese samurai saw Jesus with pigtails on the crucifix, but he did not come across Jesus with a topknot back home in the swamp of Japan. In the swamp of Tecali he listened to the confession of a former Japanese monk who discovered Jesus among the Indians, but back in the swamp of Japan Jesus was not to be found among the Japanese speaking Japanese.

Did Endo find his answer in the swamp of Tecali, an answer he could not find in the swamp of Japan? And with that answer from the swamp of Tecali, will it now be less difficult for him to find a similar answer in the swamp of Japan? Perhaps it depends on whether the swamp of Japan has changed since the seventeenth century in the eyes of Christians in Japan. But a more important question is whether Christians and theologians in Japan have developed "a theological eye" that is capable of sighting Jesus among the Japanese — an eye different from the "German" eye or "American" eye. All Christians and theologians of the countries outside the cultural orbit of Christianity have to ask themselves a similar question. The decisive theological or christological inspiration for us has to come from the swamp of Tecali. To find the swamp of Tecali in the swamp of Japan, to discover it in the swamp of China, to sight it in the swamp of Thailand, to develop a theology of it in the swamp of Taiwan, to construct a christology of it in the swamp of India.... This remains a major theological task that must challenge us, inspire us, and excite us. The Japanese renegade monk at Tecali was very much to the point when he said to the samurai: "I have finally been able to grasp an image of Him [Jesus] that conforms to my own heart."

Jesus-Christ Is *Christa* Too

If there has to be the swamp of Tecali, there has to be *Christa*, too. If there has to be that "ugly, emaciated man" on the crucifix, there also has to be "that ugly, emaciated woman" on it. And if that "ugly, emaciated man, devoid of majesty, bereft of outward beauty, so wretchedly miserable" puzzled and haunted that Japanese samurai and set him on an unfamiliar spiritual voyage, that "ugly, emaciated woman, devoid of majesty, bereft of outward beauty, so wretchedly miserable" must also puzzle and haunt many male Christians and theologians and set them on a new theological journey.

The Christa, "created in 1975 by sculptor Edwina Sandys for the United Nations' Decade for Women, had been shown in galleries and art exhibits, but it had never before been displayed in a church." When it was unveiled at the Maundy Thursday services at the Episcopal Cathedral of St. John the Divine in Manhattan, New York, in 1984, "gasps could be heard throughout the main chapel." Why the gasps? Because "the Christa was, in fact, a Christa, complete with undraped breasts and rounded hips."

Bare breasts and bare rounded hips. These are what caused the gasps. They are two external marks of a female person. Christian piety seldom enables a believer to go beyond gazing at the externality. A woman said, perhaps in anger: "It's disgraceful. God and Christ are male. They're playing with a symbol we've believed in for all our lives." But a symbol reveals and conceals. It uncovers and covers. For all her life she had believed what the male symbol of God was supposed to reveal and uncover, but was never led to think what that same symbols may cover and conceal also. And there is something more dangerous. A symbol may lie! After all, a symbol — any symbol — is a creation of human effort conditioned and limited by historical and cultural realities. We have to develop power of imagination to expose the lies a symbol inadvertently tells as well as to appropriate the truths it may convey. But the religious establishment, as we all know, does not encourage its members to develop that power. That is why God must be male with what maleness means in a patriarchal society — power, glory, majesty, domination, and sovereignty. Christ must be male yesterday, today, and forever, world without end, with all the prerogatives of prophet, priest, and king, ordained primarily for male members of the human community. How could there, then, be no gasps when the Christa, the female Christ in stark nakedness, was unveiled in, of all places, a cathedral, the very symbol of masculine power and majesty for all these centuries?

If Christian piety tends to remain with externals, traditional Christian theology, as more and more women Christians and theologians in the West and more and more women and men Christians and theologians in the Third World have discovered, is unfortunately often skin-deep only. To the New York suffragan bishop the Christa was "a 'desecration' of Christian symbols." And he "urged parishioners to write the diocese's presiding bishop... 'if it shocks you as much as it did me.' "[19] What shocked the suffragan bishop was not the haggard face trying to contain the extreme sorrow and pain seething in Christa's heart, not the emaciated body on which centuries of injustice has been done, but the female parts of the body fully exposed to the world. What a skin-deep theology! That theology cannot penetrate into the heart of Christa. It is not capable of experiencing the tremendous anguish that almost bursts that naked body. It cannot even understand that nakedness is a silent but powerful indictment against the world of men who reduce women to be objects of their sexual whims. No wonder Christa shocked the suffragan bishop and his skin-deep theology.

But a symbol, even a Christian symbol, can exhaust its power. A symbol — each and every symbol — has a history. It is born, functions vigorously for a certain period of time, grows impotent, and is replaced. A symbol, including a religious symbol, has a social history. It cannot be understood in separation from the society in which it functions. A symbol also has a cultural history. It is explained by a culture that gives birth to it and explains that culture it affects and shapes. It of course has a spiritual history. It nourishes the human spirit and enables it to aspire to something noble and worthy, but it can also terribly distort it and drive it to the verge of insanity.

A symbol, in short, has a human history. And it grows and wanes as mistakes committed by human beings in history are exposed, as secrets hidden in the depths of history come to light, and as visions nurtured in the womb of history erupt. In the history of symbols, then, we perceive the history of God with humanity. Ultimately, that history cannot be expressed in ordinary everyday language. It is the realm of apocalyptic language. And we know from our Bible how mysterious, fascinating, and gripping that language can be. It is human language compressed into the images and symbols that demand not just knowledge but wisdom, not merely intellect but heart, not only reason but intuition to comprehend.

Since the history of God with humanity is an open history, symbols that testify to it must be open, too. A closed symbol is a contradiction in terms. It betrays the nature of symbols. It renders symbols into plain language. That is the end of symbols as symbols. Those persons offended by the Christa do not know what they are doing to symbols. Symbolism of the Christa did not "desecrate" Christian symbolism. It forced open the "Christian" symbol of maleness and exposed it to the history of God with women as well as men, and not just with men. It compelled the Christian church to take the full consequences of God's creation of women as well as men, including the ordination of women. It revealed a fundamental weakness and deficiency in traditional androcentric Christian theology — a theology incapable of dealing with the female part of God.

The Christa, the symbol of the *female* Christ, has restored history to women. She is a powerful portrait of God's image in women. As a Korean woman puts it:

> Christa: female Christ in suffering. She was just like laborers. Her body was so thin that I could feel pain from her body, but her face was different. Her face was smiling even though she was on the cross, she could see the glory of God in her. So many women are suffering like Christa even now. Christa, she is a symbol of new humanity of women. From the suffering, life comes out again. This means that God is still suffering with the people, male and female. God is suffering with women who are oppressed in the society and in the family and even in themselves. Christa receives all the suffering of all women, so women should stand up and walk with joy and love into the world for peace.
>
> I feel sorry for those men [and women] who could not accept Christa. I pray for them to open their eyes to see God's image in Christa too.[20]

A symbol that evokes such a deep spiritual awareness must have a rich history behind it and will create an equally rich history in the future. The symbolism of the Christa has just begun to exert its power on the faith and theology of the Christian community.

"God's image in Christa" cannot but revolutionize our human psyche conditioned by centuries of male domination. It cannot but change our society shaped by the long traditions of patriarchism. And "God's image in Christa" will have to transform our Christian faith. It will have to create a room, a big room, in our Christian theology for the God of women as well as the God of men. That revolution, that transformation, that creation, has already begun, and no power on earth, much less the power of traditional theologians, is able to thwart it. In and through the Christa, God declares that God is not to be thwarted any more from being fully God — the God of women as well as men, the God who bears sufferings of women as well as those of men, the God who sets women as well as men free to fulfill God's purpose of creation.

How that image of God in women has suffered! Christa is the story of suffering women. Christa has been suffering since the days when women were held inferior to men. No one knows when that began, but one thing is certain: Christa has had a long, long history. That history in China goes back at least to the third century B.C.E. when a woman poet lamented:

How sad it is to be a woman!
Nothing on earth is held so cheap.
Boys stand leaning at the door
Like gods fallen out of heaven.
Their hearts brave the Four Oceans,
The wind and dust of a thousand miles.
No one is glad when a girl is born;
By her the family sets no store.[21]

Women have been held so cheap for more than two thousand years in China. When there was a famine, girls either starved to death first or were sold. When there was a war, women were raped and enslaved. And when the Chinese government decreed a one-child-per-family policy to curb the population explosion in the recent past, many baby girls were secretly murdered to make room for a baby boy yet unborn. It is the same in India today. "Of the more than 1000 cases reported from Bombay," it is noted, "not a single case of abortion of a male fetus was reported, whereas 97 percent of the fetuses identified [by means of amniocentesis used for sex determination] as female have been aborted."[22] Little wonder the ancient Chinese woman poet said that nothing on earth is held so cheap as women.

Those Christians, bishops, theologians, shocked by the naked body of Christa have not heard that woman poet in the third century B.C.E. lament: "How sad it is to be a woman!" Of course, they could not recognize her as Christa. They have not seen the silent tears of those poor Indian mothers having an abortion not because of health reasons or family planning, but solely because the fetus in their wombs is female. How could they, then, perceive Christa in those Indian mothers? But Christa is every woman disfigured, raped, battered, discarded. Christa is every girl murdered in order for her family to have a son. Christa is every female fetus aborted to make room for a male fetus in the mother's womb.

"Where is Christ?" asks Yong Ting Jin from Malaysia in a meditation. "When can one see Christ? With whom is Christ present today?" To these questions some voices answer:

VOICE 1 [*working-class woman, forty years old, has three children, works in the same factory as her husband*]: I feel broken. I can't go on with this. God, why do I have to work as hard as my husband? My hands hurt, my body is worn out. I am always tired. God, where are you? Are you on the T.V., are you in the marketplace, are you in the assembly line?

VOICE 2 [*black woman in South Africa, thirty years old, lives in a barracks with two young children. Her husband is working in a gold mine and only comes home once a year*]: God, why are you white? I am black. My suffering is black, my hopes are black. My job is white. As a black woman I can only work as a teacher being unmarried. They have also taken my husband away from me. God, I want to paint you black. God, why are you white?

VOICE 3 [*prostitute, thirty years old, brought up in an orphanage*]: God, do you look further than my miniskirt and leather boots? Do you see my suffering? I sell my body. I am no more than flesh. A toy for men. God, I hate you, you are like them. God, what do you really look like?[23]

Christa is that forty-year-old over-worked woman. Christa is that thirty-year-old black woman who wants to paint God black. Christa is that thirty-year-old prostitute who sells her body. And God is Christa as well as Christus. We now know where Christa-Christus is, so we also know where God is. We now know who Christa-Christus is, so we also know who God is.

And Christa is that woman sitting in a pew waiting for her church to come to its senses and embrace Christa in tears of repentance, in anticipation of a new vision of God. That woman in a pew is saying:

> I sit in a pew
> Waiting.
> The Human
> Becomes Divine.
> The bread...
> Perhaps kneaded by a woman's hands.
> The wine...
> Perhaps women worked in the vinery.
> But when the Human
> becomes Divine
> a woman's hands are taboo!
> "You shall not touch
> the Divine!"
>
> The Divine became human,
> Penetrated a woman's womb.
> (Patriarch had no place!)
> Like soft petals enfolding
> a crystal dewdrop,
> The seed nestled
> in a female form.
>
> "You shall not touch
> the Divine!"

The mother's hands held the child.
They soothed, they comforted,
they created security.
The hands were always there
as surely as the setting sun
reveals itself with every dawn.

"You shall not touch
the Divine!"

The battered body
taken off the cross...
Women's hands gently
perform the burial rites.
The crimson blood
must surely stain those hands.
Women's hands —
caring hands.

"You shall not touch
the Divine!"

I sit in a pew
Waiting.[24]

Now that Christa has entered the church, and not just in galleries and art exhibits, the waiting must be over. There is nothing Christa cannot touch, even the bread and wine for the sacrament in memory of Christa-Christus. There is nothing Christa cannot do, even celebrating the broken body of Christa-Christus. For that Christa-Christus is you and me, a woman and a man who suffers and hopes, who dies and rises again. As a woman said, contemplating the Christa: "When I look at the Christa, I see *me*. That is me on that cross."[25]

Redemptive Power of Death

That ugly, emaciated man on the crucifix, that ugly, emaciated Indian with pigtails on the cross, that ugly, emaciated woman nailed to it, call to mind those hymns of insuperable beauty and masterful artistry dedicated to the "suffering servant" in Second Isaiah, the "servant songs" (Isa. 42:1–4; 49:1–6; 50:4–9; 52:13–53:12). These poems take us through the extraordinary pilgrimage of the servant. The servant is "God's chosen one" (42:1) who "will make justice shine on every face" (42:3) and "plant justice on earth" (42:4). The servant is firm in the faith that God "named me from my mother's womb (49:1)... to restore the tribes of Jacob, to

bring back the descendants of Israel" (49:6). The servant's mission, however, goes far beyond Israel and Judah, for God "will make the servant
a light to the nations, to be God's salvation to earth's farthest bounds"
(49:6). What a sublime vision! And what a stupendous mission! A vision
such as this inspires confidence. And a mission such as this summons our
courage. The servant is prompted to declare:

> Who dare argue against me? Let us confront one another.
> Who will dispute my cause? Let them come forward.
> The Lord God will help me;
>   who then can prove me guilty?
> They will all wear out like a garment,
> the moths will eat them up.
>
> (Isa. 50:8–9)

The servant is defiant. Those opposed to the servant are challenged "to
take part in a legal contest."[26] The servant is utterly sure of the outcome of
the contest. Before our mind's eye stands the servant taking the opponents
to task, testifying to God's salvation for Israel and for the nations.

But, as it turns out, the servant has not won victory. When we come
to the fourth and last song, we are confronted with the servant reduced
to a pitiful sight. What we hear is almost a dirge, majestic but mournful, magnificent but tragic. It induces sighs and moves one to tears. That
noble vision of the servant has vanished. That grandiose mission of the
servant has been aborted. And at this point the song reaches the height of
incomparable sublimity and passion. The servant now

> had no beauty, no majesty to draw our eyes,
> no grace to make us delight in him [NEB.]
> He was despised and rejected by people;
> as a man of sorrows, and acquainted with grief;
> and one from whom people hide their faces,
> he was despised, and we esteemed him not [RSV].
>
> (Isa. 53:2c–3)

Is this the servant extolled in the earlier songs? Is this the servant aflame
with a divine vision and stirred with a grand mission? This servant and
that servant — they seem as different as heaven and earth (*t'ien jan chi
pieh*, to use a Chinese phrase). Do we not see in this humiliated servant
"that ugly, emaciated man" on the crucifix?

The song turned dirge goes on and invites us to lament with it the
tragic fate that has fallen on the servant:

> Surely he has borne our griefs
>   and carried our sorrows;

> yet we esteemed him stricken,
>> smitten by God, and afflicted.
> But he was wounded for our transgressions,
>> he was bruised for our iniquities;
> upon him was the chastisement that made us whole,
>> and with his stripes we are healed.
>
> (Isa. 53:4–6, RSV)

Who is this servant of God? Students of the Hebrew Scriptures have racked their brains over the question. Bible critics have exhausted their ingenuity to find an answer. Christian theologians have spent endless hours to solve the mystery. But is the question meant to be so elusive? Does it have to remain a puzzle forever?

The words of the song are in fact not words. They draw a picture. They paint a portrait. They form a four-foot bronze statue of Christa unveiled in the Episcopal Cathedral of St. John the Divine in New York. That servant is Christa — a suffering woman. That servant is Christus — a suffering man. That servant is Jesus-Christ and Jesus-Christ is that servant. And what a redemptive power gets released from the suffering and death of the servant, from that Jesus hyphenated with Christ, from that ugly, emaciated woman called Christa, from that ugly, emaciated man called Christus! For upon every Christa-Christus "was the chastisement that made us whole." With the stripes of every Christa-Christus "we are healed." This is the decisive meaning of the suffering and death of Jesus, the suffering and death of women, men, and children, the suffering of us all. That death condemns the sins of the world. It purifies the world ravaged by human greed and insanity. It makes a new heaven and a new earth (Rev. 21:1) not a matter of choice, but a matter of the divine imperative.

Could it be that thoughts such as these were in Jesus' mind when he said the bread was his body to be broken and the wine was his blood to be shed for many, perhaps implying in behalf of many, and even in solidarity with many (Mark 14:24; pars. Matt. 26:28, Luke 22:20)? As has been pointed out, "conceptions of the atoning power of death play a large part in the thought of Jesus' contemporaries. Every death has atoning power — even that of a criminal if he dies penitent."[27] This seems also what is meant in the totally different religious tradition of Buddhism, which says that one's death can be transformed if it is dedicated to "the benefit and ultimate happiness of others."[28] This atoning and transforming power of death must be the power of resurrection, the power of life that overcomes the power of sin and death, that empowers us to live in the presence of death in anticipation of a full life in God. This power of life is the power of the reign of God. The reign of God! This will be the next station of our "christological" journey in the second volume.

NOTES

1. See Joachim Jeremias, *The Eucharistic Words of Jesus*, trans. Norman Perrin (London: SCM Press, 1966), pp. 84–86.

2. Ibid., p. 219.

3. Ibid.

4. Ibid.

5. Joachim Jeremias, *New Testament Theology: The Proclamation of Jesus*, trans. John Bowden (New York: Charles Scribner's Sons, 1971), p. 291.

6. See *A Concise Greek-English Dictionary of the New Testament*, prepared by Barclay M. Newman, Jr. (London: United Bible Societies, 1971), p. 187a.

7. Ibid.

8. "The Inmate in Solitary," by Clement John; see *Judiciary under Siege* (Hong Kong: International Affairs–CCA, 1983), p. 135.

9. Shusaku Endo, *Silence*, trans. William Johnston (Tokyo: Kodansha International Ltd., 1982).

10. Shusaku Endo, *The Samurai*, trans. van C. Gessel (New York: Vintage Books, 1982).

11. Ibid., p. 159.

12. Ibid., p. 167.

13. Ibid., p. 159.

14. Ibid., p. 119.

15. Ibid., pp. 119–122.

16. Ibid., p. 221.

17. Ibid., p. 222.

18. Endo, *Silence*, p. 292.

19. Information and quotations in these three paragraphs are from *Time*, May 7, 1984, p. 44.

20. Quoted in "Reflections on the Christa," *Journal of Women and Religion* (Berkeley, Center for Women and Religion), vol. 4, no. 2 (Winter 1985), p. 49.

21. Quoted by Soon Man Rhim in *Women of Asia: Yesterday and Today* (New York: Friendship Press, 1983), p. 51, from Katie Curtin, *Women in China* (New York/Toronto: Pathfinder Press, 1975), p. 13.

22. See R. P. Ravindra, "What Is Amniocentesis?" in *Stree* (July 1986), p. 9.

23. From "Order of Worship," prepared by Yong Ting Jin for Christology consultation, September 27–October 3, 1986, organized by CCA. The "Order of Worship" was reproduced in *In God's Image* (Singapore, c/o CCA), December 1986, pp. 14–16.

24. A poem by Ranjini Rebera from Australia. See *In God's Image*, p. 38.

25. Quoted by Edwina Hunter in "Reflections on the Christa, from a Christian Theologian," in "Reflections on the Christa," p. 30.

26. Claus Westermann, *Isaiah 40–66: A Commentary*, trans. David M. G. Stalker (London: SCM Press, 1968), p. 231.

27. Jeremias, *The Eucharistic Words of Jesus*, p. 231.

28. Sogyal Rinpoche, *The Tibetan Book of Living and Dying* (New York: HarperCollins, 1992), p. 219.

Index of Scriptural References

235

LUKE (cont.)

14:12–14, *198*
15:11–32, *75*
15:13, *76*
15:20, *76*
16:23, *186*
17:6, *84*
17:21, *185*
18:15–17, *83*
18:31–32, *142*
19:1–10, *138*
19:45, *140*
19:45–46, *134, 140*
19:47, *141*
19:47a, *134*
20:9–18, *139*
20:19, *142*
22:14, *191*
22:19, *212, 215*
22:20, *232*
22:21, *192*
22:24–27, *149*
22:42, *73, 84, 113*
22:44, *142*
23:2, *127, 138*
23:13–16, *82*
23:26, *94*
23:32, *216*
23:35–37, *84*
23:46, *120*
23:47, *120*
23:49, *193*
24:18, *127*

JOHN

1:1, *104*
1:14, *185*
1:43–51, *16*
7:11, *83*
9:2, *49, 50*
9:3, *50*
10:2–4, *67*
11:1–44, *12, 86*
11:25, *13*
11:33, *13*
11:34, *13*
11:38, *13*
11:50, *82*

12:24, *134*
14–17, *65*
14:1, *65*
14:20, *65*
15:5, *66*
16:32–33, *66*
21:25, *116*

ACTS

1:8, *19*

ROMANS

1:22–23, *33*
5:8, *215*
8:14–17, *92*
8:22, *8*
11:13–15, *80*
16:7, *195*

1 CORINTHIANS

1:18, *80*
1:23, *80, 94*
1:24, *80*
5:21, *77*
13:12, *102*
15:7, *195*
15:14–15, *97*

PHILIPPIANS

2:6–8, *58*
2:8, *85*

HEBREWS

11:8–9, *162*
12:1, *15*
13:8, *x*

JAMES

2:16–17, *169*
5:11, *43*

REVELATION

21:1, *232*

General Index

CPSIA information can be obtained at www.ICGtesting.com
Printed in the USA
LVOW11s1300110516

487760LV00003B/114/P